REMOVING THE MASK:
GIFTEDNESS IN POVERTY

PAUL D. SLOCUMB, Ed.D.
RUBY K. PAYNE, Ph.D.

REMOVING THE MASK:
GIFTEDNESS IN POVERTY

RFT

PUBLISHING CO.

Slocumb, Paul D., & Payne, Ruby K.
        Removing the Mask: Giftedness in Poverty
Paul D. Slocumb & Ruby K. Payne ©2000. 380 pp.
        Bibliography pp. 373-380
        ISBN 1-929229-00-3

1. Education   2. Sociology   3. Title

Contents

Acknowledgments   vii

Introduction   ix

Chapter One:
     The Paradigm   1

Chapter Two:
     Environmental Opportunities   17

Chapter Three:
     Weighing the Opportunities   43

Chapter Four:
     Student Production   75

Chapter Five:
     Informant Data   97

Chapter Six:
     Cognitive/Language Skills   135

Chapter Seven:
     Designing for Equity   155

Chapter Eight:
     Curriculum for the Gifted from Poverty   177

Chapter Nine:
    Nurturing and Keeping the Gifts   211

Chapter Ten:
    The Systemic Challenge   245

Chapter Eleven:
    Conclusion—Opportunity Knocks   261

Research Notes   267

Appendix   308

Bibliography   371

Acknowledgments

A very special thanks to ...

Dr. Ruby Payne, author of *A Framework for Understanding Poverty* and co-author of this book, for encouraging me to write about giftedness in poverty. Because of her work, the quest to find giftedness behind the mask of poverty has begun in earnest.

Dr. Sandra Kaplan, who has been my colleague, friend, and mentor for more than 20 years. Her encouragement and sharing of knowledge continue to inspire me.

Diane Hochstein, vice president of training for Intellectual Development Systems, for giving me new lenses through which to see the world and myself. It was but a beginning.

The prekindergarten and kindergarten teachers at L.F. Smith Elementary in Pasadena, Texas, for piloting the *Environmental Opportunities Profile*.

Dr. Janet Penner, director of curriculum in the Pearland school district, for field-testing the *Rating Superior Students from Diverse Backgrounds*, and Charlotte Larsen, G/T specialist, for always being there to open doors.

The staff and students of the Lamar school district in Rosenberg, Texas, who challenged me, as their instructional leader, to meet the diverse needs of the students in that community. The search for answers began a journey that is still in progress. A special "thank you" goes to the G/T facilitators of Lamar for their willingness to search for more efficient ways to identify and address the needs of the gifted from diverse backgrounds.

The many members of the Texas Association for the Gifted and Talented for allowing me to serve in a leadership role of this organization. I am honored to have been among so many scholars who share a commitment to gifted children everywhere.

The hundreds of students, teachers, and administrators with whom I have had the opportunity to work, for they have been my true teachers. In every workshop and seminar I conduct, they teach me.

Dr. Theresa Monaco, professor, University of Houston, Houston, Texas, for giving me the opportunity to teach graduate courses in curricula for the gifted. Teaching teachers has forced me to articulate my own learning.

Dan Shenk, for his skills as an editor—and for his commitment to quality and excellence.

Dr. Janel Miller, for her commitment to and support of me as a person and a professional. Because of her, adversity and my roots in poverty have meaning and purpose.

And all my love to ...
the one who is always in my corner, Dr. Bonny Cain, my wife, colleague, confidante, and friend, for her unwavering support and commitment. She has always been among the first to recognize, appreciate, and remind me of my own gifts and talents.

Paul D. Slocumb, Ed.D.

Dear Reader,

When I first read Ruby Payne's book, *A Framework for Understanding Poverty*, I knew I had found some labels and explanations for things that I had personally and professionally experienced in my life. Having worked in the field of gifted education for many years, I also knew that many school districts have struggled to identify gifted and potentially gifted students from low socioeconomic backgrounds. Over the years I have read the literature and listened to a variety of consultants on meeting the needs of gifted students from diverse backgrounds. For every proposed answer, there seemed to be "Yes, but...," followed by five more questions.

As Dr. Payne has conducted workshops across the United States on the subject of poverty, she has been questioned repeatedly about gifted students from poverty. She shared this information with me and suggested that we pursue it. Having worked in a school district with a diverse population, I knew the difficulties in identifying gifted students from diverse backgrounds. I too had struggled with the identification process, as well as keeping the students in the program once they were identified.

Having the opportunity to be a curriculum auditor, doing evaluations of gifted programs in a variety of school districts, and having done a dissertation on achieving and non-achieving kindergarten students by doing home visits, I also knew that equity was a key issue. School districts, under the guise of fairness, were omitting their students from poverty in the gifted program while increasing their numbers of students from poverty in other special programs. Opportunities in the home environment were not there, and yet students were being assessed as though they were all from middle-class America. In working with Dr. Payne, I found the pieces of the puzzle coming together. This work is a first step in looking at students' gifts and talents in a context of opportunities afforded within the home environment. Their giftedness is shaped differently and, therefore, must be examined differently. The gifted from poverty do not come to school with middle-class experiences and values; programs thus must be adjusted to accommodate the experiences and values that are fostered in the culture of poverty. This work addresses two major questions:

1. How do I identify gifted students from low socioeconomic environments?

2. Once the district has identified them, how do school officials design and implement programs that will meet these students' needs and keep them in the program?

Removing the Mask: Giftedness in Poverty is for the practicing professional who is committed to finding and serving the best and the brightest from the culture of poverty.

Paul D. Slocumb, Ed.D.

Chapter One:

The Paradigm

Rick
Age: 10

Rick lives with his grandmother and his twin brother Mick in a suburb of a major city. The two boys have been living with their grandmother since they were 11 months old. Their father is her son. According to Grandma, "He sees the boys when he feels like it—usually once or twice a month." The father gives no financial support. Rick's mother lives in the city. She sees Rick and his brother once or twice a year. The boys usually spend a night or two with her when she comes to get them.

Rick's grandmother works at a local hospital in the housekeeping department. She completed the 9th grade in school. She makes approximately $14,500 a year. She has worked at the hospital for 11 years. She receives food stamps and Medicaid. Both of these benefits are to end this year. She says there are too many forms to be completed (to keep the food stamps and Medicaid) that she couldn't fill out. Rick and his brother participate in the free-lunch program at school.

Rick has been in the same school for more than two years. He attends an extended-day class to help him improve his grades and performance on the state competency test. The program is funded with Title I money. He started kindergarten when he was 5. He was retained in 3rd grade.

No adult men live in the household. Rick's grandmother is the only adult female in the household. Rick has regular chores at home. He does the dishes each night. His bedtime is 9 p.m. on school nights. On weekends he is allowed to stay up until 2 or 3 a.m. watching television. It is his "payback" for the 9 p.m. bedtime during the school week. Rick has never spent the night more than 50 miles away from home.

The small house in which the three live is decorated in neutral tones. Rick and his brother have some books, but they are books for younger children. No newspapers or magazines are received in the home. His grandmother does speak in formal register. Rick is a member of the dominant ethnic and economic group on his school campus.

CHAPTER ONE:

THE PARADIGM

"There's nothing so unequal as the equal treatment of unequals."
-Felix Frankfurter, U.S. Supreme Court Justice

When an identification process imposes criteria on students as though they all come to school having had the same opportunities, they are being treated equally. They are not, however, being treated equitably.

Equal: "as great as; the same as; like or alike in quantity, degree, value; of the same rank, ability, merit; evenly proportioned or balanced" (p. 481).

Equity: "the quality of being fair or impartial; that which is fair and just; the application of the dictates of conscience or the principles of natural justice to the settlement of controversies" (p. 482).

- Webster's Encyclopedic Unabridged Dictionary of the English Language, (1997)

In most public-school settings, students must meet an arbitrarily set, minimum birth-date range in order to start school, and readiness to learn is a non-issue. Students in a public-school setting rarely come to school equally equipped to learn. Yet school systems make the assumption that all of them are ready to begin the learning process at the same point. Programs such as prekindergarten and Head Start readily acknowledge that students in fact do not come to school equally equipped to learn. These programs, however, are not mandatory. Therefore, students from poverty enter public school and are placed side by side with students whose backgrounds are much more advantaged.

Treating all students equally in the identification of gifted students all too often results in the extreme under-identification of an entire segment of the student population who come to school quite "unequal."

 These "unequals" enter a system governed by an unwritten code calling for all students to be alike. At first, this practice appears to be not only fair but ideal. Treating all students equally, however, results in singular identification processes. Gifted/talented identification processes are one example that, to varying degrees, disregards the backgrounds of the students. Once identified, the students enter a singular program design that ignores the multiplicity of factors that have contributed to the differences in the students themselves. This disregard of differences creates inequity.

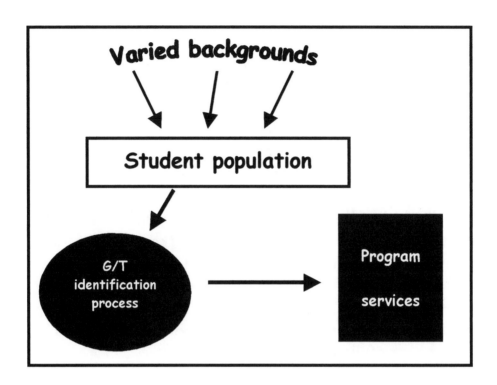

Equity in programs designed to identify and serve potentially gifted/talented students is two-pronged. The first prong is the identification process. The second prong is in the program design—that is, the manner in which the identified gifted students from poverty receive services once the students are identified.

Gifted/talented students from poverty cannot be identified or served as though they were from non-poverty households.

To identify gifted students from poverty necessitates educators including in the identification process those environmental factors that contribute to the students' readiness to learn. After the identification process has occurred, schools must structure services for those students in a manner commensurate with their needs. Not addressing both of these issues results in inequity.

Generally, in the identification process a criterion exists to assess students' abilities in relationship to those criteria. The educators identify those who meet the criteria; the identified students enter the program for the gifted/talented and begin receiving services. Most of these identification processes for gifted/talented programs are highly competitive. This is so because of the following:

1. The process is designed to select an identified number of students from the larger population using criteria that are heavily dependent on standardized test scores.

2. Students who come from economically advantaged households usually score better on standardized tests because they have more access to abstract language within the home environment.

3. Parents who come from middle- and upper-middle-income households are usually goal-oriented, wanting more educational and financial opportunities for themselves and their children.

AND

4. Parents perceive that the **best teachers** are **teaching the best students** in the **best program** and **"I want the best for my child."**

Identifying students in this manner may appear to be equal, but it is not equitable. What educators ultimately identify is not giftedness but rather opportunity.

By not examining students' foundational experiences, the effect of such foundational experiences gets assessed without looking at the causes. It is essential to examine the underlying causes and effects of those learning, social, and emotional behaviors as masked and observed in school.

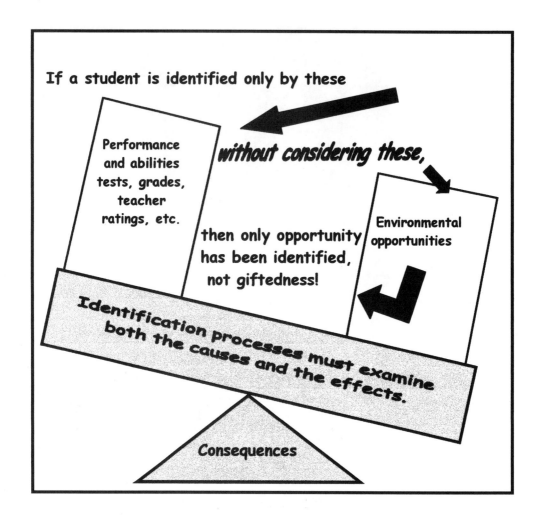

If a student is identified only by these

Performance and abilities tests, grades, teacher ratings, etc.

without considering these,

then only opportunity has been identified, not giftedness!

Environmental opportunities

Identification processes must examine both the causes and the effects.

Consequences

Treating individuals differently in order to establish equity is not new. Competitive sports events have long acknowledged the need for equity. Golfers have handicapping scores. Women golfers have "red tees" that reduce the distance between the tee and the green. Female basketball players use a smaller basketball than the one that male basketball players use.

Competitive-performance events attempt to level the playing field in order to achieve equity. Students who receive private music lessons may find themselves in the symphonic band while those who do not have the private lessons are only skilled enough, by comparison, to be in concert band. Symphonic bands compete against only other symphonic bands. The following diagram depicts this process.

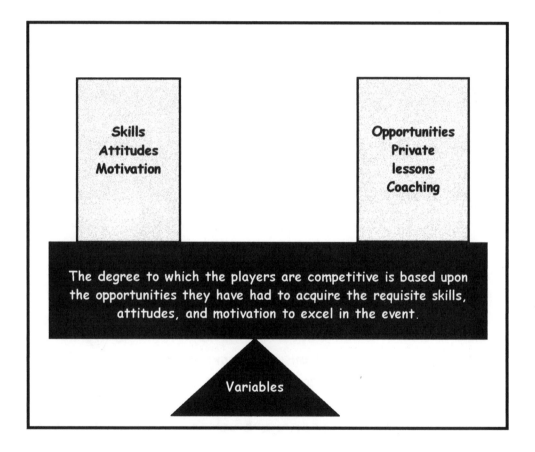

Foundational opportunities greatly impact the skills, attitudes, and motivation of the competitors. These factors, however, are not the sole elements that dictate the category in which they compete. In events in which size and gender are significant factors in the competition, competitors are placed in categories with comparable players. For example, weightlifters, boxers, and wrestlers compete with those of like gender and size. A heavyweight does not compete with a middleweight. Choirs, drama groups, and bands from high schools with small enrollments compete with one another while students in large schools also compete with one another.

Competitive events that don't account for differences in gender, physical size, or physical strength of the players are those events in which size, gender, and strength are not a factor. Skeet competition allows men and women to compete with one another because it is the power of the gun and the accuracy of the shooter that are the critical elements—not size, gender, or physical strength of the competitor. The power of the racecar or the strength of the horse is a factor so significant that it makes the person driving the car or riding the horse of lesser consequence, comparatively speaking.

Typically, identification processes for the gifted/talented do pit students from more advantaged backgrounds against students from less advantaged backgrounds, even though the opportunities within the students' environment make them unequal. Identical treatment of unequals in this situation produces a system that is inequitable.

Identifying the Inequities

Before the identification paradigm can shift from equal to equity, educators must identify and address the sources of the inequity. The sources of the inequity for students from poverty are rooted in the home and the resources available to the student. Having access to resources increases the probability that young children will perform better in school. The presence of these resources within the home environment is vital to the students' skills, attitudes, and motivation. The resources that are pivotal to this development appear below. A more detailed discussion of each of these resource categories is included in the next chapter.

RESOURCES

- **Financial**
- **Emotional**
- **Mental**
- **Spiritual**
- **Physical**
- **Support systems**
- **Relationships/role models**
- **Knowledge of hidden rules**

(Discussion of these resources is included in Chapter Two and also in Payne, 1998, p. 16.)

These resources, or the lack thereof, contribute significantly to the opportunities that students do or do not have in their early, formative years. Impoverished backgrounds contribute to lesser skill and lower production levels. This "lack of" is clearly exhibited and most definitively judged in school settings.

Poverty is "the extent to which an individual does without resources" (Payne, 1998, p. 16). This lack of resources sets the stage for the variations and differences one sees in students. When identifying the potentially gifted student, this lack of resources frequently manifests itself in students through the following:

- Score lower on standardized test.
- Behave differently from their peers from middle-class households.
- Appear unmotivated, lacking goals and planning skills.
- Lack social skills necessary to resolve conflicts.
- Lack many skills that society regards as basic academic skills.

Educators not understanding the causes behind these symptoms tend to exclude bright students coming out of poverty for consideration as potentially gifted students. Their brightness is often hidden behind the mask of poverty. Traditionally, most identification processes for the gifted do not look beyond the mask. The mask becomes a "What you see is what you get" scenario.

Screening all students as if they have had backgrounds that are equal ignores the factors that have contributed to the vast differences that impact their lives. Competitive events acknowledge the differences between the competitors where clearly agreed-upon factors can unfairly skew the competition in favor of one over another. Recognition of the same inequity must be applied to any process in which children are identified for a program intended to serve their specific needs. This modification of process, be it gifted identification or a boxing division, brings equity to the competition. How can a student from an impoverished background possibly compete with the student who has had the resources to attend quality preschool programs; travel; and have access to children's books, computers, and educational toys?

Equity does not eliminate the student who comes from an advantaged background. It does, however, allow for the student who comes from the disadvantaged background to compete for inclusion on a team that limits the number of team members.

An appropriate way to check systemically for equity is for a school district to do the following:

- Ascertain the percentage of identified gifted/talented students who are from low socioeconomic and non-low socioeconomic backgrounds.

- Compare those percentages to the overall percentages in the larger school population.

In other words, if 60% of the students on a campus come from low-income families, then approximately 55 to 65% of the identified gifted students should be from low-income families. The numbers represented within the identified gifted/talented population should be relatively proportionate to the larger school population. Vastly disproportionate representation from the "free and reduced lunch" population and non-"free and reduced lunch" population identified as gifted/talented would be an indicator that the identification process lacks equity.

For educators to change this paradigm and achieve equity, they must consider the differences between the students from poverty and those from environments with more opportunities. Only then can equity in the identification process become a reality. After schools address the equity issue, they must address the issue of services. If schools continue to design services as though one size fits all, then schools will not achieve a fully equitable program for gifted/talented students.

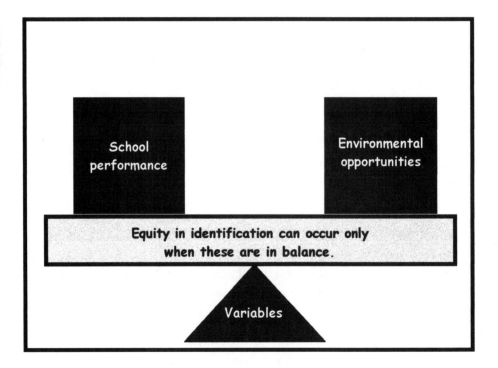

The Challenge

To address the needs of the gifted from poverty, schools must:

- Develop and adopt an identification process that considers the environmental opportunities of the students.

- Develop a program and instructional design that acknowledges and addresses the differences between gifted students from poverty and non-poverty households.

Chapter Two:

Environmental Opportunities

Maya Angelou

Maya Angelou, a renowned poet, author, director, lecturer, and university professor, grew up in segregated Stamps, Arkansas. At age $7\frac{1}{2}$ Maya went to live with her mother in St. Louis. While living there, her mother's boyfriend raped her. After young Maya told her family what had happened, the man was found kicked to death. She stopped talking. She later wrote, "I thought my voice killed him, so I stopped speaking at that moment. I stopped for six years."

She returned to Stamps to live with her grandmother, who patiently waited for Maya to speak. Grandmother, a poor, semi-literate black woman who grew up in a small town in the South, was a loving support system. Young Angelou learned to read and write, and her Uncle Willie taught the youngster her "times tables." Willie's right side was paralyzed, but his left side was strong, and he stood her by the pot-bellied stove in their general store and quizzed her. Maya said, "I learned my times tables exquisitely … If awakened in the middle of the night, I could do my times tables."

In spite of poverty and enormous psychological obstacles, the once silent Maya Angelou now speaks multiple languages and has achieved great things because of the human resources she had within the home environment. As a young child she learned to read, write, and perform mathematical calculations. Without such a support system, she may have been doomed to a very different world.

How much has history been affected because opportunities for students with great potential have not been presented? Are some of the world's problems still unsolved because of the untapped potential of children trapped by poverty?

CHAPTER TWO:

ENVIRONMENTAL OPPORTUNITIES

When a school does not truly identify all gifted/talented students from all segments of the population, the school has compromised equity. In the name of fairness—treating all students alike—students from poverty have been unfairly omitted from programs for gifted/talented students. School systems must develop an identification process for the gifted/talented that takes this into account.

To do this, examination of the home environment must be an integral part of the identification process. Tests and other identification measures that don't consider the home environment do little more than rearrange an existing ineffective and inequitable identification process.

Students from enriched backgrounds typically perform better
in school than those from poverty, as measured by standardized
achievement and intelligence tests. Schools must establish a
process that offsets what is measured in school with what
exists in the home environment.

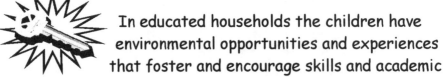 In educated households the children have
environmental opportunities and experiences
that foster and encourage skills and academic
performance to a level higher than students who don't have
such opportunities. The diagram below illustrates this inequity.

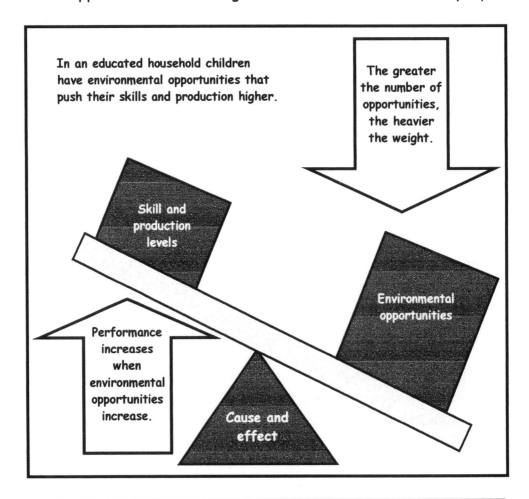

In an educated household children
have environmental opportunities that
push their skills and production higher.

The greater
the number of
opportunities,
the heavier
the weight.

Skill and
production
levels

Environmental
opportunities

Performance
increases
when
environmental
opportunities
increase.

Cause and
effect

The more opportunities available, the higher the performance levels. The greater the number of opportunities in the home environment, the greater the impact these opportunities have on academic performance. Thus, performance levels are higher.

The higher the level of education in the household, the more abstract the processes and procedures in the household. With less education, household members tend to operate at a more concrete level. The following diagram depicts this hierarchy in relationship to education.

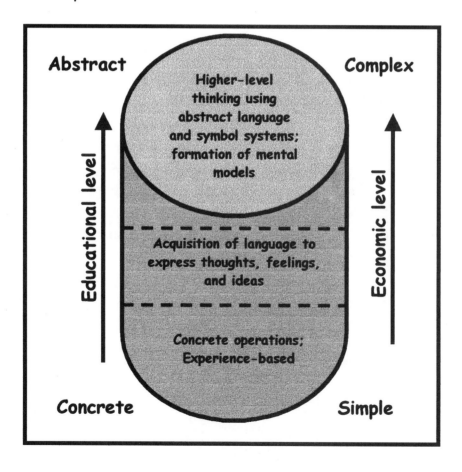

This diagram is not suggesting that higher levels of education produce wealth, but rather that education protects against poverty. Students from educated households are exposed to more abstract uses of language, more complex planning processes and procedures, schemas to organize space, precise use of words and phrases to describe objects and tasks, assignment of abstract values to time, and labeling part-to-whole relationships. Such exposure allows students to develop mental models, which serve as tools to get meaning from things they read, hear, and experience in school and in the outside world.

Low levels of education in a household produce concrete and underdeveloped abilities. Students from uneducated households typically are exposed to concrete uses of language, short phrases and limited word choice, concrete uses of numbers and language, simple processes, and random classification systems. Students from these environments don't develop mental models for generalizing about what they read, hear, and experience. The information these students take into their brain is not as readily organized in a way that allows for learning to transfer to new situations. The result is concrete and simple processes for dealing with a complex world filled with complex information, tasks, and processes. Without the mental models, the higher-level thinking processes remain out of reach. This concrete world becomes the foundation on which the school must build.

In poor, uneducated households the children have limited access to opportunities that have a positive impact on their skill and production levels. Students who grow up in an environment in which the adults in the household don't label and categorize as a means of organizing and giving meaning to the world cannot possibly understand a teacher who says, "This is noun." Abstract terms to label abstract language don't make sense to students who haven't had the opportunity to develop the mental models within the home environment to process such information.

Resources in the home environment for students from poverty are frequently lacking in both quantity and quality. As a result, students don't get identified as gifted/talented since their skills aren't those that are typically measured and/or valued by schools steeped in middle-class norms.

Without opportunities within the household environment, skill levels are typically lower. With lower skill production, the lower are the chances that the student will be considered for the school's gifted/talented program.

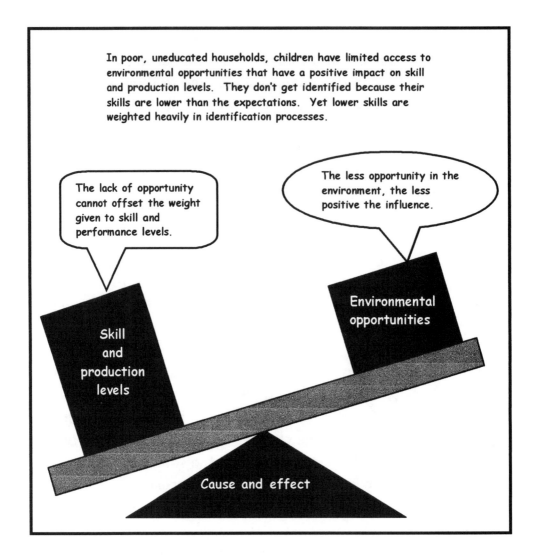

In traditional identification processes, schools assign a greater weight to the skill and performance levels. In doing this, they are weighting the lack of opportunity within the home environment because the skill and performance levels for this segment of the population are usually lower. By not acknowledging the environmental differences, skill and performance levels prevail, regardless of cause and effect. It becomes a lose/lose cycle for the student.

Student from poverty: "The school considers what I don't have (skill and performance levels) more than those opportunities within the environment that have shaped my skill and performance levels."

Student from non-poverty: "The school considers my environmental opportunities because they are reflected in my skill and performance levels."

This is not an intelligence issue; it is an opportunity issue. One solution might be to answer the following question: What would the production levels of a student from poverty look like if his/her home environment had been comparable to the non-poverty students?

Value systems and attitudes about learning are acquired first in the home environment. The presence of children's books and parents reading communicate to young children the value and joy in reading. Oral-language patterns using formal English-language patterns pave the way for children to read, write, and communicate effectively in middle-class institutions. Safe and clean environments and warm, affectionate parents help children develop a personal confidence that they are worthy and safe in this world. Schedules and routines help children develop personal, social, and emotional boundaries. Children raised with predictable schedules and routines understand cause-and-effect relationships, and they develop the ability to predict and to understand the meaning of consequences.

In looking at poverty, it's important to understand that poverty isn't mainly about money. As stated in Chapter One, poverty is **"the extent to which an individual does without resources"** (Payne, 1998, p. 16). These resources include the following:

FINANCIAL: Having the money to purchase goods and services.

EMOTIONAL: Being able to choose and control emotional responses, particularly to negative situations, without engaging in self-destructive behavior. This is an internal resource and shows itself through stamina, perseverance, and choices.

MENTAL: Having the mental abilities and acquired skills (reading, writing, computing) to deal with daily life.

SPIRITUAL: Believing in divine purpose and guidance.

PHYSICAL: Having physical health and mobility.

SUPPORT SYSTEMS: Having friends, family, and backup resources available to access in times of need. These are external resources.

RELATIONSHIPS/ROLE MODELS: Having frequent access to adult(s) who are appropriate, who are nurturing to the child, and who don't engage in self-destructive behaviors.

KNOWLEDGE OF HIDDEN RULES: Knowing the unspoken cues and habits of a group.

Such resources within the home environment increase significantly the opportunities and probability that the student will be successful in school. The more the home environment lacks these resources, however, the more likely the student will struggle in school. More importantly, this "lacking environment" leaves the student feeling unempowered rather than empowered as a learner. Most young children are keenly aware of what they can and cannot do in relationship to other children.

Students from middle class receive benefits not only from home environments, they also are exposed to other enriched environments. In middle-class America (where typically both parents work outside the home), quality day care is a key factor in young children's readiness for school learning. Often being on welfare, or working only for minimum wage, prevents parents in poverty from accessing quality day-care services. At best, they access the Head Start and federally funded preschool programs.

Multiple children, single parents, and welfare become powerful limitations to the development of young children. Survival is far more important than books, educational games, and puzzles in the home. The issue is not love and caring; the issue is survival.

The struggle inherent in survival permeates every aspect of the life of the family in poverty. It controls not only the physical resources, but the emotional resources as well. Education can become the lifeline that can help economically poor students break the cycle of poverty—but only if their education opens up a world of "more" and not "less" because of their background.

The Differences

What is the major difference between the students from poverty and those from more advantaged environments? The difference lies in the opportunities typically inherent in the students' environments. These opportunities may or may not be tangible, but all of them in some way contribute to models that the student references for thinking, believing, and behaving.

The resources available to the student can impact learning either positively or negatively. The following chart illustrates some of the possible results.

Resources	Result of sufficient resources	Result of insufficient resources
Financial	Health care, books, toys, computers, vacations, transportation, food, shelter	Lack of prenatal care; poor nutrition; lack of physical space for adequate motor development; lack of experiences through toys and play for children; unemployment; basic necessities lacking
Emotional	Task commitment; persistence; ability to reason through and verbalize situations and solve problems, articulate feelings; ability to control anger and behavior	Impulsive behavior; lack of causal reasoning; lack of language to express feelings; physical punishment of children for misbehavior; may curse at children when scolding them
Mental	Ability to read, write, and compute; presence of books, magazines, puzzles, and games; ability to function with day-to-day tasks, learning new things as needed; can problem-solve	Absence of books, puzzles; parents unable to read to children; dependence on television for entertainment and information; limited job possibilities; poor problem-solving skills; little experience with abstract reasoning; decisions made on basis of likes and dislikes
Spiritual	Environment of hope, empowerment, inner strength, self-worth, purposefulness	Personal efforts perceived to be insignificant; feelings of hopelessness
Physical	Healthy; able to perform daily routines; ability to work	Poor health; diets high in sugar and fats; poorly developed sensory motor and ocular motor systems; adults miss work and

		have no sick-leave benefits
Support systems	Friends and relatives available to help in times of need; ability to hire help when needed; can find answers when needed; physical and emotional support available from others	Quality day care unavailable; older children caring for younger children; high stress levels because there is no help; feelings acted out rather than verbalized and dealt with logically and rationally; lack of knowledge about how to deal with institutions
Relationships/ role models	Presence of nurturing adults; feelings of love, caring, and safety; attitude of "I can"	Feelings of being isolated; unable to find answers; feelings of abandonment and victimization; unable to show affection toward others; distrust of others
Hidden rules	Adheres to rules of social class; is accepted by social class to which he/she belongs; can adapt and survive in social situations; knows expectations of group	Unable to understand rules in workplace; loses jobs; difficulty in communicating with social-service organizations because of lack of understanding of "rules"; distrust of institutions

Without the availability of these resources in the home, the effects of poverty on student achievement and behavior enter the classroom and put these students at a significant disadvantage.

For students from more advantaged backgrounds, the presence of these resources produces a positive set of circumstances that has a positive carryover into the school. The more resources present in the home, the more the student benefits.

Since school is a middle-class institution, students from middle-
and upper-middle-class environments have a definite edge.
These students are usually surrounded by support systems not
available to students from poverty. Teachers readily recognize
the confident students who can verbalize wants and needs in a
pleasing manner that fits the hidden rules of middle class.

Teachers don't always recognize the strengths of students
from poverty. They verbalize wants and needs in a manner that
is incompatible with the hidden rules of middle class. The
hidden rules of poverty are not the rules that are typically
valued or understood in schools. Payne (1998, p. 59) identifies
these hidden rules for people from wealth, middle class, and
poverty as follows:

Hidden Rules Among Poverty, Middle Class, and Wealth

Category	Poverty	Middle class	Wealth
Possessions	People	Things	One-of-a-kind objects, legacies, pedigrees
Money	To be used, spent	To be managed	To be conserved, invested
Personality	Is for entertainment; sense of humor is highly valued	Is for acquisition and stability; achievement is highly valued	Is for connections; financial, political, social connections are highly valued
Social emphasis	Social inclusion of people they like	Emphasis is on self-governance and self-sufficiency	Emphasis is on social exclusion
Food	Key question: Did you have enough? Quantity	Key question: Did you like it? Quality important	Key question: Was it presented well? Presentation

	important		important
Clothing	Valued for individual style and expression of personality	Valued for its quality and acceptance into norm of middle class; label important	Valued for its artistic sense and expression; designer important
Time	Present most important; decisions made for moment based on feelings or survival	Future most important; decisions made against future ramifications	Traditions and history most important; decisions made partially on basis of tradition and decorum
Education	Valued and revered as abstract but not as reality	Crucial for climbing success ladder and making money	Necessary tradition for making and maintaining connections
Destiny	Believes in fate; cannot do much to mitigate chance	Believes in choice; can change future with good choices now	Noblesse oblige
Language	Casual register; language is about survival	Formal register; Language is about Negotiation	Formal register; language is about networking
Family structure	Tends to be matriarchal	Tends to be Patriarchal	Depends on who has money
World view	Sees world in terms of local setting	Sees world in terms of national setting	Sees world in terms of international view

Love	Love and acceptance conditional, based upon whether individual is liked	Love and acceptance conditional and based largely upon achievement	Love and acceptance conditional and related to social standing and connections
Driving force	Survival, relationships, entertainment	Work, achievement	Financial, political, social connections

What Does It Look Like in School?

Hidden rules come with students to the classroom and are manifested in a variety of ways. The contrast can be readily observed in any classroom that consists of students from poverty, middle class, and wealth.

Possible Manifestations in School of Hidden Rules Among Poverty, Middle Class, and Wealth

Category	Poverty	Middle class	Wealth
Possessions	Sticks up for friends; doesn't "rat" on friends; "don't say nuthin' about my momma"	Gives gifts to express appreciation	Gives expensive gifts; place item was purchased is important
Money	Spends money; shares money with friends	Saves money for things; doesn't share money	Never talks about money; having money is a given
Personality	Class clown; jokester; uses casual-register language in colorful way; verbally loud	Displays social graces: "please," "thank you," "yes ma'am"	People acknowledged and valued by their titles and family connections

Social emphasis	Includes only people in group he/she likes; nonconforming; being with friends more important than homework	Self-disciplined, responsible; wants to please	Circulates primarily within circles of wealth
Food	Will take food from others; wants more	Won't eat what isn't liked	Won't eat cafeteria food; preference for gourmet foods
Clothing	Makes personal statement with clothing and hair	Wears what is fashionable	Wears designer clothes; artistic statement
Time	Tardy to class; what's happening with friends takes precedence over everything	Punctual; plans for homework, play, television	Follows schedules and traditions
Education	Can't see relevance of school to his/her world	Motivated; crucial to be successful and please teacher	Strives to go to "right" school; prestigious
Destiny	"Not my fault"; little sense of choice; "they don't like me"	Makes choices to receive certain payoffs	Follows in steps of family; obligation to social class and family status
Language	Casual register; may use profanity/vulgarity to express feelings and emotions	Formal register; able to verbalize thoughts and feelings	Formal register; engages in name-dropping; extensive vocabulary
Family structure	"Don't call Mom, Auntie, Memaw"; doesn't have phone	Don't call/tell my dad	"Don't embarrass family name"

World view	Immediate neighborhood is his/her reference point	Reference point reflects national perspective; knows U.S.	Reference point is international; vacations in foreign countries; has vacation homes
Love	Shows affection to people he/she likes; grades and discipline records unimportant	Associates with other students who succeed in school	Associates with other students from "good" families
Driving force	Goes to school to be with friends and to entertain	Strives to achieve in school; wants good grades	"I go to school with ... or at ... "

Non-poverty students purchase presents for the teacher at holiday and birthday times. Their manner of dress reflects the fashion of the day, and the supplies needed for school are available. When a project is due, the parents are there to assist the student and the teacher. When the field trip occurs, one parent is there is help the teacher with the group. Mother volunteers to make the cookies for the Christmas party, and Dad agrees to help out at a booth for the fall festival. The student's desk contains the flashy pencils, the newest and biggest box of Crayola crayons with the built-in sharpener, and unique and clever items from the local office-supply store. When the student plays Pocahontas in the school play, there is an elaborate beaded costume that Mother made, along with the elaborate headdress acquired when the family vacationed last summer in Arizona. Mom, Dad, grandparents, and other family members are present with the video camera to preserve this moment.

Students from poverty cannot afford the presents for the teacher and in all likelihood will cause a disturbance when the teacher begins to open her presents in hopes that no one notices he/she has not brought a gift. Mother will not send homemade cookies to the school in a nice little tray with a colorful bow on it. If enough food stamps were available, some Oreos might be purchased at the local convenience store, only to be partially consumed by the student on his way to school. Neither Mother nor Dad will participate in the fall festival, but the student may show up alone, without money to spend, only to be the disruptive student who is constantly "horsing around" and being a general nuisance. Assigned projects will not be completed because Mother doesn't have a car or the money to go to Wal-Mart to buy the poster board. The student's desk is in disarray, and school supplies are missing, lacking, or broken. The special box of Crayola crayons found in the desk belongs to another class member. The child gets to be an Indian brave in the Thanksgiving play, dressed in his grocery-sack vest, made at school under the supervision of the teacher, fringed with scissors at the bottom, colored brightly with crayons, and crowned with a construction paper headdress. Schools proudly maintain, however, that they treat all students alike, fairly, and equally.

When the resources are limited in the environment and survival is the priority, the school's request for the "extras" appears unnecessary to the parent who lives in poverty. Among these unrealistic requests are:

- School supplies that go beyond pencil and paper.
- Specific food requests for the class party.

- Chaperones for the class field trip.
- Collections of objects, such as household objects, leaves, insects, etc., for the science lesson.
- Stories and photos related to family history, vacations, and family traditions.
- Projects that require additional materials and resources.
- Trips to the local library or museum—or use of a home computer.
- Show and tell: "What I Did During My Summer Vacation," "What I Got for Christmas," "My Birthday Party," "My Family Tree."

Students who don't have the resources within their home environments are juxtaposed against students who do. Without an understanding of the students from poverty, their talents go undetected, overshadowed by the lack of resources and other behaviors rooted in poverty.

The Uses of Language

 A crucial part of student achievement is the use of language. Students from poverty manifest language abilities differently from middle-class students—in three major ways:

1. Registers of language
2. Discourse patterns
3. Story structure

Registers of Language

Basing her analysis on the work of Martin Joos (1967), Ruby Payne (1998, p. 42) describes five registers of language, as follows:

Register	Explanation
Frozen	Language that is always the same, predictable: Lord's Prayer, wedding vows, etc.
Formal	The standard sentence syntax and word choice of work and school. Has complete sentences and specific word choice.
Consultative	Formal register when used in conversation. Discourse pattern not quite as direct as formal register.
Casual	Language between friends and is characterized by a 400- to 800-word vocabulary. Word choice general and not specific. Conversation dependent upon non-verbal assists. Sentence syntax often incomplete.
Intimate	Language between lovers or twins. Language of sexual harassment.

Dr. Maria Montano-Harmon (1991) found that the majority of students in her study of minority and poor students have access only to casual register at home. The lack of formal register puts students from poverty at a severe disadvantage in school. Standardized tests and all reading material are in formal register. Teachers and administrators communicate in formal register.

The inability to use formal register places the students from poverty in an oral and written world that uses a language they don't understand. It's not uncommon to hear teachers of young children comment on students' lack of language skills. Translated, this assessment means "I don't understand what my students are trying to say, and they don't seem to understand me." This is because the students talk in casual register, and the teacher talks in formal register. It's also related to patterns of discourse.

Discourse Patterns in Formal and Casual Register

Formal register is more direct than casual register. The pattern in formal register is to get to the point. In casual register the pattern is much more circular. Students using casual register tend to talk around a situation, wandering from topic to topic without ever seeming to get to the point. Students who don't have access to formal language get very frustrated in trying to communicate their thoughts, feelings, and ideas. Likewise, teachers become frustrated when they tell a student over and over what they want from the student and yet the student doesn't appear to "get it."

Story Structure

Formal-register story structure has a beginning, middle, and end. It is chronologically sequenced, and the most important part of the story is plot. In casual-register story structure, the story begins with the end of the story, or the part that has the most emotional appeal. The story then proceeds in vignettes with audience participation. The story ends with a comment about the characters and their value. The most important part of the story is characterization (Payne, 1998, pp. 45-46).

Implications for Identifying Gifted Students from Poverty

Inherent in most identification processes for gifted/talented is a heavy reliance on students' facility with language. Given that most students from poverty communicate and think in casual register—and that their patterns of discourse are typically not linear—standardized assessment measures are not going to reflect their true potential. In their quest for equity, school personnel must apply this knowledge of language uses to the identification process.

In summary, a gifted/talented identification process must take into account the following critical factors if schools are going to identify gifted students from poverty backgrounds.

1. Lack of resources contributes to the thinking, believing, and behaving patterns of students from poverty—socially, emotionally, and academically.

2. The hidden rules of poverty govern the students' reactions to other people, situations, and their personal decision-making.

3. Casual register limits students' abilities to perform in an academic setting that operates in formal register.

4. Communications by students from poverty, oral and written, often appear illogical by middle-class standards because of structure and concrete use of language.

Implications for Equity in the Identification of Gifted Students from Poverty

For students from poverty ...

- Standardized tests will not accurately measure their abilities.

- Survival in poverty is very concrete; survival in school is very abstract.

- Knowledge and experiences brought to school will reflect the lack of many of the resources enjoyed by non-poverty students.

Chapter Three:

Weighing the Opportunities

"I did like Josh, and I think that if a child as smart and as caring as Josh is now a 'child from hell,' it is because nobody took the time to nurture him. It is more a matter of circumstance than character. Josh and too many other twelve-year olds have their chance decreased, not because they are bad or destructive, but simply because they lack the opportunities and the encouragement children require. Children like Nichole have parents and teachers who have taught and encouraged her to think ahead, to problem solve, to be self-motivated; who have helped her with homework, corrected bad behavior, and supported her in swimming and dance lessons. When she is interested in something, we are there to help her find and develop her gifts and talents. When she has questions or worries, we are there to talk about them.

"It is possible that Josh will never know these things or ever have these chances. He will not receive these same opportunities for growth. Among the middle class, we find the perpetuation of the American dream: my kids will do at least as well as I did. Among the homeless and the poor, the inheritance is often a legacy of poverty and failure if the family has lived this way for generations. These kids all step up a rung, too; they will usually progress and be a little better off than their parents, but they will not catch up without intervention—especially the intervention of education. If kids don't know how to make choices and how to think critically, they don't have a chance."

- Stacy Bess, *Nobody Don't Love Nobody*
(pp. 169-170), 1994

CHAPTER THREE:

WEIGHING THE OPPORTUNITIES

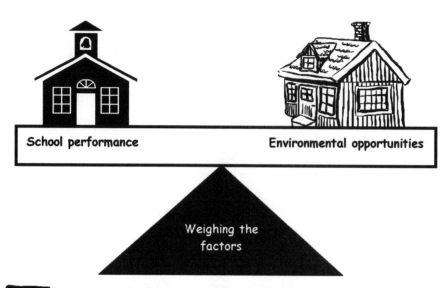

School performance   Environmental opportunities

Weighing the factors

To change the identification paradigm, current practices must change. They must ...

Move from ⟶   ⟶ Move to

Move from	Move to
• Cut-off scores	• Preponderance of evidence
• Questioning admittance	• Providing support
• Relying on quantitative measures	• Relying on qualitative measures
• Recommendations	• Perceptions
• Nominations	• Whole-class screening
• Equality	• Equity
• Reliance on school work	• Consideration of environmental factors

To determine the impact of the home environment on students from poverty and non-poverty households, school personnel look at the home and determine which factors within that environment exist that impact learning positively or negatively. It's important to determine the degree to which home environment has shaped the performance of poverty and non-poverty students. If Johnny is compared to Mary, and they come from very different home environments—one with an abundance of resources and the other with limited resources—schools are comparing apples to oranges in the identification process, rather than apples to apples.

Why is it important to look at the home environment?

- **To identify the presence and absence of resources in the home that impact student achievement.**

- **To help separate the issues of giftedness versus opportunity.**

- **To help separate enriched experiences from innate abilities.**

- **To extract from the identification process those elements within the home environment that contribute to**

> **giftedness being packaged differently from norm.**
>
> • **To assess the degree and dimension to which the student has had the opportunity to think abstractly.**

The *Environmental Opportunities Profile* (Slocumb & Payne, 1999), which appears later in this chapter, is such an instrument. When giftedness is being identified, this instrument sets the stage for an "apples to apples" comparison of students. A representative of the school interviews the student's primary caregiver. The interviewer asks questions focusing on things within the home environment that influence student achievement. According to Garcia (1994), the following three areas are part of the identification process:

- **Student Production**
- **Informant Data**
- **Cognitive/Language Skills**

These areas represent qualitative data rather than quantitative data. School personnel compile the qualitative data and juxtapose those data against the information collected about the home environment using a *Preponderance of Evidence* grid to record the data (Slocumb & Payne, 1999). This form also appears at the end of this chapter.

The school uses these two instruments to collect information about the students' home environment and the students' performance in school.

Environmental Opportunities Profile	Preponderance of Evidence
Definition: An instrument used to interview the primary caregiver. The questions on this instrument receive a point value ranging from 1 to 3 points and correlate with the three types of qualitative data collected in the school. The areas are: • **Student Production** • **Informant Data** • **Cognitive/Language Data**	**Definition:** A grid used to record the qualitative student performance data collected in school. Data collected in the home also are recorded on this grid. The data reflect three areas related to student performance. The areas are: • **Student Production** • **Informant Data** • **Cognitive/Language Data**

This identification process allows school personnel to view the traditional (test scores) and non-traditional information (checklists, ratings, interviews, etc.) collected within the context of the

school. For example, if a student from a privileged background
were asked, "Who is George Washington?" the student would
probably say he was a president or the first president of the
United States. A student from poverty, when asked the same
question, might say George Washington is the name of a street
in his neighborhood or the name of a person.

> **Is one student brighter than the
> other one, or are both students
> reflecting the opportunities and
> experiences they have had within
> the home environment?**

Administering the EOP

Through an interview of the student's primary caregiver, school
personnel collect information related to the student's home
environment. The instrument design lends itself to school
personnel conducting the interview in the home or via the
telephone. Slocumb and Payne designed the *Environmental
Opportunities Profile* (Slocumb & Payne,
1999) to work with problems inherent in
poverty conditions. Specifically, visits to
homes in high-poverty neighborhoods can
be unsafe for school employees. The
telephone becomes an alternative method
of retrieving this information. When there is no telephone in
the home, school officials usually have an emergency number

they can use to reach the parent. The school may also obtain information needed on the *Environmental Opportunities Profile* (EOP) at the time the child enrolls in school. The school enrollment process is an ideal time to administer the EOP to all of these groups.

Because parents of students from poverty frequently do not see institutions as helpful, and having their child in a program for the gifted is not seen as a plus, setting a tone of confidence and trust is very important. Explaining to parents that the school is seeking additional information that will help the school better meet their child's needs is the first step. The child's classroom teacher, building principal, counselor, nurse, social worker, librarian, or a specialist in the gifted/talented are each possibilities for conducting the interview. Parent volunteers, however, should not be used. The information the school seeks is confidential. Conveying to the parent that this information is confidential helps build trust between the school and the parent.

A good interviewer is a person who:

- Is at ease in the situation.

- Puts the parent or caregiver at ease.

- Takes into account answers by parent/caregiver in phrasing subsequent questions.

- Asks questions in such a way as to avoid putting the interviewee on the defensive.

If the interviewee becomes defensive, he/she may try to second-guess the interviewer as to what is the "right" or "expected" response. The goal is to be objective and accepting as opposed to approving or disapproving. This is essential if school personnel are to find out how this person feels and what he/she does with the child rather than what he/she may think the school wants him/her to say.

Parents usually aren't nervous about being interviewed, but interviewers sometimes are. The interviewer needs to spend some time at the beginning of the interview getting acquainted with the parent and the child. The general tone of the interview should be that of two friendly people, who like to talk about children, sitting down together and doing exactly that. This warm-up period offers a good opportunity to say something nice about the child, and it helps break the ice so that both parties feel more comfortable.

Collecting Information on Foster Children and Adopted Children

Some students who come from poverty may be living in foster homes. It isn't uncommon for some students from poverty to live in multiple foster homes within a school year. In this event, the interviewer should get as much information as the foster parent can share. If the foster parent reports only on the home environment within the foster setting, significant information about the student's background may be overlooked. Likewise, if the student has been in the foster setting since he/she was quite young, school personnel may consider the foster environment the norm for that student. In some cases, and depending on the age of the student and circumstances, the student may be the source for some of the information.

The same is true of an adopted child. The information would depend on the length of time the student has been in the adoptive setting. The interviewer from the school writes down all relevant information. Some children may be living with a relative for a variety of reasons. Unless the relative has had the child for an extended period of time, the interviewer needs to inquire about the child's previous background and use that information on the EOP.

Meet the Kids

The following is a summary of four interviews. Manuel is in 2nd grade, Joe is in 4th grade, Krystal is in 3rd grade, and Sasha is in 6th grade. These scenarios will be used in the appropriate sections in subsequent chapters to illustrate how an interviewer would complete the EOP.

Scenario #1: Manuel
Birthday: May 31   Age: 8
Person interviewed: The father

Manuel lives with his mother and father. He has a younger sister who is in kindergarten. Manuel was in the bilingual program in kindergarten and 1st grade. He exited the bilingual program at the end of 1st grade. He is currently in an English as a Second Language class. He was in a full-day kindergarten program.

His father works for an auto body-repair shop. He has had the same job since 1989. He graduated from high school in the community where he now lives and works. He speaks formal English fluently. He is the sole provider of the family's income. He has no medical benefits. His salary is less than $20,000 a year. The family has one vehicle. The father usually comes home for lunch each day. Manuel participates in the school's free-lunch program.

Manuel's mother completed school at the highest grade level available in Mexico City, Mexico. She speaks and writes Spanish. She is currently learning English by attending an evening program in Manuel's school that teaches non-English-speaking adults English while also teaching parenting skills. She comes to the school one evening a week with her two children. The children are provided books, and the parents are taught how to help their child with school-related work while the parents are learning English. Manuel's mother is a stay-at-home mom. She does not drive a car. Her family of origin still lives in Mexico, and Manuel's family visits there about once a year.

Manuel's parents have lived in the same home for 12 years. It's a three-bedroom house with two bathrooms, a dining room, kitchen and family room combination, and a two-car garage. The living area has a ceiling fan that has three lights. There is also a lamp in the room.   The drapes are usually open during the day. The walls of the home are white. The drapes are green and yellow. The furniture is beige and brown. The light fixture above the kitchen table has four light bulbs.

At the end of Manuel's kindergarten year, the school district rezoned the attendance zones to his school. After Manuel attended his newly assigned school for six weeks, his father requested that Manuel be transferred back to his current school. The district allows for, even encourages, families to keep their children in the same school if they will provide transportation. Manuel's parents chose to keep him at his current school because, as his father stated, "The teachers at his school are more like parents than teachers. I like the school. I think it is better."

Manuel is expected to be in bed each night at 9:30 p.m.; however, this varies on occasion. The family almost always eats together, but the time varies because of Father's work. Dinner is usually between 5 p.m. and 7:30 p.m.

Manuel has more than 20 children's books because of the school's evening program that he attends with his mother. The family does not subscribe to a newspaper or magazine. His *father purchases a newspaper occasionally to get the coupons. They dropped their subscription to the local paper because it became too expensive.*

Manuel has not missed a day of school this year. In 1st grade he missed four days. Manuel's Reading grade the last six weeks was an 86. His grades are in the A, B, and C range. Social Studies was his lowest grade this year. As a 1st-grader in a bilingual classroom, his Iowa Test of Basic Skills scores (English version) were 40th percentile in Reading, 30th percentile in Language, and 59th percentile in Mathematics. When he was in the 1st grade, Manuel took the Ravens test. His age score was the 92nd percentile.

Campus Data

28% African-American	**59% Hispanic**
12% Anglo	**78% free lunch**

36% mobility rate

Scenario #2: Joe
Birthday: July 15   Age: 9
Person interviewed: The mother

Joe is an Anglo male in 4th grade who lives with his mother in a three-bedroom apartment. He is one of five children in the family. Joe has an older sister in 7th grade, an older brother in 5th grade, a brother in 2nd grade, and a sister in kindergarten. Joe's parents divorced when he was in 1st grade. He hasn't seen his father since he moved out. His mother currently has a male friend who stays with them occasionally. Joe's mother was born *in the state where she currently lives and attended school in the community where she now lives. She dropped out of school in 11th grade. She currently does domestic work for the apartment complex where they live. She has no medical benefits. Joe's mother makes less than $15,000 a year, but she does receive a housing discount due to working for the apartment's owner. Joe participates in the free-lunch program at school.*

Joe has been attending the same elementary school since prekindergarten. Last year on the state competency test he mastered all the reading objectives and math objectives. He received academic recognition because he mastered all the objectives tested. Joe's end-of-year average in 1st grade was one C, two D's, and three B's. In 2nd grade he was in the Title I program and made three C's and four B's. In 3rd grade he made three C's, one D, and two B's. He wasn't in the Title I program in 3rd grade. His lowest performance area on his report cards from 1st grade through mid-year of 4th grade has always been Language Arts. He is not a discipline problem in school. Joe's attendance in school has been fairly consistent. He missed three days in 1st grade, five in 2nd grade, nine in 3rd grade, and two days as a 4th-grader. Joe's 3rd-grade teacher said his grades would be better if he "tried harder; he doesn't do his homework as he should." Because of his performance on the state competency test last year, the principal placed him in a class this year that includes seven identified gifted children.

Joe shares a bedroom with his brothers. The apartment has beige walls, and the furniture is brown and the carpet is brown. During the day the blinds are usually lowered to help keep the electric bill down. The living room has one overhead light, and the kitchen has a light above the kitchen table. The living room did have two lamps, but the children broke the lamps while "horsing around." Joe occasionally spends the night with a friend in the same apartment complex, but he has never been more than 50 miles away from home.

Joe usually watches television until 10 p.m. before going to bed. Some of the family members eat at the kitchen table, and some eat in the living room in front of the TV. His mother reported, "Joe done real good in school. He passed everything, and he don't get in no trouble." The children have some books at home that they check out at the school library. They don't buy books because they're too expensive. The family doesn't receive a daily newspaper or magazine. They do, however, receive an advertisement circular that is distributed free throughout the community. Only English is spoken in the home.

Campus Data

53% African-American	26% Hispanic
21% Anglo	85% free lunch
45% mobility rate	

Scenario #3: Krystal
Birthday: April 16   Age: 8
Person interviewed: The sitter

Krystal is an African-American female in 3rd grade who lives with her mother and father in a five-bedroom house. She is one of two children in the family. Krystal has an older brother in 5th grade. Krystal's parents both work outside the home.

Mother is a physician, and Dad is an attorney. Their combined income exceeds $150,000 a year. Because Krystal's parents work long hours, a full-time nanny resides in the home. Krystal has attended the same school for the past two years.

Krystal's father has his own law firm, and her mother has an independent medical practice in a neighboring community. Both of her parents were born in the United States. She and her family live in a spacious home of approximately 6,000 square feet. The family takes a skiing trip every Christmas, and they take a one-week vacation during the summer as a family. Krystal and her brother also go to a summer camp for two weeks in July.

Krystal has her own room. She has a telephone, a computer, and a TV/VCR. The home has a variety of books and reading materials, including the daily newspaper. Because of their parents' schedule, the children eat together. The nanny prepares their dinner and supervises the children's bedtime and homework schedule.

The nanny is a high school graduate and has two years of college. She is 28 and has been with Krystal and her brother for one year. Prior to her hiring, the children had the same nanny for three years. Formal English is spoken in the home.

Campus Data

60% Anglo	**15% African-American**
10% Asian	**7% Hispanic**
8% other	**15% mobility rate**
5% free lunch	

Scenario #4: Sasha
Birthday: September 29   Age: 11
Person interviewed: The mother

Sasha is an Anglo female in 6th grade. She is an only child. Her mother and father divorced when Sasha was 3. The father sees Sasha every other weekend and on specified school holidays. He lives approximately one hour from Sasha. He is a high school graduate and currently works as a mechanic for a local dealership. He pays $800 a month in child support. He also carries Sasha on his company's insurance program. He has remarried and has two children with his current wife. Sasha's mother has no medical coverage.

Sasha's mother has an interior decorating business that she started three years ago. Following high school graduation, she worked for a local department store as a salesperson, then worked her way up to being a consultant for them in the drapery department, attending special training and taking some courses. She describes herself as a "self-made" person. Her income last year was between $30,000 and $40,000. She calls on most of her clients in the evening. When Sasha was younger, her mother hired a sitter to come in the evening, but now that Sasha is older she stays at home alone. Sasha says she has a daily schedule that she follows most of the time. Her mother does call her between appointments when she works later. At this time her mother is not in a relationship with anyone. Since the divorce, she has had one serious relationship, but it didn't work out.

Sasha and her mother live in the house her mother had when she was married to Sasha's dad. The house has approximately 1,800 square feet. It is nicely decorated. Her mother subscribes to several magazines that are related to her work. Most of the books in the home also are related to interior designing. Sasha doesn't have any books of her own. She does, however, check out books at the school library. Her mother doesn't subscribe to the daily newspaper. There is a computer in the home, and Sasha has her own phone and TV. Although this is Sasha's first year at the middle school, she attended the same elementary school K-5.

Sasha has spent the night away from home a few times when she visits her grandmother. Her grandmother lives in another state.

Campus Data

35% Anglo	*40% Hispanic*
15% African-American	*10% Asian*
60% free lunch	*25% mobility rate*

Complete an EOP on at least two of
these students.

Joe
Manuel
Krystal
Sasha

REMEMBER ...

When in doubt,
err on the side of the student.

Environmental Opportunities Profile

Developed by Ruby K. Payne, Ph.D., and Paul D. Slocumb, Ed.D.
©RFT Publishing Co., 1999

Date of interview_____ Name of interviewer_____

Name of student_____ Grade level_____

School_____ Teacher_____

Person interviewed_____ Relationship to student_____

Address_____

City_____ ZIP_____ Day phone #_____

Evening phone #_____ Emergency #_____

Additional notes from interview:

Total number of people in household:
_____
Range of family's annual income:
____Less than $10,000
____$10,000 to $20,000
____$20,000 to $30,000
____$30,000 to $40,000
____$40,000 to $50,000
____$50,000 to $75,000
____More than $75,000

Environmental Opportunities Profile
Developed by Ruby K. Payne, Ph.D., and Paul D. Slocumb, Ed.D.
©RFT Publishing Co., 1999

Section I: Student Production	Criteria	Rating
Item 1: Number of years of schooling of primary caregiver, particularly mother **Question:** How many years were you in school, starting with 1st grade?	• 16+ years of schooling • 12-15 years of schooling • Less than 12 years of schooling	☐ 1 point ☐ 2 points ☐ 3 points
Item 2: Number of years at same school **Question:** How long has your child gone to this school?	• Has or will spend two or more years in same school • Is and/or plans to be in same school for one year • Moves during year; is unlikely to stay for entire school year	☐ 1 point ☐ 2 points ☐ 3 points
Item 3: Child/family have medical/health benefits **Question:** Does your family have medical/health benefits that include child?	• All members are covered • Only employed parent(s) are covered • No members are covered	☐ 1 point ☐ 2 points ☐ 3 points
Item 4: Number of years in same job; stability of income **Question:** Do you and/or other adults in the household work outside the home? How long have you/they worked there?	• One or more adults are employed and have been consistently employed for two or more years with same company or type of work • One or more adults are employed and	☐ 1 point ☐ 2 points

	have been for at least one year with same company or type of work	
	• No adult is employed or has been employed for more than six months with same company or type of work on full-time basis	☐ 3 points
Item 5: Identified as LD, ED, ADHD, ADD, 504, Title I, bilingual, etc. **Question:** Does your child receive any special services at school, such as with reading or math from a special teacher, in Special Education, special tutoring, etc.?	• No learning conditions identified	☐ 1 point
	• Identified learning problems; interventions appear effective; parents pleased with student's progress	☐ 2 points
	• Learning problems identified; interventions appear ineffective; parents displeased with progress	☐ 3 points
Subtotal of Section I =		
Section II: Informant Data	**Criteria**	**Rating**
Item 6: Parents born in United States **Question:** Were you and your spouse born in the United States?	• Both parents born in United States	☐ 1 point
	• One parent born in United States	☐ 2 points
	• Neither parent born in United States	☐ 3 points
Item 7: Support system in home—number of adult males in household	• One or more adult males live in	☐ 1 point

Question: How many adult men live in your house?	household, consistently and fairly constantly • One adult male on fairly permanent basis; if divorced, father exercises visitation rights regularly	☐ 2 points
	• No adult males in household, or males are not in household on regular basis	☐ 3 points
Item 8: Support system in home—number of adult females in household **Question:** How many adult women live in the household?	• One or more adult females live in household, consistently and fairly constantly	☐ 1 point
	• One adult female on fairly permanent basis; if divorced, mother exercises visitation rights regularly	☐ 2 points
	• No adult females in household, or females are not in household on regular basis	☐ 3 points
Item 9: Support system in household—number of adults in household **Question:** How many children are in the household and how many adults (ratio of children to adults)?	• Child/adult ratio is one-to-one or better	☐ 1 point
	• Child/adult ratio is two children to one adult	☐ 2 points
	• Child/adult ratio is three or more children to one adult	☐ 3 points

Item 10: Amount of light in home **Question:** Do you have lots of light in your house? Do you open the curtains during the day?	• Window coverings are open during day; three or more light fixtures and/or lamps are in major rooms in house	☐ 1 point
	• Window coverings partially open; overhead light or lamp per room	☐ 2 points
	• Window coverings closed; one or less low-wattage light bulb is used; light often comes from TV	☐ 3 points
Item 11: Use of color in home décor **Question:** What colors are in your house? Describe the colors of your walls, pictures, and furniture.	• Light-colored walls with contrasting colors in drapes and furnishings	☐ 1 point
	• Neutral shades and décor; colors complement or blend rather than contrast	☐ 2 points
	• Darker décor; random use of medium-to-dark nondescript color	☐ 3 points
Item 12: Is older or younger than classmates **Question:** When was your child born? Did he/she start kindergarten when he/she was 5? Has he/she ever been retained?	• Overage—has been retained, started school late, or has birthday within first two months of school	☐ 1 point
	• Same age range as classmates	☐ 2 points
	• Underage—has birthday one or two months prior to start date of school	☐ 3 points

Item 13: Qualifies for and/or receives free or reduced lunch **Question:** Does your child take part in the free-or-reduced lunch program at school? (Note: If this is a sensitive question to ask, check school records.)	• No assistance • Reduced lunch • Free lunch	☐ 1 point ☐ 2 points ☐ 3 points
Item 14: Child is member of dominant racial or ethnic group of campus (dominant means 50% or more of students belong to that group) **Question:** Check school records	• Member of dominant group • There is no dominant group; no group has 50% or more • Not member of dominant group	☐ 1 point ☐ 2 points ☐ 3 points
Item 15: Child is member of dominant economic group of campus **Question:** Check school records	• Member of dominant group • There is no dominant group; no group has 50% or more • Not member of dominant group	☐ 1 point ☐ 2 points ☐ 3 points
Item 16: There are general time frames for meals, TV, going to bed, taking bath, etc. **Question:** Do you have a set time that you make your child take a bath? Go to bed? Watch TV? Do homework? Etc.	• Time frames exist and are consistently followed • Time frames exist for most and are often followed • Time frames vary or are nonexistent and are inconsistently followed	☐ 1 point ☐ 2 points ☐ 3 points

Item 17: Child has spent night 50 miles or more away from home with parent or other family member **Question:** Has your child ever been 50 miles or more away from home with you or another family member and stayed overnight? If so, how many times?	• Frequently—more than once a year • Occasionally—once a year (such as family vacation) • Never	☐ 1 point ☐ 2 points ☐ 3 points
Subtotal of Section II =		

Section III: Cognitive/Language Skills	Criteria	Rating
Item 18: Significant relationships **Question:** Who is the primary caregiver of the child?	• Two or more significant relationships • At least one significant relationship • None	☐ 1 point ☐ 2 points ☐ 3 points
Item 19: Number of children's books in home **Question:** How many books does your child have that are for him/her? (Note: Books should have been purchased for him/her.)	• Two or more books per year of age • One book per year of age • Less than one book per year of age	☐ 1 point ☐ 2 points ☐ 3 points
Item 20: Presence of newspapers or magazines in home **Question:** Do you purchase newspapers or magazines on a regular basis?	• Daily newspaper and two or more magazines • Weekend newspaper or tabloid purchased on regular basis; magazines purchased at store	☐ 1 point ☐ 2 points

	• No systematic access to newspapers or magazines	☐ 3 points
Item 21: Formal register is used at home (in any language) **Question:** Observe for use of language	• Spoken and written formal register (in any language) used by all adult household members	☐ 1 point
	• Formal register spoken by all adult household members, but not written	☐ 2 points
	• Casual register used by one or more of household adults; very little writing of any kind	☐ 3 points
Item 22: Speaks language other than English **Question:** What languages are spoken in the home? (Observation)	• All adults in household speak English	☐ 1 point
	• At least one adult speaks at least one language fluently	☐ 2 points
	• Language acquisition delayed, or no dominant language; poor grammatical structures used orally	☐ 3 points
Subtotal of Section III =		
Total of Sections I, II, and III =		

At the end of each chapter on Student Production, Informant Data, and Cognitive/Language Skills, the applicable section of the EOP is completed using the scenarios about Manuel, Joe, Tiffany, and Sasha as examples.

Preponderance of Evidence

The *Preponderance of Evidence* grid is divided into four major sections. These sections represent the different types of data that are collected in the school. These are:

- **Student Production**
- **Informant Data**
- **Cognitive/Language Skills**
- **Standardized Testing Data**

The next three chapters provide an in-depth look at each of these areas and the role each plays in the identification process. Student Production, Informant Data, and Cognitive/Language Skills are first examined in the context of the school environment using portfolios, interviews, rating scales, samples of students' work, and other qualitative data.

The *Environmental Opportunities Profile* (EOP) provides information that also reflects these same areas. Included at the end of each chapter on Student Production, Informant Data, and Cognitive/Language Skills, the applicable section of the EOP is completed using the scenarios about Manuel and Joe as examples.

The following diagram shows the parallel relationship between what is measured in school against what exists within the home.

Information Related to Student Performance That Is Collected in School			
Categories →	Student Production	Informant Data	Cognitive / Language Skills
Instruments and measures →	• Portfolios • Spatial and Problem-solving abilities • Math replications • Reading replications	• Slocumb-Payne Teacher Perception Inventory • Student interview • Peer Perception Inventory	• Reading samples • Math samples • Writing samples
Factors in the Home Environment Examined to Determine the Impact of Environment on School Performance			
Categories →	Student Production	Informant Data	Cognitive / Language Skills
Instruments and measures →	• EOP: Interview of primary caregiver	• EOP: Interview of primary caregiver	• EOP: Interview of primary caregiver

The *Preponderance of Evidence* grid is used to record all the identification information the school collects. This instrument follows.

Preponderance of Evidence
Environmental Opportunities Profile
Developed by Paul D. Slocumb, Ed.D., and Ruby K. Payne, Ph.D.
©RFT Publishing Co., 1999

I. Student Production

A. Math replication

3	2	1

B. Story replication

3	2	1

C. Spatial/problem-solving

3	2	1

D. Portfolios

	3	2	1	Avg.
Critical thinking				
Creative thinking				
Total				

II. Informant Data

A. Slocumb-Payne Teacher Perception Inventory

12	8	4

B. Peer Perception Inventory

5+=12	4 = 5	3 = 6	2 = 4

II. Informant Data, continued

C. Student interview

12	8	4

III. Cognitive/Language Skills

A. Writing sample

4	3	2	1

B. Reading sample

4	3	2	1

C. Mathematics sample

4	3	2	1

SUMMARY OF DATA

	I	II	III	IV	Totals
A.					
B.					
C.					
D.		NA	NA	NA	Totals
Subtotal				NA	
EOP Points					
Totals					
Valid (Y/N)					
G/T (Y/N)					

NA = Not applicable

IV. Standardized Testing Data

A. Standardized data			
%ile	%ile	&ile	%ile
4	3	2	1

B. Academic recognition: state competency tests	
Yes = 3	No = 0

C. Mastery of all state competency subtests	
Yes = 3	No = 0

Anecdotal comments:

_____
_____
_____
_____
_____
_____
_____
_____
_____
_____
_____
_____
_____
_____
_____
_____
_____
_____
_____
_____
_____
_____
_____
_____
_____
_____
_____

Chapter Four:

Student Production

You are here.

Preponderance of Evidence
Environmental Opportunities Profile
...ped by Paul D. Slocumb, Ed.D., and Ruby K. Payne, Ph.D.
©RFT Publishing Co., 1999

I. Student Production

A. Math replication

3	2	1

B. Story replication

3	2	1

C. Spatial/problem-solving

3	2	1

D. Portfolios

	3	2	1	Avg.
Critical thinking				
Creative thinking				
Total				

II. Informant Data

A. Slocumb-Payne Teacher Perception Inventory

12	8	4

B. Peer Perception Inventory

5+=12	4 = 5	3 = 6	2 = 4

II. Informant Data, continued

C. Student interview

12	8	4

III. Cognitive/Language Skills

A. Writing sample

4	3	2	1

B. Reading sample

4	3	2	1

C. Mathematics sample

4	3	2	1

SUMMARY OF DATA

	I	II	III	IV	
A.					
B.					
C.					
D.		NA	NA	NA	Totals
Subtotal			NA		
EOP Points					
Totals					
Valid (Y/N)					
G/T (Y/N)					

NA = Not applicable

CHAPTER FOUR:

STUDENT PRODUCTION

This chapter addresses the use of work students produce and create in school as part of an identification process. These products become part of a portfolio that includes examples of the student's best work over time. This chapter provides suggested guidelines and methods that can be used in compiling student portfolios so the portfolio is an effective means of identifying gifted/talented students from poverty. The instruments included in Section I of the **Preponderance of Evidence** grid are included in the Appendix.

The chapter then focuses on the home environment where those environmental factors that enhance student production in school are identified using the **Environmental Opportunities Profile** (EOP). Manuel and Joe's personal information will be used in this and subsequent chapters to illustrate specific sections of the EOP.

Student Production in School Environment

Student Production (Garcia, 1994) is a qualitative assessment strategy for looking at a student's abilities over time. One viable and popular means of doing this is the use of a portfolio. One format for implementing portfolios was developed by Sandra Kaplan (n.d.-a) for the Texas Education Agency. Used with a target student population, for whom it was difficult to collect accurate quantitative data, school personnel saw it as a useful tool with students from diverse backgrounds. Data included in the portfolio are typically collected during a two- to four-month period, providing a sense of the student's development over time. A committee of teachers then evaluates the portfolios using criteria that focus on critical and creative thinking. Kaplan (n.d.-a) suggests that the criteria include the following:

- Unusual presentation of an idea.

- Work advanced beyond age or grade level.

- Complex or intricate presentation of an idea.

- In-depth understanding of an idea or skill.

- Resourceful and/or clever use of materials.

- Evidence of support of research for the idea.

- Work organized to communicate effectively.

- Evidence of high interest and perseverance.

Since no standardized means exist for rating the portfolios, the committee's discussion of the student's work is assessed using the norms of the campus population. Using a three-point-scaled rubric for each of the categories, committee members enter the results on the **Preponderance of Evidence** grid. The grid for this section of the **Preponderance of Evidence** form would appear as follows:

Portfolios				
	3	2	1	Average
Creative thinking				
Critical thinking				
Total				

The categories on the **Preponderance of Evidence** form in this section could be modified, depending on the categories the school or district chooses to include. The point distribution, however, must match the corresponding section on the **Environmental Opportunities Profile**. For example, if the maximum number of points that can be earned for Student Production on the EOP is 15 points, then the **Preponderance of Evidence** section for Student Production can earn only a maximum of 15 points. It's critical to give the same maximum number of points for Student Production in both school and home. This allows one to be weighed against the other to determine the degree of influence the home environment has had on school performance.

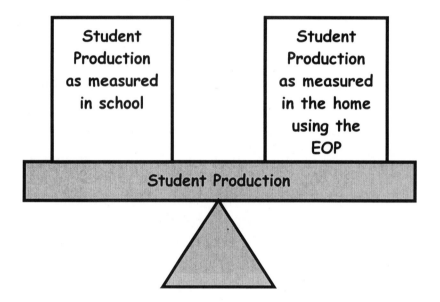

Whatever means the district chooses to collect examples of Student Production, the goal is to obtain samples of student work that demonstrate his/her performance over time. Areas that are useful are those that reflect a student's ability to problem-solve, be creative, be a critical thinker, and perform basic reading and math replications.

When properly implemented, the portfolio can be a valuable tool in the assessment of students from all populations in the identification of gifted/talented students (Johnsen, Ryser, &

Dougherty, 1993). Paulson and Paulson (1991) note that when evaluating portfolios the focus should be on what is observed about a student's ability, not whether there is rater agreement on what is observed. Because the portfolio makes limited use of language and allows the student to self-select examples of his/her best work, the probability of students from poverty emerging is greatly increased.

Gifted students tend to exhibit higher cognitive functioning at an earlier age. Because of this, another method of evaluating students' products involves what has been termed generic products (García, 1994). Using this process, students receive instruction for a particular activity prior to doing work independently. The screening and selection committee then compares the products at a given grade level or school site. The products are designed to require advanced problem-solving skills in order to show the differences among students. Modeling activities and strategies becomes an important factor for students from poverty who frequently come from backgrounds that have not modeled such learning behaviors.

García (1994) describes a lesson used in a summer-school program for gifted students from disadvantaged backgrounds. Students were required, in a limited amount of time, to make as many categories as possible using geometric shapes of different colors, sizes, and thicknesses. Another activity required students to create a figure using toothpicks and jellybeans. The finished products were then compared to those other children had created within the school environment. Ultimately, a committee ranked a student's response in comparison to his/her peers at a specific grade level and school site. This allows a local norm to evolve.

An excellent source for local districts in the construction of portfolios is **Portfolios: Enriching and Assessing All Students** (Kingore, 1993, p. 64). Planned experiences should be designed to elicit specific behaviors characteristic of gifted students. The planned experiences should create opportunities for gifted students to display the degree and dimension to which they have the following attributes:

- Unusual understanding and use of language
- Critical and creative thinking abilities
- Curiosity about ideas, events, and how things work
- Ability to see relationships and detect patterns
- Questioning attitude
- Sense of humor
- Ability to learn at a faster rate
- Empathy and sensitivity towards others

School district personnel can incorporate four to six planned experiences as part of the identification process.
These planned experiences work best when school personnel implement the activities on a regular basis, providing students enough practice to feel comfortable with the type of planned experiences being implemented. Because some teachers may not offer students opportunities to display their creative thinking abilities on a regular basis, students frequently need opportunities to practice activities in which creativity is fostered. Students who feel that all assignments have "the correct answer" may have difficulty believing that an assignment does not have a right or wrong answer to it. Giving students ample opportunities to practice more open-ended

assignments increases the probability that students will take the academic risks that are necessary to show their giftedness.

It's important to recognize that because of their limited opportunities within the environment, students from poverty may manifest gifted behaviors differently from middle-class students. Students from poverty might manifest the degree and dimension to which they have some of the above-mentioned behaviors as follows:

- **Use of language:** Vocabulary may be limited to casual register; sentence structure may lack cause-and-effect relationships; use of figurative language may reflect comparisons to people and entertainers.

- **Critical thinking:** May not possess ability to plan, but is intrigued with the idea of planning; discerns patterns in human behavior but not in ideas.

- **Curiosity:** Curious and independent; asks questions that are focused on relationships; extensive memory about people and conversations; questions things related to fairness issues.

- **Divergent thinker:** Incorporates unexpected or unusual points of view through oral language, manipulatives, and art.

- **Sense of humor**: Application of finely tuned sense of humor; creates original jokes; humor often reflects imitations of people and events; tells stories; mimics accurately.

- **Intense sensitivity**: Demonstrates a strong sense of justice as defined by poverty; fairness issues; identifies with the anti-hero, sees the anti-hero as the victim.

- **Rate of learning**: When shown how to do things that the student considers meaningful, he/she learns quickly.

The rubrics used in assessing the production of students from poverty should reflect the unique manifestations of the abilities of students from poverty.

In school systems with diverse populations, establishing and using a local norm is a key component. Because attendance zones within school systems often focus on geographical boundaries that keep the school close to the neighborhood, it's common to have more of the lower-socioeconomic students clustered together on a campus rather than distributed among multiple schools. Generational poverty tends to be concentrated in certain areas of town. Situational poverty could occur within middle-class neighborhoods because of an illness, loss of a job, or divorce. These situational conditions, however, tend to be temporary and don't greatly impact the overall composition of the school. Using a local norm at the campus level is a vital piece of the equity issue. It's analogous to allowing students in the symphonic band to compete for the first-chair position. The symphonic-band member does not compete for first-chair position with members of the concert band.

Student Production in Home Environment

Information secured from an interview of the primary caregiver that is related to Student Production includes the following:

- Number of years of schooling of the primary caregiver, particularly the mother.
- Number of years the student has been in the same school.
- Availability of health and medical benefits for the family and the child.
- Stability of income for the family.
- Special services a student may be receiving within the school, such as Special Education, 504, Title I, etc.

Each item on the EOP has criteria for rating the environmental conditions on a scale of 1 to 3. Examining a student's production within the school while keeping the student's background in mind allows the selection committee to better assess the weight of influence the home environment has had on the performance of the student.

The Student Production section of the EOP of Manuel, Joe, Krystal, and Sasha would show the following point distributions (see charts on ensuing pages).

Scenario #1: Manuel

Section I: Student Production	Criteria	Rating
Item 1: Number of years of schooling of primary caregiver, particularly mother **Question:** How many years were you in school, starting with 1st grade?	• 16+ years of schooling • 12-15 years of schooling • Less than 12 years of schooling	❏ 1 point ✓ 2 points ❏ 3 points
Item 2: Number of years at same school **Question:** How long has your child gone to this school?	• Has spent or will spend two or more years in same school • Is and/or plans to be in same school for one year • Moves during year; is unlikely to stay for entire school year	✓ 1 point ❏ 2 points ❏ 3 points
Item 3: Child/family have medical/health benefits **Question:** Does your family have medical/health benefits that include the child?	• All members are covered • Only employed parent(s) are covered • No members are covered	❏ 1 point ❏ 2 points ✓ 3 points
Item 4: Number of years in same job; stability of income **Question:** Do you and/or the other adults in the household work outside the home? How long have you/they worked there?	• One or more adults are employed and have been consistently employed for two or more years with same company or type of work • One or more adults are employed and have been for at least one year with same company or type of work • No adult is employed or has been employed for more than six months with same	✓ 1 point ❏ 2 points ❏ 3 points

	company or type of work on full-time basis	
Item 5: Identified as LD, ED, ADHD, ADD, 504, Title I, bilingual, etc. **Question:** Does your child receive any special services at school, such as with reading or math from a special teacher, in Special Education, special tutoring, etc.?	• No learning conditions identified • Identified learning problems; interventions appear effective; parents pleased with student's progress • Learning problems identified; interventions appear ineffective; parents displeased with progress	❏ 1 point ✓ 2 points ❏ 3 points
	Subtotal of Section I =	9

An Analysis of Student Production: Manuel

Manuel's home environment reflects some strengths that will help him in school. His father is a high-school graduate, and his mother attended school in Mexico, completing the highest grade level that was available to her. The parents have made a conscious effort to have their child in the current school; therefore, he is unlikely to change schools. This adds stability to Manuel's schooling. No family members have medical coverage, but the father has worked for the same company for a number of years.

Even though Manuel was in a bilingual program, he appears to be making satisfactory progress. Since the mother is attending classes to learn English, and the father speaks English, Manuel's language development will probably continue. His mother attending classes at the school to learn English, coupled with the parents' initiative to keep Manuel in the same school because of the teachers in the school, show the value they place on school and learning. Manuel would receive 9 points on the EOP in the Student Production section.

Scenario #2: Joe

Section I: Student Production	Criteria	Rating
Item 1: Number of years of schooling of primary caregiver, particularly mother **Question:** How many years were you in school, starting with 1st grade?	• 16+ years of schooling • 12-15 years of schooling • Less than 12 years of schooling	❑ 1 point ❑ 2 points ✓ 3 points
Item 2: Number of years at same school **Question:** How long has your child gone to this school?	• Has spent or will spend two or more years in same school • Is and/or plans to be in same school for one year • Moves during year; is unlikely to stay for entire school year	✓ 1 point ❑ 2 points ❑ 3 points
Item 3: Child/family have medical/health benefits **Question:** Does your family have medical/health benefits that include the child?	• All members are covered • Only employed parent(s) are covered • No members are covered	❑ 1 point ❑ 2 points ✓ 3 points
Item 4: Number of years in same job; stability of income **Question:** Do you and/or the other adults in the household work outside the home? How long have you/they worked there?	• One or more adults are employed and have been consistently employed for two or more years with same company or type of work • One or more adults are employed and have been for at least one year with same company or type of work	❑ 1 point ✓ 2 points

	• No adult is employed or has been employed for more than six months with same company or type of work on full-time basis	❑ 3 points
Item 5: Identified as LD, ED, ADHD, ADD, 504, Title I, bilingual, etc. **Question:** Does your child receive any special services at school, such as with reading or math from a special teacher, in Special Education, special tutoring, etc.?	• No learning conditions identified	❑ 1 point
	• Identified learning problems; interventions appear effective; parents pleased with student's progress	✓ 2 points
	• Learning problems identified; interventions appear ineffective; parents displeased with progress	❑ 3 points
	Subtotal of Section I =	**11**

An Analysis of Student Production: Joe

Unlike Manuel, Joe's home environment reflects greater deprivation. His mother dropped out of school, she has worked in the same job for a year and a half, and the family has no medical coverage. Joe has, however, attended the same school since 1st grade. Joe received Title I services for one year and appears to be making progress. Even though his grades have fluctuated somewhat, his performance on the state competency test indicates that he is mastering the reading and mathematics objectives. Joe would receive 11 points on the EOP in the Student Production section.

Scenario #3: Krystal

Section I: Student Production	Criteria	Rating
Item 1: Number of years of schooling of primary caregiver, particularly mother **Question:** How many years were you in school, starting with 1st grade?	• 16+ years of schooling • 12-15 years of schooling • Less than 12 years of schooling	✓ 1 point ❑ 2 points ❑ 3 points
Item 2: Number of years at same school **Question:** How long has your child gone to this school?	• Has spent or will spend two or more years in same school • Is and/or plans to be in same school for one year • Moves during year; is unlikely to stay for entire school year	✓ 1 point ❑ 2 points ❑ 3 points
Item 3: Child/family have medical/health benefits **Question:** Does your family have medical/health benefits that include the child?	• All members are covered • Only employed parent(s) are covered • No members are covered	✓ 1 point ❑ 2 points ❑ 3 points
Item 4: Number of years in same job; stability of income **Question:** Do you and/or the other adults in the household work outside the home? How long have you/they worked there?	• One or more adults are employed and have been consistently employed for two or more years with same company or type of work • One or more adults are employed and have been for at least one year with same company or type of work • No adult is employed, or has been employed for more than six months with same company or type of work on	✓ 1 point ❑ 2 points ❑ 3 points

	full-time basis	
Item 5: Identified as LD, ED, ADHD, ADD, 504, Title I, bilingual, etc. **Question**: Does your child receive any special services at school, such as with reading or math from a special teacher, in Special Education, special tutoring, etc.?	• No learning conditions identified • Identified learning problems; interventions appear effective; parents pleased with student's progress • Learning problems identified; interventions appear ineffective; parents displeased with progress	✓ 1 point ❑ 2 points ❑ 3 points
	Subtotal of Section I =	**5**

An Analysis of Student Production: Krystal

Krystal's parents are college graduates. The nanny who resides with Krystal and her brother also has a high-school diploma, plus some college. Krystal has attended the same school for the last two years. She comes from a stable family that has sufficient income and health benefits. Her parents have job stability. Krystal is not in any special programs at school. Krystal would receive 5 points on the EOP in the Student Production section.

Scenario #4: Sasha

Section I: Student Production	Criteria	Rating
Item 1: Number of years of schooling of primary caregiver, particularly mother **Question**: How many years were you in school, starting	• 16+ years of schooling • 12-15 years of schooling • Less than 12 years of schooling	❑ 1 point ✓ 2 points ❑ 3 points

with 1st grade?		
Item 2: Number of years at same school **Question:** How long has your child gone to this school?	• Has spent or will spend two or more years in same school • Is and/or plans to be in same school for one year • Moves during year; is unlikely to stay for entire school year	✓ 1 point ❑ 2 points ❑ 3 points
Item 3: Child/family have medical/health benefits **Question:** Does your family have medical/health benefits that include the child?	• All members are covered • Only employed parent(s) are covered • No members are covered	❑ 1 point ✓ 2 points ❑ 3 points
Item 4: Number of years in same job; stability of income **Question:** Do you and/or the other adults in the household work outside the home? How long have you/they worked there?	• One or more adults are employed and have been consistently employed for two or more years with same company or type of work • One or more adults are employed and have been for at least one year with same company or type of work • No adult is employed, or has been employed for more than six months with same company or type of work on full-time basis	✓ 1 point ❑ 2 points ❑ 3 points
Item 5: Identified as LD, ED, ADHD, ADD, 504, Title I, bilingual, etc. **Question:** Does your child receive any special services at school, such as with reading or math from a special teacher, in Special Education, special tutoring,	• No learning conditions identified • Identified learning problems; interventions appear effective; parents pleased with student's progress • Learning problems identified; interventions appear	✓ 1 point ❑ 2 points ❑ 3 points

etc.?	ineffective; parents displeased with progress	
	Subtotal of Section I =	**7**

An Analysis of Student Production: Sasha

Sasha has attended schools in the same district since kindergarten. Her mother is a high school graduate and has some post-high-school training. Though Sasha's father carries medical insurance on Sasha, her mother has no health benefits. If Sasha's mother were to become seriously ill, the stability of the family would be in jeopardy. Sasha has not received any special services in the school. Sasha would receive 7 points on the EOP in the Student Production section.

Students who demonstrate above-average to exceptional performance on work collected at school, while at the same time receiving a high score on the EOP in the area of Student Production, show an ability to learn in spite of enormous obstacles. This is the case with Joe. Joe's performance on the state competency test, despite his limited resources, is a remarkable achievement. It also demonstrates the powerful potential influence of schooling on the student from poverty.

The first step in hypothesizing about the possible degree to which the environment has impacted the student's performance is to look at the home. Student Production in school—as evidenced by products, portfolios, etc.—is juxtaposed against the observations of what is found in the home as revealed on the EOP. The following diagram illustrates this concept.

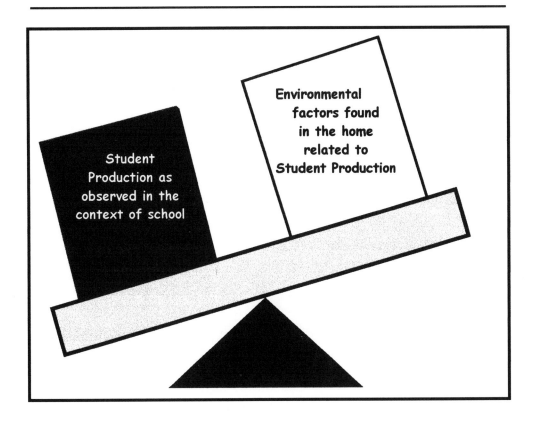

Home environmental factors are powerful influences on Student Production. School performance is typically lower because opportunities within the home do not enhance school performance.

Assessing Student Production

When assessing Student Production, remember ...

- Factors in the home environment affect Student Production at school; therefore, they must be a factor in the identification process.

- Before collecting samples of work, teachers should model the activities and strategies for students from poverty and make sure all needed materials are available.

- Members of the selection committee must examine portfolios of students from poverty in the context of how they might manifest gifted behaviors differently.

- Local campus norms should be developed as part of the assessment of student production.

Chapter Five:

Informant Data

Preponderance of Evidence
Environmental Opportunities Profile
Developed by Paul D. Slocumb, Ed.D., and Ruby K. Payne, Ph.D.
©RFT Publishing Co., 1999

I. Student Production

A. Math replication		
3	2	1

B. Story replication		
3	2	1

C. Spatial/problem-solving		
3	2	1

D. Portfolios				
	3	2	1	Avg.
Critical thinking				
Tot				

II. Informant Data

A. Slocumb-Payne Teacher Perception Inventory		
12	8	4

B. Peer Perception Inventory			
5+=12	4 = 5	3 = 6	2 = 4

II. Informant Data, continued

C. Student interview		
12	8	4

III. Cognitive/Language Skills

A. Writing sample			
4	3	2	1

B. Reading sample			
4	3	2	1

C. Mathematics sample			
4	3	2	1

SUMMARY OF DATA

	I	II	III	IV	
A.					
B.					
C.					
D.		NA	NA	NA	Totals
				NA	
EOP Points					
Totals					
Valid (Y/N)					
G/T (Y/N)					

NA = Not applicable

CHAPTER FIVE:

INFORMANT DATA

This chapter focuses on the use of Informant Data as a qualitative means of assessing student performance. Informant Data consist of eliciting valuable information from parents, peers, and teachers. This chapter looks at instruments and measures that educators may use to obtain this information at school and then, employing the EOP, looks at home environmental factors that allow school personnel to assess the degree to which the environment has impacted school. At the end of the chapter, Manuel, Joe, Krystal, and Sasha are used to illustrate the influence of the home environment on what teachers and others observe about students in school.

Informant Data in School Environment

Three instruments recommended for use in collecting Informant Data using the *Preponderance of Evidence* process are:

- **Slocumb-Payne Teacher Perception Inventory**
- **Peer Perception Inventory**
- **Student Interview**

Various methods and instruments have been developed for use with each of these groups. Specific ones are included, but school personnel may opt to use others so long as they allow for perceptions from a variety of sources.

Slocumb-Payne Teacher Perception Inventory

The most prevalent use of informant data in the identification process has been the use of teacher rating scales, specifically *Scales for Rating the Behavioral Characteristics of Superior Students* (Renzulli, Smith, White, Callahan & Hartman, 1976). Though training in the use of this instrument is essential, frequently the training does not occur because of time constraints within most educational systems. As a result, most teachers view the use of rating instruments as a means of "recommending" or "not recommending" a student for inclusion in the gifted/talented program.

Rating systems are perceptional inventories; they are not recommendation instruments. A teacher's perception of a student in an instructional context is significant. For example, a teacher's management style and types of instructional opportunities afforded students greatly contributes to his/her perception of the student. A student in a classroom that doesn't foster creative processes, unusual ideas, and original products is not likely to be perceived by his/her teacher as highly creative or particularly bright. The teacher who does most of the talking in the class, versus a teacher who allows students to do most of the talking, may not perceive a student who speaks out as highly verbal. He/she is most likely to perceive the student as one who is unable or unwilling to pay attention, follow directions, or be quiet. Such negative perceptions result in a low student rating on a teacher rating scale.

To assess more accurately a teacher's perception of a student's behavioral characteristics, a rating scale is needed that forces the teacher to look at both the positive and negative manifestations of giftedness. Many students from poverty manifest the same attributes of giftedness as advantaged students; however, their manifestations may not be recognized because they are not couched in middle-class values and norms.

Gifted Attribute: Large Storehouse of Knowledge	
Educated household	Uneducated household
A student from an educated household may have a large storehouse of knowledge about many things to which he/she has been exposed, such as ...	A student from an uneducated household may have a large storehouse of knowledge about many things to which he/she has been exposed, such as ...
• Space	• Singers

• Architecture • Politics • Art • Music • Science • Places the student has visited	• Athletes • Who has the largest collection of videos • What can or cannot be purchased with food stamps • Who can protect others in the neighborhood • Other information related to entertainment, relationships, and survival

Does the student from poverty have any less of a "storehouse of knowledge" than the student from the educated household, or is it packaged differently because of economic and cultural differences and opportunities?

Slocumb-Payne Teacher Perception Inventory, A Rating Scale for Superior Students from Diverse Backgrounds (Slocumb & Payne, 1999) is an instrument designed to help teachers look at both the positive and negative manifestations of giftedness. The instrument asks teachers to read two descriptors related to the same attribute.

One descriptor is of a gifted attribute as it might be manifested in a middle-class context. The corresponding descriptor depicts the gifted attribute as it might be manifested in a lower-socioeconomic environment—or how it might be manifested in a less positive context. The teacher selects the descriptor that most closely aligns with his/her perception of the student. He/she then rates the student on a scale of 1 to 4. Presented in this manner, a teacher's rating of students from educated and uneducated households could be numerically equal. An example of one of the descriptors from this instrument, which is included toward the end of this chapter, follows.

Perception of attributes	Seldom or never	Occasionally	Frequently	Almost always	Frequently	Occasionally	Seldom or never	Perception of attributes
1. Curious about information; inquisitive; does not accept information at first glance; questions and pushes for more information	1	2	3	4	3	2	1	1. Obnoxious with questions; likes to "stump" people with hard questions; likes questions with "shock value"; questions authority; unwilling to follow rules

Factoring both the negative and positive manifestations of giftedness increases the probability that the student from poverty will be treated equitably in the identification process.

Peer Perception Inventory

Student perceptions of other students are another valuable source of information. The *Peer Perception Inventory* (Slocumb & Payne, 1999) asks students to name classmates who would be good at finding a lost puppy, getting the computer working, finding the words to a popular song, knowing the steps to a dance, the secrets to winning at a video game, repairing a backpack, or telling an entertaining story. The 15 items reflect many of the strengths, interests, and values of students from poverty. The frequency of times a student's name appears determines the point value that is entered on the *Preponderance of Evidence* form. For example, if five of a student's classmates wrote his/her name as the person they would go to for learning the steps to a dance, or the person you would go to for help with your math, etc., the student would receive 12 points on Section II-B of the *Preponderance of Evidence* grid.

Student Interview

The Student Interview provides students themselves the opportunity to respond to different scenarios designed to elicit creative problem-solving responses. Students are rated on a scale of 1 to 3 using a rubric. Criteria are given to guide the interviewer in his/her overall assessment of each student's responses. Questions that may be used in the Student Interview also appear at the end of this chapter.

Informant Data in Home Environment

Informant Data also are collected in the context of the home using the *Environmental Opportunities Profile* (EOP). The information collected represents factors that contribute significantly to the student behaviors teachers observe in school. Questions are asked that relate to the following:

- Support system in the home; ratio of adults to children.
- Age of the child in relationship to the peer group.
- Use of color and light in the home.
- Free-and/or-reduced lunch recipient.
- Member of the dominant racial or ethnic group of the school.
- Use of the time within the home environment; structure for meals, TV viewing, etc.

For each of the questions, the primary caregiver's response receives a point value of 1 to 3 points. The total points in the Informant Data category on the EOP (36 points) coincide with the Informant Data points received on the Slocumb-Payne Teacher Perception Inventory (12 points), Peer Perception Inventory (12 points), and the Student Interview (12 points) for a total of 36 points.

Different lenses give different perspectives.

When examining Informant Data ...

- **Students from poverty manifest gifted behaviors in the context of their experiences just as middle-class students do.**

- **Teachers' perceptions of students are usually couched in middle-class values and norms.**

- **Gifted behaviors for students from poverty must be looked at from a different perspective.**

- **Perceptions evolve based on a context in which the person doing the rating works with the student. That context usually controls the perception.**

Manuel, Joe, Krystal, and Sasha

Using scenarios of Manuel, Joe, Krystal, and Sasha from Chapter Three, the Informant Data section of the EOP would show the following point distributions.

Scenario #1: Manuel

Section II: Informant Data	Criteria	Rating
Item 6: Parents born in United States **Question:** Were you and your spouse born in the United States?	• Both parents born in United States • One parent born in United States • Neither parent born in	☐ 1 point ✓ 2 points ☐ 3 points

	United States	
Item 7: Support system in home—number of adult males in the household **Question:** How many adult men live in your house?	• One or more adult males live in household, consistently and fairly constantly • One adult male on fairly permanent basis; if divorced, father exercises visitation rights regularly • No adult males in household, or males are not in household on regular basis	✓ 1 point ❑ 2 points ❑ 3 points
Item 8: Support system in home—number of adult females in the household **Question:** How many adult women live in the household?	• One or more adult females live in household, consistently and fairly constantly • One adult female on fairly permanent basis; if divorced, mother exercises visitation rights regularly • No adult females in household, or females are not in household on regular basis	✓ 1 point ❑ 2 points ❑ 3 points
Item 9: Support system in household—number of adults in the household **Question:** How many children are in the household and how many adults (ratio of children to adults)?	• Child/adult ratio is one-to-one or better • Child/adult ratio is two children to one adult • Child/adult ratio is three or more children to one adult	✓ 1 point ❑ 2 points ❑ 3 points
Item 10: Amount of light in home	• Window coverings are open during day; three or more	✓ 1 point

Question: Do you have lots of light in your house? Do you open the curtains during the day?	light fixtures and/or lamps are in major rooms in house • Window coverings partially open. Overhead light or lamp per room • Window coverings closed. One or less low-wattage light bulb is used. Light often comes from TV.	☐ 2 points ☐ 3 points
Item 11: Use of color in home décor **Question:** What colors are in your house? Describe the colors of your walls, pictures, and furniture.	• Light-colored walls with contrasting colors in drapes and furnishings • Neutral shades and décor, colors complement or blend rather than contrast • Darker décor; random use of medium-to-dark nondescript color	☐ 1 point ✓ 2 points ☐ 3 points
Item 12: Is older or younger than classmates **Question:** When was your child born? Did he/she start kindergarten when he/she was 5? Has he/she ever been retained?	• Overage—has been retained, started school late, or has birthday within first two months of school • Same age as classmates (November through May) • Underage—has birthday one or two months prior to start date of school	☐ 1 point ✓ 2 points ☐ 3 points
Item 13: Qualifies for and/or receives free or reduced lunch **Question:** Does your child take part in the free-or-reduced lunch	• No assistance • Reduced lunch • Free lunch	☐ 1 point ☐ 2 points ✓ 3 points

program at school? (Note: If this is a sensitive question to ask, check school records.)		
Item 14: Child is member of dominant racial or ethnic group of campus (dominant means 50% or more of students belong to that group) **Question:** Check school records	• Member of dominant group • There is no dominant group; no group has 50% or more • Not member of dominant group	✓ 1 point ❑ 2 points ❑ 3 points
Item 15: Child is member of dominant economic group of campus **Question:** Check school records	• Member of dominant group • There is no dominant group; no group has 50% or more • Not member of dominant group	✓ 1 point ❑ 2 points ❑ 3 points
Item 16: There are general time frames for meals, TV, going to bed, taking bath, etc. **Question:** Do you have a set time that you make your child take a bath? Go to bed? Watch TV? Do homework? Etc.	• Time frames exist and are consistently followed • Time frames exist for most things and are often followed • Time frames vary or are nonexistent and are inconsistently followed	❑ 1 point ✓ 2 points ❑ 3 points
Item 17: Child has spent a night 50 miles or more away from home with parent or other family member	• Frequently—more than once a year • Occasionally—once a year (such as family vacation)	❑ 1 point ✓ 2 points

Question: Has your child ever been 50 miles or more away from home with you or another family member and stayed overnight? If so, how many times?	• Never	❏ 3 points
	Subtotal of Section II =	19

An Analysis of Informant Data: Manuel

Manuel's father was born in the United States; his mother was born in Mexico. Both of his parents live with him. Manuel has the benefit of having both an adult female and adult male as role models. With only two children in household, there is a one-to-one ratio of adults to children in the home. This allows for more attention from adults than in households where there are more children than adults. The drapes are usually open during the day and there is sufficient lighting in the home. The home is decorated in neutral tones. Manuel has a May 31st birth date, making him in the age range with his classmates. He is on free lunch. The dominant groups in the school are Hispanic and students who participate in the school's free-lunch program. Manuel belongs to both of these groups. Though time frames exist within the home for watching television, eating, and going to bed, the schedules are not followed consistently. Manuel takes trips to Mexico with his family at least once a year to visit relatives. Manuel's EOP points are 19 out of a possible 36.

Scenario #2: Joe

Section II: Informant Data	Criteria	Rating
Item 6: Parents born in United States **Question:** Were you and your spouse born in the United States?	• Both parents born in United States • One parent born in United States • Neither parent born in United States	✓ 1 point ❑ 2 points ❑ 3 points
Item 7: Support system in home—number of adult males in household **Question:** How many adult men live in your house?	• One or more adult males live in household, consistently and fairly constantly • One adult male on fairly permanent basis; if divorced, father exercises visitation rights regularly • No adult males in household, or males are not in household on regular basis	❑ 1 point ❑ 2 points ✓ 3 points
Item 8: Support system in home—number of adult females in household **Question:** How many adult women live in household?	• One or more adult females live in household, consistently and fairly constantly • One adult female on fairly permanent basis; if divorced, mother exercises visitation rights regularly • No adult females in household, or females are not in household on regular basis	✓ 1 point ❑ 2 points ❑ 3 points

Item 9: Support system in household—number of adults in the household **Question:** How many children are in the household and how many adults (ratio of children to adults)?	• Child/adult ratio is one-to-one or better • Child/adult ratio is two children to one adult • Child/adult ratio is three or more children to one adult	❑ 1 point ❑ 2 points ✓ 3 points
Item 10: Amount of light in home **Question:** Do you have lots of light in your house? Do you open curtains during the day?	• Window coverings are open during day; three or more light fixtures and/or lamps are in major rooms in house • Window coverings partially open; overhead light or lamp per room • Window coverings closed; one or less low-wattage light bulb is used; light often comes from TV	❑ 1 point ❑ 2 points ✓ 3 points
Item 11: Use of color in home décor **Question:** What colors are in your house? Describe the colors of your walls, pictures, and furniture.	• Light-colored walls with contrasting colors in drapes and furnishings • Neutral shades and décor, colors complement or blend rather than contrast • Darker décor; random use of medium-to-dark nondescript color	❑ 1 point ❑ 2 points ✓ 3 points
Item 12: Is older or younger than classmates **Question:** When was your child born? Did	• Overage—has been retained, started school late, or has birthday within	❑ 1 point

he/she start kindergarten when he/she was 5? Has he/she ever been retained?	first two months of school • Same age as classmates (November through May) • Underage—has birthday one or two months prior to start of school	❏ 2 points ✓ 3 points
Item 13: Qualifies for and/or receives free or reduced lunch **Question:** Does your child take part in the free-or-reduced lunch program at school? (Note: If this is a sensitive question to ask, check school records.)	• No assistance • Reduced lunch • Free lunch	❏ 1 point ❏ 2 points ✓ 3 points
Item 14: Child is member of dominant racial or ethnic group of campus (dominant means 50% or more of students belong to that group) **Question:** Check school records	• Member of dominant group • There is no dominant group; no group has 50% or more • Not member of dominant group	❏ 1 point ❏ 2 points ✓ 3 points
Item 15: Child is member of dominant economic group of campus **Question:** Check school records	• Member of dominant group • There is no dominant group; no group has 50% or more • Not member of dominant group	✓ 1 point ❏ 2 points ❏ 3 points
Item 16: There are general time frames for meals, TV, going to bed, taking bath, etc.	• Time frames exist and are consistently followed • Time frames exist for most	❏ 1 point ❏ 2 points

Question: Do you have a set time that you make your child take a bath? Go to bed? Watch TV? Do homework? Etc.	things and are often followed • Time frames vary or are nonexistent and are inconsistently followed	✓ 3 points
Item 17: Child has spent a night 50 miles or more away from home with parent or other family member Question: Has your child ever been 50 miles or more away from home with you or another family member and stayed overnight? If so, how many times?	• Frequently—more than once per year • Occasionally—once per year (such as family vacation) • Never	❑ 1 point ❑ 2 points ✓ 3 points
	Subtotal of Section II =	30

An Analysis of Informant Data: Joe

Joe lives with his mother who was born in the United States. His father was born in the United States, but Joe's father is really not part of his life. Joe doesn't have the benefit of any male role models. The adult/child ratio is one adult to five children. The apartment in which Joe lives is done in shades of brown, and the window coverings are usually drawn to save electricity. Lighting in the apartment is limited. Joe was born in July, making him younger than most students in his grade. The dominant group in the school is African-American. Joe is Anglo; therefore, he is not a member of the dominant racial or ethnic group. He is, however, one of the 85 percent who participates in the free-lunch program, making him a member of the dominant economic group in the school. Joe is allowed to stay up late, and the family doesn't have an established routine for eating, watching television, or going to bed. Joe has never been 50 miles away from home to spend the night. Joe's EOP points are 30 out of a possible 36.

Scenario #3: Krystal

Section II: Informant Data	Criteria	Rating
Item 6: Parents born in United States **Question:** Were you and your spouse born in the United States?	• Both parents born in United States • One parent born in United States • Neither parent born in United States	✓ 1 point ❑ 2 points ❑ 3 points
Item 7: Support system in home—number of adult males in household **Question:** How many adult men live in your house?	• One or more adult males live in household, consistently and fairly constantly • One adult male on fairly permanent basis; if divorced, father exercises visitation rights regularly • No adult males in household, or males are not in household on regular basis	✓ 1 point ❑ 2 points ❑ 3 points
Item 8: Support system in home—number of adult females in household **Question:** How many adult women live in the household?	• One or more adult females live in household, consistently and fairly constantly • One adult female on fairly permanent basis; if	✓ 1 point ❑ 2 points

	divorced, mother exercises visitation rights regularly.	❏ 3 points
	• No adult females in household, or females are not in household on regular basis	
Item 9: Support system in household—number of adults in the household **Question:** How many children are in the household and how many adults (ratio of children to adults)?	• Child/adult ratio is one-to-one or better	✓ 1 point
	• Child/adult ratio is two children to one adult	❏ 2 points
	• Child/adult ratio is three or more children to one adult	❏ 3 points
Item 10: Amount of light in home **Question:** Do you have lots of light in your house? Do you open curtains during the day?	• Window coverings are open during day; three or more light fixtures and/or lamps are in major rooms in house	✓1 point
	• Window coverings partially open; overhead light or lamp per room	❏ 2 points
	• Window coverings closed; one or less low-wattage light bulb is used; light often comes from TV	❏ 3 points
Item 11: Use of color in home décor **Question:** What colors are in your house? Describe the colors of your walls, pictures, and furniture.	• Light-colored walls with contrasting colors in drapes and furnishings	✓ 1 point
	• Neutral shades and décor, colors complement or blend rather than contrast	❏ 2 points
	• Darker décor; random use of medium-to-dark nondescript color	❏ 3 points

Item 12: Is older or younger than classmates **Question:** When was your child born? Did he/she start kindergarten when he/she was 5? Has he/she ever been retained?	• Overage—has been retained, started school late, or has birthday within first two months of school • Same age as classmates (November through May) • Underage—has birthday one or two months prior to start of school	✓ 1 point ❑ 2 points ❑ 3 points
Item 13: Qualifies for and/or receives free or reduced lunch **Question:** Does your child participate in free-or-reduced lunch program at school? (Note: If this is a sensitive question to ask, check school records.)	• No assistance • Reduced lunch • Free lunch	✓ 1 point ❑ 2 points ❑ 3 points
Item 14: Child is member of dominant racial or ethnic group of campus (dominant means 50% or more of students belong to that group) **Question:** Check school records	• Member of dominant group • There is no dominant group; no group has 50% or more • Not member of dominant group	❑ 1 point ❑ 2 points ✓ 3 points
Item 15: Child is member of dominant economic group of campus **Question:** Check school records	• Member of dominant group • There is no dominant group; no group has 50% or more • Not member of dominant group	✓ 1 point ❑ 2 points ❑ 3 points

Item 16: There are general time frames for meals, TV, going to bed, taking bath, etc. Question: Do you have a set time that you make your child take a bath? Go to bed? Watch TV? Do homework? Etc.	• Time frames exist and are consistently followed • Time frames exist for most things and are often followed • Time frames vary or are nonexistent and are inconsistently followed	✓ 1 point ❑ 2 points ❑ 3 points
Item 17: Child has spent a night 50 miles or more away from home with parent or other family member Question: Has your child ever been 50 miles or more away from home with you or another family member and stayed overnight? If so, how many times?	• Frequently—more than once a year • Occasionally—once a year (such as family vacation) • Never	✓ 1 point ❑ 2 points ❑ 3 points
	Subtotal of Section II =	**14**

An Analysis of Informant Data: Krystal

Krystal's parents were born in the United States. Both parents and a nanny reside in the home. Krystal has supporting adults in her life. She lives in a spacious home that is nicely decorated. She is within the average age range of her classmates. She does not receive free lunch. Since very few students in her school receive free lunch, she is a member of the dominant economic group of the school. Her school has a 15 percent

African-American population; therefore, Krystal is not a member of the dominant racial group at her school. Krystal's EOP points are 14 out of a possible 36.

Scenario #4: Sasha

Section II: Informant Data	Criteria	Rating
Item 6: Parents born in United States **Question:** Were you and your spouse born in the United States?	• Both parents born in United States • One parent born in United States • Neither parent born in United States	✓ 1 point ❑ 2 points ❑ 3 points
Item 7: Support system in home—number of adult males in household **Question:** How many adult men live in your house?	• One or more adult males live in household, consistently and fairly constantly • One adult male on fairly permanent basis; if divorced, father exercises visitation rights regularly • No adult males in household, or males are not in household on regular basis	❑ 1 point ✓ 2 points ❑ 3 points
Item 8: Support system in home—number of adult females in household **Question:** How many adult women live in the household?	• One or more adult females live in household, consistently and fairly constantly • One adult female on fairly permanent basis; if divorced, mother exercises visitation rights regularly	✓ 1 point ❑ 2 points

	• No adult females in household, or females are not in household on regular basis	❏ 3 points
Item 9: Support system in household—number of adults in the household **Question:** How many children are in the household and how many adults (ratio of children to adults)?	• Child/adult ratio is one-to-one or better • Child/adult ratio is two children to one adult • Child/adult ratio is three or more children to one adult	✓ 1 point ❏ 2 points ❏ 3 points
Item 10: Amount of light in home **Question:** Do you have lots of light in your house? Do you open curtains during the day?	• Window coverings are open during day; three or more light fixtures and/or lamps are in major rooms in house • Window coverings partially open; overhead light or lamp per room • Window coverings closed; one or less low-wattage light bulb is used; light often comes from TV	✓1 point ❏ 2 points ❏ 3 points
Item 11: Use of color in home décor **Question:** What colors are in your house? Describe the colors of your walls, pictures, and furniture.	• Light-colored walls with contrasting colors in drapes and furnishings • Neutral shades and décor, colors complement or blend rather than contrast • Darker décor; random use of medium-to-dark nondescript color	✓ 1 point ❏ 2 points ❏ 3 points

Item 12: Is older or younger than classmates **Question:** When was your child born? Did he/she start kindergarten when he/she was 5? Has he/she ever been retained?	• Overage—has been retained, started school late, or has birthday within first two months of school • Same age as classmates (November through May) • Underage—has birthday one or two months prior to start date of school	✓1 point ❑ 2 points ❑ 3 points
Item 13: Qualifies for and/or receives free or reduced lunch **Question:** Does your child take part in the free-or-reduced lunch program at school? (Note: If this is a sensitive question to ask, check school records.)	• No assistance • Reduced lunch • Free lunch	✓ 1 point ❑ 2 points ❑ 3 points
Item 14: Child is member of dominant racial or ethnic group of campus (dominant means 50% or more of students belong to that group) **Question:** Check school records	• Member of dominant group • There is no dominant group; no group has 50% or more • Not member of dominant group	❑ 1 point ❑ 2 points ✓ 3 points
Item 15: Child is member of dominant economic group of campus **Question:** Check school records	• Member of dominant group • There is no dominant group; no group has 50% or more • Not member of dominant group	❑ 1 point ❑ 2 points ✓ 3 points

Item 16: There are general time frames for meals, TV, going to bed, taking bath, etc. Question: Do you have a set time that you make your child take a bath? Go to bed? Watch TV? Do homework? Etc.	• Time frames exist and are consistently followed • Time frames exist for most things and are often followed • Time frames vary or are nonexistent and are inconsistently followed	❑ 1 point ✓ 2 points ❑ 3 points
Item 17: Child has spent a night 50 miles or more away from home with parent or other family member Question: Has your child ever been 50 miles or more away from home with you or another family member and stayed overnight? If so, how many times?	• Frequently—more than once a year • Occasionally—once a year (such as family vacation) • Never	❑ 1 point ✓ 2 points ❑ 3 points
	Subtotal of Section II =	19

An Analysis of Informant Data: Sasha

Sasha's parents were born in the United States. Though her father doesn't live with her, Sasha sees him on a regular basis. The child/adult ratio is one-to-one. Sasha's home is nicely decorated, and the space is sufficient for two people. She has a September birth date, making her older than her classmates. She doesn't receive free lunch; however, the majority of the students at her school are on free lunch. As a result, Sasha is not a member of the dominant economic group of the school. She also is not a member of the dominant racial group of the school. Though her mother is gone many nights because of her work, she does call and check on Sasha and remind her of her homework. Sasha, however, is left to set her own schedule. Sasha doesn't spend the night away from home very much, but she does travel to see her grandmother once a year. Sasha's EOP points are 19 out of a possible 36.

A Comparison of Manuel, Joe, Krystal, and Sasha

Of the four students, Joe's deprivation is greatest. He lives in a smaller environment with fewer resources than Manuel, Krystal, and Sasha. Manuel has the advantage of having adults in his life on a daily basis. Though Manuel's and Sasha's home routines are not consistently followed, they are nevertheless more predictable than are Joe's. Being one of five children with one adult earning less than $15,000 a year makes Joe's life very unpredictable. Though Manuel doesn't have access to more money than Joe does, the number of people who are dependent on that income is less. Manuel and Krystal both have a father who has been consistently employed. Krystal, Joe, and Sasha have parents who are purchasing a home. That economic factor adds stability and predictability to their lives.

Of the four, Krystal has the greatest opportunities within the home. Her family vacations twice a year, and she attends a summer camp. Sasha and Manuel do have stable lives; however, Manuel has a greater support system than Sasha does. Manuel has a mother who stays at home. Sasha is left on her own while her mother works.

Joe is not so fortunate. The EOP points for Manuel, Joe, Krystal, and Sasha reflect the opportunities that exist within their individual home environments. Manuel and Sasha have loving and caring parents who are employed. Their life, however, can change drastically if anything happens to their primary caregiver. With no medical coverage, one major illness could put the family in a situational condition of poverty. Of the four students, Joe is in the greatest need with the fewest resources within the home.

Slocumb-Payne Teacher Perception Inventory
A Scale for Rating Superior Students from Diverse Backgrounds

Developed by Paul D. Slocumb, Ed.D., and Ruby K. Payne, Ph.D.
©RFT Publishing Co., 1999

Student's name_____ Date_____

School_____Grade_____Age_____

Teacher/person completing this form_____

How long have you known this student? _____years _____months

Directions: This scale is designed to obtain a teacher's perception of a student's characteristics as a potentially gifted/talented student. This is not a recommendation form; it is a perception of a student within the context of a classroom or school. Since each classroom is as unique as the teacher conducting that classroom, one teacher's perception of a student may vary considerably from that of another.

The items are derived from the research literature dealing with characteristics of gifted and creative persons. A considerable number of individual differences can be found within any student population; therefore, the profiles are likely to vary a great deal. There is no right answer to any question.

Each descriptor item in each row should be read from the left and from the right, and then circle the applicable number that best describes your perception of the student as he/she relates to that descriptor. **You are to circle only one number in each row.** Each descriptor is designed to be "two sides of same coin." Persons completing this instrument may find it helpful to first read the descriptor on the left, then the one on the right, and then place a check mark beside the descriptor that best aligns with your perception of the student under consideration. Then, using that descriptor, circle the number that most closely describes your perception of the student in relation to the descriptor.

One descriptor item per row (either the one on the left or the right) is to be rated as follows:

- 1 = Seldom or never
- 2 = Occasionally
- 3 = Frequently
- 4 = Almost always

Slocumb-Payne Teacher Perception Inventory
A Scale for Rating Superior Students from Diverse Backgrounds
Developed by Paul D. Slocumb, Ed.D., and Ruby K. Payne, Ph.D.
©RFT Publishing Co., 1999

Perception of attributes	Seldom or never	Occasionally	Frequently	Almost always	Frequently	Occasionally	Seldom or never	Perception of attributes
1. Curious about information; inquisitive; doesn't accept information at first glance; questions and pushes for more information	1	2	3	4	3	2	1	1. Obnoxious with questions; likes to "stump" people with hard questions; enjoys questions with "shock value"; questions authority; unwilling to follow rules
2. Stubborn; avoids tending to other things that need to be done just because he/she is not through with his/her priority	1	2	3	4	3	2	1	2. Sticks to task; gets job done; doesn't give up easily even when things are difficult
3. Finds it hard to wait for others; unwilling to do detail work; shows reluctance to do some assignments because he/she already "knows" content or skill	1	2	3	4	3	2	1	3. Learns at faster rate than his/her peer group; absorbs more with less practice; able to accelerate his/her learning; displays eagerness to do work
4. Understands subtleties of language in his/her primary language; uses language in powerful way; displays unique sense of humor; able to use language to build personal relationships	1	2	3	4	3	2	1	4. "Smart mouth"; master at put-downs of others; uses humor in destructive manner; unable to relate to peers because his/her sense of humor isn't as sophisticated; class clown

5. Thirsts for knowledge; seeks answers to questions; motivated to do research to find answers to questions; likes rhetorical questions; curious about ideas	1	2	3	4	3	2	1	5. Shows little interest in what is to be learned; wants to pursue only those things that spark his/her curiosity; is more curious about people than events
6. Has difficulty completing tasks; unaware of deadlines; oblivious to those around him/her; very focused on and committed to his/her priorities	1	2	3	4	3	2	1	6. Commits to long-range projects and tasks; focused; goal-oriented; strives to meet high standards
7. Loves ambiguity and dislikes being given specific directions and/or parameters; unable to be specific with other people who need specific direction; comes across as highly creative/inventive	1	2	3	4	3	2	1	7. Able and willing to ascertain and solve problems; does not need specific directions; may set own goals that surpass teacher's expectations
8. Deeply interested in many things; is good at many things; loves to learn new things	1	2	3	4	3	2	1	8. Unable to make decisions—or makes decisions quickly without regard for consequences; may hop from one thing to another without experiencing closure in anything; appears random
9. Develops high standards and expectations of self; self-starter who needs little supervision; has self-control	1	2	3	4	3	2	1	9. Perfectionist; nothing is ever good enough; can't finish something because it still isn't correct; may display low self-image about academic performance

10. Has trouble listening while others talk; interrupts others to point of rudeness; talks at inappropriate times; may be reluctant to write; very expressive in casual register	1	2	3	4	3	2	1	10. Excellent facility with language; can elaborate on thoughts and ideas; uses formal register when communicating with others
11. Highly developed social conscience; concern for social issues and problems; awareness of global issues; has internal locus of control	1	2	3	4	3	2	1	11. Overconcern for social problems and issues to extent that depression results; doomsday view of life; overwhelmed with despair in world/community; sees self as victim
12. Able to comprehend complex ideas and thoughts; able to learn advanced and more complex content	1	2	3	4	3	2	1	12. Out of touch with reality, day-to-day routines; bored by simpler things in life; unwilling or unable to abide by basic requirements and/or rules
13. Unwilling to learn facts to support generalizations; can be great "talker" but is unable to produce because work lacks substance	1	2	3	4	3	2	1	13. Sees patterns in things; can transfer learning to new situations; sees big picture; discovers new information; supports generalizations with facts/details
14. Makes connections; sees relationships between/among diverse ideas and events	1	2	3	4	3	2	1	14. Difficult to stay focused because of random thoughts/ideas; highly creative but perceived as "weird" by peers
15. Shows clever, unique responses to questions and problems; often responds with humor or offers "silly" response to questions	1	2	3	4	3	2	1	15. Generates large number of ideas or solutions to problems and questions; often offers unusual, unique, clever responses

16. Appreciates color; likes to doodle and draw; has affinity for graffiti	1	2	3	4	3	2	1	16. Sensitive to beauty; tunes in to aesthetic characteristics of things
17. Uninhibited in expressions of opinion; sometimes radical and spirited in disagreement; tenacious	1	2	3	4	3	2	1	17. Uninhibited in expressions of opinion; sometimes appears radical and disagreeable; may show anger when disagreeing with others
18. High risk-taker in academic endeavors; adventurous and speculative in his/her thinking	1	2	3	4	3	2	1	18. Risk-taker; dares to break rules and then challenges authority when caught; unafraid to challenge others
19. Criticizes openly; unwilling to accept authoritarian rules and procedures; orally and openly condemns them; may irritate others	1	2	3	4	3	2	1	19. Criticizes constructively in socially acceptable manner; unwilling to accept authoritarian pronouncements without critical examinations
Add each column; enter totals here								
Sum total of all 7 columns								

Student Interview
Developed by Paul D. Slocumb, Ed.D., and Ruby K. Payne, Ph.D.
©RFT Publishing Co., 1999

Student_____ D.O.B. _____Grade level__

Teacher_____ School_____

Interviewer_____ Date of interview_____

OVERALL RATING: 1   2   3

1. One day when you arrive at school, you discover that your teacher
   is ill and will be out of school for the remainder of the school
   year. Your new substitute teacher enters the room. Much to your
   surprise, your new teacher is a robot. Your robot teacher says
   that she can do many things that your regular teacher couldn't do.
   How would you like your robot teacher to be different from your
   regular teacher? What would you like your robot teacher to do
   that your regular teacher does not do? (Listen for connection to
   technology, sense of fairness, magic, personification, humor.
   Push the student to elaborate his/her answers.)

2. You turn the television on and there is a movie on. The movie is
   about you. Tell me what you think is happening in that movie about
   you. It's your movie; you can make it do anything you want. (Push
   for a plot to be revealed. Does his/her story have other
   people, things, or ideas out of the ordinary?)

3. If you could fix one thing in your neighborhood, what would you
   fix and how would you go about fixing it? (Listen for scope and
   abstraction. With older and/or more affluent children,
   substitute town, state, United States, or world for
   neighborhood.)

4. Would you consider yourself an "expert" on a subject that is not taught in school? Why are you an "expert" in this? How did you become an expert? **(If students do not understand what an expert is, explain it to them. Ask probing questions if the student can't think of anything (example: "What is something your friends always ask you to do because they know you can do it better than anyone else?").**

5. What is the easiest way for you to learn something new? **(Push for an elaboration of a method or rate of learning.)**

6. Have you ever been bored? Tell me about what happens when you get bored. How do you handle it? **(Listen for creative ways in which he/she handles boredom. Listen for problem-solving strategies.)**

7. You just won a new television set. This TV is different from some others. You can schedule the shows you want to watch between 7 and 8 o'clock each night without using a VCR. You also can make them last 15 minutes, 30 minutes, 45 minutes, or one hour in length without commercials. Which shows would you want to watch during that hour on Monday night? What about on Tuesday night? Wednesday night? Etc. **(If the student names the same shows for several days, stop the questioning. Listen for a theme as to the types of shows the student is selecting. Ask the student if he/she would always watch them in the same order.)**

8. What do you think being gifted means? Can you give me the names of at least two people whom you believe to be gifted? These can be people you know, people you have read about, or even people who are not alive anymore. Describe for me why you think they are gifted. **(If the student doesn't have a personal definition of gifted, talk about gifted people as those who**

have some exceptional abilities. You can use fairy tales or fictional characters as examples.)

9. Your two best friends are having a problem. They are mad at each other. You like them both and want the three of you to play like you used to. How would you go about getting your two best friends to stop being mad at each other and be best friends again? **(Listen for problem-solving strategies. Ask other questions that will cause the student to speculate on possible strategies he/she might use. Example: "Well, what if that didn't work? What would you try next?")**

10. If you could invent one thing that would help another person, what would you invent and why? **(Listen for a creative response that shows an awareness of others and their needs. The student could refer to a group rather than an individual.)**

Remember ...

In conducting the student interview, make it as conversational as possible.

- Set the student at ease by asking questions about him/her and his/her family.

- Try to get the student to elaborate on his/her answers.

- Probe for more. Ask clarifying questions.

Peer Nomination
(Elementary)

NOTE: The Peer Nomination process works best in a classroom that is heterogeneously grouped. Students who are grouped homogeneously (no matter how low the students appear academically) will perceive some of the other students in the class as their best resource when answering the questions. Campuses that practice such grouping configurations will probably have a larger percentage of students from poverty included in those classes. For this reason, students in these classrooms should still have the opportunity to nominate their peers.

For younger children, a grid that includes the names of the students across the top with the questions down the left side of the grid works best. This allows younger children to put an X in a box without them struggling with the spelling the other students' names.

Think about the other students in your class. Who would you go ask if ...

1.   You wanted the best ideas about how to find a lost puppy?

2.   You wanted to get the computer working?

3.   You needed advice about a friend?

4.   You needed all the words to a popular song?

5.   You needed to know the steps to a dance?

6.   You didn't have lunch money?

7.   You needed to know what happened on the last three episodes of a TV show?

8.   You needed help with your math?

9.   You needed a good drawing?

10.   You needed someone who could help you win an argument with someone else?

11.   You needed the secrets to winning a video game?

12.   You needed your backpack fixed?

13.   You needed a personal problem explained to the teacher?

14.   You wanted to hear a good story?

15.   You wanted someone to make you laugh?

Chapter Six:

Cognitive/Language Skills

Preponderance of Evidence
Environmental Opportunities Profile
Developed by Paul D. Slocumb, Ed.D., and Ruby K. Payne, Ph.D.
©RFT Publishing Co., 1999

I. Student Production

A. Math replication

3	2	1

B. Story replication

3	2	1

C. Spatial/problem-solving

3	2	1

D. Portfolios

	3	2	1	Avg.
Critical thinking				
Creative thinking				
Total				

II. Informant Data

A. Slocumb-Payne Teacher Perception Inventory

12	8	4

B. Peer Perception Inventory

5+=12	4 = 5	3 = 6	2 = 4

II. Informant Data, continued

You are here.

D. Student interview

	8	4

III. Cognitive/Language Skills

A. Writing sample

4	3	2	1

B. Reading sample

4	3	2	1

C. Mathematics sample

4	3	2	1

SUMMARY OF DATA

	I	II	III	IV	
A.					
B.					
C.					
D.		NA	NA	NA	Totals
				NA	
EOP Points					
Totals					
Valid (Y/N)					
G/T (Y/N)					

NA = Not applicable

CHAPTER SIX:

COGNITIVE/LANGUAGE SKILLS

Language strongly influences one's perception of another's abilities. The more formal the language, the more articulate and larger the vocabulary, the brighter the person is perceived to be. Students from educated households have usually had an exposure to language that has expanded their vocabulary and has taught them formal register by example (Montano-Harmon, 1991; Payne, 1998). For students from uneducated households, the opportunities for an extended vocabulary are greatly diminished, and the spoken vocabulary to which the student is exposed is more frequently in casual register. This chapter looks at the cognitive and language skills of students from poverty. This chapter also explores the significance that standardized testing has for students from poverty. Factors within the home environment also are examined as they contribute to the performance of students in cognitive and language skill development in school.

In assessing a student's performance in the cognitive/language category, educators may gather a sample of a student's abilities in the areas of reading, writing, and mathematics. Teachers can use a rubric that outlines expected proficiencies in order to assess students' performance in the areas of writing, reading, and mathematics. Categories that may be useful in measuring each of these appear in the subsequent chart.

Cognitive/Language Skills		
Reading	**Writing**	**Mathematics**
• Fluency • Constructive use of language • Motivation to read • Applications of reading strategies to get meaning from print	• Organization and structure • Language control • Support and elaboration • Staying focused on topic	• Conceptualizing mathematical problems and solutions • Logical reasoning • Cause-and-effect relationships

The *Environmental Opportunities Profile* (EOP) also examines the support base within the home environment that fosters the development of cognitive and language abilities. Areas addressed include:

- Number of significant relationships within the home.

- Number of children's books available.

- Presence of newspapers and magazines.

- Use of formal and casual register.

- Language spoken in the home.

Students who lack resources within the home environment receive more points on the EOP than do those who have the resources. This allows those who are charged with selecting the gifted/talented students to assess the measured performance within the school in the context of the opportunities that exist within the home environment. The question is: "Have the opportunities within the home environment enhanced or limited the student's performance in school?"

An examination of the home environments of Manuel, Joe, Krystal, and Sasha shows this impact. The EOP for these four students on the Cognitive/Language Skills section follows.

Scenario #1: Manuel

Section III: Cognitive/Language Skills	Criteria	Rating
Item 18: Significant relationships **Question:** Who is the primary caregiver of the child?	• Two or more significant relationships • At least one significant relationship • None	✓ 1 point ❑ 2 points ❑ 3 points
Item 19: Number of children's books in home **Question:** How many books does your child have that are for him/her? (Note: Books should have been purchased for him/her.)	• Two or more books per year of age • One book per year of age • Less than one book per year of age	❑ 1 point ❑ 2 points ✓ 3 points
Item 20: Presence of newspapers or magazines in home **Question:** Do you purchase newspapers or magazines on a regular basis?	• Daily newspaper and two or more magazines • Weekend newspaper or tabloid purchased on regular basis; magazines purchased at store • No systematic access to newspapers or magazines	❑ 1 point ❑ 2 points ✓ 3 points
Item 21: Formal register is used at home (in any language) **Question:** Observe for use of language	• Spoken and written formal register (in any language) used by all adult household members • Formal register spoken by all adult household members, but not written • Casual register used by one or more of household	✓ 1 point ❑ 2 points ❑ 3 points

	adults; very little writing of any kind	
Item 22: Speaks language other than English **Question:** What languages are spoken in the home? (Observation)	• All adults in household speak English • At least one adult speaks at least one language fluently • Language acquisition delayed, or no dominant language; poor grammatical structures used orally	❑ 1 point ✓ 2 points ❑ 3 points
	Subtotal of Section III =	10

An Analysis of Cognitive/Language Skills: Manuel

Manuel's greatest resource is the presence of both a mother and father in the household. The books he has in the home belong to the school; therefore, he has not grown up surrounded by written language. Just about the only time a newspaper is purchased is to access coupons. His father speaks and writes English and uses formal register when speaking to others. His mother, though she is in the process of learning English, speaks and writes Spanish. Out of a maximum of 15 points, Manuel received 10 in the Cognitive/Language section of the EOP.

Scenario #2:   Joe

Section III: Cognitive/Language Skills	Criteria	Rating
Item 18: Significant relationships	• Two or more significant relationships	❑ 1 point

Question: Who is the primary caregiver of the child?	• At least one significant relationship • None	✓ 2 points ❏ 3 points
Item 19: Number of children's books in home **Question:** How many books does your child have that are for him/her? (Note: Books should have been purchased for him/her.)	• Two or more books per year of age • One book per year of age • Less than one book per year of age	❏ 1 point ❏ 2 points ✓ 3 points
Item 20: Presence of newspapers or magazines in home **Question:** Do you purchase newspapers or magazines on a regular basis?	• Daily newspaper and two or more magazines • Weekend newspaper or tabloid purchased on regular basis; magazines purchased at store • No systematic access to newspapers or magazines	❏ 1 point ❏ 2 points ✓ 3 points
Item 21: Formal register is used at home (in any language) **Question:** Observe for use of language	• Spoken and written formal register (in any language) used by all adult household members • Formal register spoken by all adult household members, but not written • Casual register used by one or more of household adults; very little writing of any kind	❏ 1 point ❏ 2 points ✓ 3 points
Item 22: Speaks language other than English **Question:** What languages	• All adults in household speak English	✓ 1 point ❏ 2 points

are spoken in the home? (Observation)	• At least one adult speaks at least one language fluently • Language acquisition delayed, or no dominant language; poor grammatical structures used orally	❑ 3 points
	Subtotal of Section III =	**12**

An Analysis of Cognitive/Language Skills: Joe

The only significant adult in Joe's life is his mother. Money is not spent on books. The only books to which Joe has access are his textbooks and those from the school library. The family doesn't subscribe to any newspapers or magazines. His mother doesn't communicate in formal register as evidenced by her saying, "He don't get in no trouble." Only English is spoken in Joe's home. Out of a maximum of 15 points, Joe received 12 points in the Cognitive/Language section of the EOP.

Scenario #3: Krystal

Section III: Cognitive/Language Skills	Criteria	Rating
Item 18: Significant relationships **Question:** Who is the primary caregiver of the child?	• Two or more significant relationships • At least one significant relationship • None	✓ 1 point ❑ 2 points ❑ 3 points
Item 19: Number of children's books in home	• Two or more books per year of age	✓ 1 point

Question: How many books does your child have that are for him/her? (Note: Books should have been purchased for him/her.)	• One book per year of age • Less than one book per year of age	❑ 2 points ❑ 3 points
Item 20: Presence of newspapers or magazines in home **Question:** Do you purchase newspapers or magazines on a regular basis?	• Daily newspaper and two or more magazines • Weekend newspaper or tabloid purchased on regular basis; magazines purchased at store • No systematic access to newspapers or magazines	✓ 1 point ❑ 2 points ❑ 3 points
Item 21: Formal register is used at home (in any language) **Question:** Observe for use of language	• Spoken and written formal register (in any language) used by all adult household members • Formal register spoken by all adult household members, but not written • Casual register used by one or more of household adults; very little writing of any kind	✓ 1 point ❑ 2 points ❑ 3 points
Item 22: Speaks language other than English **Question:** What languages are spoken in the home? (Observation)	• All adults in household speak English • At least one adult speaks at least one language fluently • Language acquisition delayed, or no dominant language; poor grammatical structures	✓ 1 point ❑ 2 points ❑ 3 points

	used orally	
	Subtotal of Section III =	**5**

An Analysis of Cognitive/Language Skills: Krystal

Krystal comes from an educated household. She has a mother, father, and nanny. She is surrounded by books, computers, daily newspapers, and other resources that her parents are capable of providing. Formal-register language is used in the home by both parents and the nanny. Out of a maximum of 15 points, Krystal received 5 points in the Cognitive/Language section of the EOP.

Scenario #4: Sasha

Section III: Cognitive/Language Skills	Criteria	Rating
Item 18: Significant relationships **Question:** Who is the primary caregiver of the child?	• Two or more significant relationships • At least one significant relationship • None	❏ 1 point ✓ 2 points ❏ 3 points
Item 19: Number of children's books in home **Question:** How many books does your child have that are for him/her? (Note: Books should have been purchased for him/her.)	• Two or more books per year of age • One book per year of age • Less than one book per year of age	❏ 1 point ❏ 2 points ✓ 3 points
Item 20: Presence of newspapers or magazines in home	• Daily newspaper and two or more magazines	❏ 1 point

Question: Do you purchase newspapers or magazines on a regular basis?	• Weekend newspaper or tabloid purchased on regular basis; magazines purchased at store	❑ 2 points
	• No systematic access to newspapers or magazines	✓ 3 points
Item 21: Formal register is used at home (in any language) Question: Observe for use of language	• Spoken and written formal register (in any language) used by all adult household members	✓ 1 point
	• Formal register spoken by all adult household members, but not written	❑ 2 points
	• Casual register used by one or more of household adults; very little writing of any kind	❑ 3 points
Item 22: Speaks language other than English Question: What languages are spoken in the home? (Observation)	• All adults in household speak English	✓ 1 point
	• At least one adult speaks at least one language fluently	❑ 2 points
	• Language acquisition delayed, or no dominant language; poor grammatical structures used orally	❑ 3 points
	Subtotal of Section III =	10

An Analysis of Cognitive/Language Skills: Sasha

Sasha has somewhat limited resources in her home environment. She lives in a single-parent household. No daily newspaper comes to the home, and Sasha does not have access to books that are for her. Formal-register language is used in the home, and English is the language spoken in the home. Even though Sasha sees her father on regular basis, her mother is the primary caregiver and the only adult whom Sasha has ready access to on a daily basis. Out of a maximum of 15 points, Sasha received 10 points in the Cognitive/Language section of the EOP.

A Comparison of Manuel, Joe, Krystal, and Sasha

Again, Joe's deprivation is greater than Manuel's, Krystal's, and Sasha's as measured by the EOP. In this section, however, Sasha's and Manuel's deprivation is closer than was reflected in the Student Production and Informant Data sections of the EOP. This is primarily due to the absence of books and newspapers in the home, an invaluable tool in cognitive and language-skill development in young children. The fact that Manuel's and Krystal's parents did graduate from high school gives Manuel and Krystal an advantage over Joe whose mother did not graduate from high school. Manuel's and Sasha's parents also use formal-register language in daily communications, whereas Joe's mother communicates in casual register. This is significant because it models appropriate syntax for young children, and learning formal register increases the probability of doing well in school and later in the workplace. Manuel was in a bilingual program, and Joe was in the school's Title I program. Krystal and Sasha have never received any special services.

Joe's school performance also shows a history of problems in reading and writing. Krystal has the most opportunities by far. Having two college graduates as parents who are employed in professional positions affords Krystal opportunities that the other three students cannot have. The lack of home opportunities in the areas of cognitive and language development in the early years is most evident in school performance.

Standardized Data

Kamin (cited in Torrance, 1982) stated that intelligence tests never would have been accepted in the United States if there had been no bias against minority populations. Research (Boyle, 1987; Gerken, 1985) has shown that intelligence tests, as well as achievement tests, are biased against children for whom English is not their primary language. However, intelligence tests are often one of the major criteria used to identify students for gifted/talented programs. Even when multiple criteria are used, qualitative data and anecdotal data tend to be overshadowed by standardized measures. Added to this problem is the cry from middle- and upper-middle-class America to use and rely upon these measures. As long as standardized tests are given a major role in the identification of gifted/talented students, the potential of many culturally different and lower-socioeconomic students will go undetected, unappreciated, and underserved.

Standardized data on the *Preponderance of Evidence* form are acknowledged; however, they don't take precedence over the qualitative data collected under each of the three major categories—Student Production, Informant Data, and Cognitive/Language Skills.

- Students who score less than one-half (33) of the total points on the EOP (66) receive a point value for their standardized scores.

These students represent that segment of the student population who have had access to resources within the home environment to perform well in school.

- Students scoring more than one-half (+33 points) the total number of points on the EOP (66) do not receive a point value for their standardized scores, as the scores are presumed invalid.

These students represent that segment of the student population who have lacked the resources within the home environment to perform well in school. Therefore, the standardized test scores for students who receive more than one-half (more than 33 points) of the total number of points available on the EOP (66 points) are not considered. Without opportunities within the home environment, students from poverty will not perform at a comparable level to those who have had an abundance of opportunities within the home environment. Therefore, standardized achievement tests and intelligence tests are not considered valid measures for students from poverty.

In the student scenarios, Joe, Manuel, and Sasha would be screened for the gifted/talented program without having their standardized test scores counting. Manuel's total points on the EOP were 38, Joe's were 53, and Sasha's were 36. All three students received more than one-half the total possible points (more than 33 points). Krystal, however, scored 24 points. Krystal's standardized test scores would be considered in the identification process.

In using the EOP, school officials have the opportunity to look at all students in relation to the resources and opportunities that are available in the home. Sasha is not on free lunch. She is not a poverty student. Because of some of her home conditions, however, she surfaces in the identification process as a student who lacks significant opportunities within the home environment. Since she is not as deprived as Joe, she would receive fewer points in the total points unless her performance in school is high enough to offset the EOP points. The higher the number of points on the EOP, the lower the other scores can be—and the student still has the possibility of qualifying for the gifted/talented program. Conversely, the lower the number of points on the EOP the higher the other scores need to be in order for the student to qualify for the gifted/talented program.

Analyzing the Data

The data collected in each of the categories (Student Production, Informant Data, Cognitive/Language Skills, and Standardized Testing Data) are totaled and entered on the **Preponderance of Evidence** data form. The corresponding categories on the **Environmental Opportunities Profile** also are totaled and entered on the **Preponderance of Evidence** data form. The following chart illustrates how consideration of the home environment begins to bring equity into the process for identifying potentially gifted students from both privileged and underprivileged backgrounds.

Two Hypothetical Students											
Non-poverty student						Poverty student					
Sub parts	I.	II.	III.	IV.	Total		I.	II.	III.	IV.	Total
A.	3	12	4	4			1	4	1	0	
B.	3	12	4	3			1	4	1	0	
C.	3	12	7	3			1	4	3	0	
D.	6						2				
Subtotal	15	36	15	10	= 76		5	12	5	0	= 22
EOP pts.	5	12	5		= 22		15	36	15		= 66
Subtotal	20	48	20	10	= 98		20	48	20	0	= 88

Minimum and maximum scores for each of the sources of information collected at school are reflected in the above chart. For the non-poverty student, it is assumed that he/she would earn the maximum number of points on school-related work (the qualitative data), and he/she would receive the minimum number of points on the EOP. It is assumed that the non-poverty student would receive the minimum number of points on the EOP because the student has the "ideal" resources and opportunities that support academic success in school.

For the poverty student, the opposite is assumed. It is assumed the student would earn the minimum number of points on school-related work while earning the maximum number of points on the EOP because of the deprivation within the home environment. The juxtaposed scores are totaled, allowing students from poverty to emerge within a competitive range with those students from more privileged backgrounds.
In the example, the student from poverty earned more than one-half the total number of available points on the EOP; therefore, his/her standardized test scores are considered invalid.

Disregarding standardized testing measures, the student from poverty and the non-poverty student have the same number of points. This brings equity to an identification process that historically has treated students equally but inequitably.

Preponderance of Evidence

In lieu of using standardized test data, educators must decide whether or not the data in each of the categories are indicative of gifted or non-gifted performance, given the environmental circumstances of the student. Using the *Preponderance of Evidence* data form, committee members must make a judgment about the student's performance in the areas of Student Production, Informant Data, and Cognitive/Language Skills. In the area of Standardized Testing Data, a student's performance is either valid or invalid, based on the points accrued on the EOP. Students who received more than one-half the total number of points (33 points) on the EOP have many factors inhibiting them from manifesting gifted behaviors on traditional achievement and intelligence tests. For those students from poverty who do well on these standardized measures and accrue more than one-half of the total available points (33 points) on the EOP, the committee should seriously consider them for inclusion in the gifted program. They would be performing at a high level despite their environmental factors.

Of the four sections of data on the *Preponderance of Evidence* data form, students should meet the criteria in at least three out of four areas. Students who receive only two out of four become a professional judgment call that the selection committee must make. The selection committee should also look at the overall performance of each student in the context of his/her environmental factors when formulating professional opinions about the student's potential giftedness.

When in doubt, it is appropriate to err on the side of the student and what is in his/her best interest.

A row also is included on the ***Preponderance of Evidence*** data-collection form that allows the selection committee to note whether or not the data in each of section are valid or invalid. This allows the selection committee to consider factors that may have invalidated some of the scores collected. For example, a student who looks at his/her neighbor for help during a math-replication activity cannot be considered as a valid indicator of his/her performance. A teacher's perception of a student who has been in the teacher's class for only a week is probably invalid. Selection committee members need the latitude, and have the responsibility to take the latitude, to invalidate scores when external factors have skewed the results.

Using a ***Preponderance of Evidence*** process in the context of environmental conditions allows all children to be considered as potentially gifted because it focuses on treating all students equitably. Equity in identification of all potentially gifted/talented students can occur only when the factors within the home environment are in balance with the performance being examined at school. Without looking closely at the opportunities within the home environment, student performance in school may be interpreted as excellent or poor when in reality it is the opportunity within the home environment that has been identified, not the ability of the student.

Chapter Seven:

Designing for Equity

Irving (Ving) Rhames
Actor

Ving Rhames grew up in Harlem, surrounded by drugs, violence, and crime. His father came and went, but his mother was always there. He never did drugs, and his mother introduced him to church.

In an interview with Gail Buchalter, Rhames said, "Growing up poor, you can't put your faith in the landlord when you don't have heat and hot water, because he's the slumlord. You feel you don't have the power to change your predicament, and that forced me and a lot of other people to look to a higher source. I think my mother also used the church as a controlling device—the fear factor was going to hell."

When Rhames was 11 he and a friend were talking to some girls. They followed the girls to a poetry class at a local youth center. It was there that Rhames learned about Paul Laurence Dunbar, James Baldwin, Langston Hughes, and other great poets. From that experience he started doing poetry readings for the Dance Theatre of Harlem.

Rhames had a teacher who told him he was gifted. He auditioned for the High School of the Performing Arts, the *Fame* school. He was accepted into the school, and that experience opened up a different world. He went on to attend Juilliard and graduated in 1983. Since then he has worked nonstop: in television soap operas, performing on and off Broadway, and in film.

Rhames goes to schools and talks to students about drugs. He spends time in homeless shelters. In 1992, Rhames was shooting a scene for the film ***The Saint of Fort Washington*** in a homeless shelter near Harlem. During the filming, one of the guys came up to Rhames and said, "Someone from the shelter wants to see you—he says he's your brother." Rhames first thought it was a joke, but it wasn't. It was his brother who had not been in touch with his family for years." He thought,

"Am I my brother's keeper?"

- **Gail Buchalter**, *Parade Magazine* (pp. 4-6), April 4, 1999

CHAPTER SEVEN:

DESIGNING FOR EQUITY

"... [I]f we spend our time judging, we may lose the opportunity to serve."
- Stacy Bess, *Nobody Don't Love Nobody* (p. x), 1994

Of the two students previously discussed, Manuel has a better chance to break the cycle of poverty. Joe also has that same possibility; however, his deprivation makes the challenges for the school greater and the likelihood of breaking the cycle less. Manuel has two parents at home; Joe has one. The adult-to-child ratio for Manuel (two adults and two children) is far better than it is for Joe (one adult and five children). Manuel's parents speak in formal register; Joe's mother speaks in casual register. Manuel's father has had the same job for a number of years, and they have lived in the same house for several years. Neither family has health benefits, which keeps the family's security on the edge. One major illness or major accident ... and the downward spiral of poverty becomes imminent.

For both boys, breaking the cycle of poverty is tied to the school. Books are not found in the home; they are in the school. English for Manuel and formal register for Joe are not in the home; they are in the school. Clear, articulated visions of hopes and dreams are not in the home; they are in the school. School is the place where their talents and abilities can be nurtured and taken to greater heights.

Without school, the limited opportunities within the home environment will only produce more of what the previous generation had, and the cycle of poverty will continue. Joe's performance on the state competency tests is a great achievement. Manuel's exit from the bilingual program in a relatively short period of time also is a great achievement. Both boys obviously have abilities. With appropriate intervention, their talents and skills can improve. Such intervention and its potential effect are between the walls of a school and within the hands of a teacher.

Achieving equity in the identification process for gifted students from poverty is but a partial solution to the issue of equity. Once students are identified for gifted services, changes within the traditional gifted/talented program need to occur in order to increase the probability that identified students from poverty will remain in, and benefit from, the program.

Several factors contribute to the "at-riskness" of gifted students from poverty in traditional programs. Among these are:

Gifted students from poverty readily recognize that their backgrounds are not equivalent to the other more affluent gifted students in the program. Feelings of inadequacy and a lowering of an already low self-image can occur.

Find more than one

Students from poverty may lack many of the resources necessary to meet the academic requirements of traditional gifted programs.

Relationships are a significant factor in the lives of students from poverty, and most of their friends are not in the program. The relinquishing of friends for academics is a huge dilemma for many gifted students from poverty. The challenge for school personnel is to help them learn how to live in an academic world and, at the same time, in a neighborhood where survival is more important and valued than intellectual pursuits.

Teachers who don't understand the hidden rules of poverty all too often spend more time trying to remove the student from the program for the gifted rather than making the programmatic adjustments and efforts necessary to keep the student in the program. The student's needs are the reason he/she should remain in the program; they are not reasons to remove the student from the program.

Because of the lack of opportunities within the home environment, gifted students from poverty often lack many of the basic academic skills expected of gifted students.

In order to increase the probability that identified gifted students from poverty are successful in programs for the gifted, the program must meet the unique needs of gifted students from poverty. Programs for the gifted must ...

Move from ...   Move to:

- Activities that are cute ...

- Activities that count.

- Pullout programs that offer part-time services for full-time needs ...

- Full-time programs that offer full-time services for full-time needs.

- Outside projects and products ...

- In-class projects and products.

- Rewarding gifts and talents ...

- Developing gifts and talents.

• Teaching only academics ...	• Teaching the value of academics.
• Acknowledging middle-class values and hidden rules ...	• Acknowledging diversity with different values and hidden rules.
• Polishing what the student brings to the learning environment ...	• Developing what the student doesn't bring to the learning environment.

The design of a school's program is often dependent on the number of gifted students on a campus and the campus' resources. Some school districts have campuses with sufficient numbers of students to have special classes of gifted students. Others have few students identified as gifted, and school personnel may cluster them in a class with non-gifted students. Still others with small numbers may be serving gifted students through a pullout resource design.

Of all the program designs, the one that is least defensible for gifted students from poverty is the pullout program. Gifted students, like any special population (and especially gifted students from poverty), have full-time needs that must be addressed on a full-time basis. Pullout programs that serve these students anywhere from one hour per week to one full day per week are insufficient.

The design of a gifted program serving gifted students from poverty needs a structure that allows the teacher the flexibility to meet the students' unique needs. The design structure enhances the opportunities for teacher and student to form a meaningful relationship. Without such a design, the likelihood of success greatly diminishes.

For significant learning to take place with these children, there must be significant relationships. The relationship between a teacher and student is more likely to occur when both parties work on that relationship on a daily basis. Because students from poverty value relationships, the student "liking" the teacher is crucial. More importantly, the student needs to know that the teacher likes and accepts him/her. In order to maximize the effectiveness of programs for serving gifted students from poverty, educators need to reconsider the design of their programs if these programs do not address these needs. Design options include the following.

Elementary-School Design Options

OPTION: In an ideal setting, a teacher would work with gifted students from poverty over multiple years. Some elementary schools have addressed this issue through "looping"—allowing the teacher to move from one grade level to the next with the students for a two- or three-year period. This allows the relationship between the teacher, the student, and the family to build.

OPTION: Schools that provide multiage classrooms can frequently accommodate children and their siblings in the same classroom. In poverty many older siblings must take care of their younger brothers and sisters. This option allows the students to feel more secure in the school environment and enables them to help one another with school-related work.

OPTION: A self-contained elementary classroom with one teacher sets the stage for meaningful relationships to develop between teacher and students. Unfortunately, many elementary schools are moving toward departmental structures that work contrary to a curriculum and program design that is more child-centered rather than adult-centered. This trend is due in large part to accountability systems that are in place in many states. As states define and impose their expectations on schools, teachers may feel fragmented in their efforts to be all things to all students. Though this feeling may be understandable, it isn't conducive to building strong relationships between young children and teachers. Neither is it conducive to a curriculum design that allows the student and the teacher flexible options during the instructional day.

OPTION: For gifted students from poverty, a self-contained classroom with multiple, identified, gifted students is preferable. Such a structure sets the stage for meaningful relationships to develop between teacher and students, as well as between students and students.

It also affords the teacher the autonomy necessary to structure his/her delivery of the curriculum based on the needs of the learners.

OPTION: Appropriately serving students from poverty necessitates a lower pupil/teacher ratio if the teacher is to have the time necessary to truly help these students. Because of the significance of relationships to students from poverty, people are often viewed as possessions. Students from poverty may, therefore, view the teacher as someone who belongs to them. Sharing the teacher with other students is difficult for some students from poverty. They demand attention: "You're **my** teacher!"

OPTION: The sooner the school begins its intervention services with students from poverty the better. Prekindergarten programs for children from poverty are a step in the right direction to minimize these children's disadvantages when they start kindergarten. Half-day kindergarten programs and non-mandatory kindergarten programs are inadequate. Full-day kindergarten programs are essential. Early intervention is critical for children from poverty.

Secondary-School Design Options

Secondary-level gifted students from poverty have many of the same needs as elementary students. For gifted students from poverty who were not identified and served at the elementary level, the demands on the teacher to help the student be successful are more complex. This is another reason the **early** identification of giftedness in children in poverty is so vital. Left unidentified and unserved, elementary gifted students from poverty develop behavioral patterns and attitudes by the time they reach the secondary campuses that are difficult to change. They frequently begin to live out a self-fulfilling prophecy that they aren't capable and able learners and that school and learning are unimportant. The home environment has communicated this concept, and all too often educators unwittingly fulfill the prophecy with their attitudes and comments.

As children move into adolescence, the importance of being with friends becomes even greater. For students from poverty, the need to be with their friends comes from powerful developmental needs, as well as from the culture of poverty. For these reasons, getting older students to initially want to be in a program for the gifted is often difficult, and getting them to perform consistently is sometimes an even greater challenge. The need for a teacher to become a "significant other" to those students is paramount. Secondary gifted students from poverty won't perform for a teacher they don't like or for a teacher they feel doesn't like them. Compounding this problem can be an administration that enforces rules that appear to the student to squelch the very things that define them: clothing, music, ability to entertain, and loud and colorful use of language. The result is a perception and feeling that "they don't like us; they have it 'in' for us."

Relationships between the school and the students also are systemic. Do students perceive the school as a place that is supportive and where the adults like them? Effective-schools literature refers to this as school climate. When students perceive the school as an adversary rather than an advocate, they respond by testing the system and its rules. Systemic practices and procedures communicate to students whether the school is an adversary or an advocate. At the secondary level this becomes a key factor in helping students from poverty stay in school and be successful in school. It's time to rethink some of the secondary practices that are "anti-me." Some secondary options that communicate advocacy and a "liking" for students include:

OPTION: Tutorials within the school day—or after-school tutorials with transportation provided.

OPTION: Provisions for assistance with homework.

OPTION: Homework practices and due dates for assignments that acknowledge that students from poverty may be working late hours outside the school day—or may be the primary caregiver while parent(s) work a second job in the evening.

OPTION: Showing support for students who must stay home on occasion to take care of younger siblings or their own children.

OPTION: Making the school and its resources (computers, library services, nursing services, etc.) available to students after school hours.

OPTION: Guidance counselors who assist students with problems and concerns instead of judging and lecturing them. Counselors must seek out these students. Waiting for them to come to the Guidance Center won't work; they won't come.

OPTION: Mentors for gifted students from poverty, such as an "Adopt-a-Student" program that allows a teacher or some other adult to work with the student throughout his/her years on that campus—to help the student make course selections, meet deadlines, explore post-high school training options, and resolve conflicts that may arise within the system.

OPTION: Partnerships between the high school and local community college. Community colleges can serve as a bridge from high school to a major university for many gifted students from poverty. Secondary gifted students from poverty may need more time to develop the skills necessary to survive in a larger, more impersonal bureaucratic structure of a university.

OPTION: Teachers who overtly convey to students that they are there to help students—and when students aren't successful the teachers communicate to students that "We failed" rather than "You failed."

OPTION: An overall tone throughout the building that all students are worthwhile, academically capable of achieving, and worthy of dignity and respect.

An example of a school establishing a significant relationship with students from poverty exists at a high school in the Midwest. With the assistance of federal grant dollars, the urban school is open for students and family members from 7 a.m. to 10 p.m. Monday through Saturday. Teachers are employed after hours to be available to help students with their homework. Computer labs are open for students and parents. Parents are encouraged to come to the school and learn new skills. The school provides GED classes, assistance with job applications, and other services for parents. A physician is housed in the school three days a week and a psychiatrist is on duty two days a week.

The principal of the school also worked with local law-enforcement officials to have a substation located near the school so that students and family members would feel safe coming to the school after hours. The principal of the school commented that, as a result of this, student performance has risen dramatically. Honors classes outnumber non-honors classes. His biggest problem is getting the students to go home at 10 o'clock in the evening.

Educators must structure schools so that staff-student relationships are nurtured and cultivated in schools. For some gifted students from poverty, many of their significant relationships are outside the school. These relationships may be with a parent, a grandparent, an aunt, or a fellow church member. For others, the school holds the key to significant relationships. Middle schools where academic teams have been implemented serve as an ideal forum on which to build relationships with students. Working together as a support team, teachers have the opportunity to help students from poverty be successful academically, socially, and emotionally. Meaningful relationships are important for all students, but for the gifted students from poverty they are absolutely essential to academic, emotional, physical, and spiritual survival.

Designing instructional programs that foster these relationships must be a priority if these students are to reach their full potential. Placing gifted students from poverty in programs that treat them as middle-class students who have resources and support systems outside the school dooms most of them to failure. What the gifted students from poverty bring to the learning environment is rooted in a home environment and a culture of poverty. These factors cannot be ignored if gifted students from poverty are to be successful.

Where to Start

The most manageable way to develop programs for gifted/talented students from poverty is for school districts to start at the primary level and move these students through the system. That isn't to say that a district should not and cannot serve gifted students from poverty in the upper grades. However, challenges are greater at the secondary level. As the number of teachers and students at the secondary level are greater than they typically are at the elementary level, it is more difficult to intervene and alter behavior patterns and attitudes. Since gifted students from poverty lack many of the preschool experiences of middle-class students, one way to begin intervening earlier is to identify a larger percentage of students at the primary grade levels and form some type of scholastic academy for these students. This could be as much as 15-25% of the total school population.

With a highly enriched curriculum in the early grades, gifted students from poverty will begin to manifest their gifts and talents in an observable fashion. At the end of the second grade, those gifted students from poverty who have participated in the Scholastic Academy in the primary years can move into the second phase of the gifted program, which may serve a smaller percentage of the students. Students who are not ready for that phase, however, should continue in the Scholastic Academy phase of the program. A diagram of the structure for such a program follows.

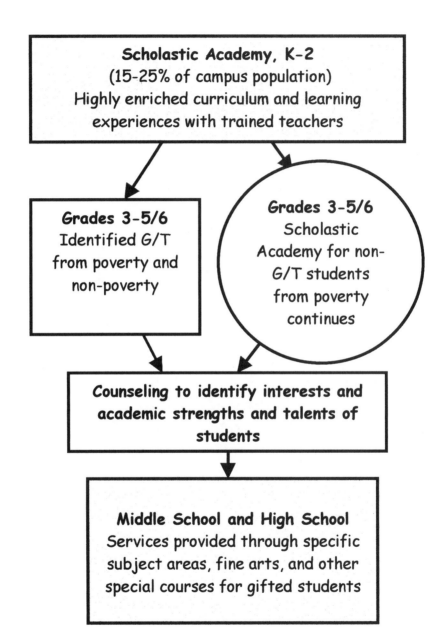

Scholastic Academy, K-2
(15-25% of campus population)
Highly enriched curriculum and learning
experiences with trained teachers

Grades 3-5/6
Identified G/T
from poverty and
non-poverty

Grades 3-5/6
Scholastic
Academy for non-
G/T students
from poverty
continues

**Counseling to identify interests and
academic strengths and talents of
students**

Middle School and High School
Services provided through specific
subject areas, fine arts, and other
special courses for gifted students

This design allows students from poverty the opportunity to acquire the necessary skills, attitudes, and behaviors that will increase the probability that they will be productive learners. This assumes that the counseling services and the instructional services are designed in a manner that addresses the issues of poverty accompanying these students. A discussion of the content of such an instructional program appears in the next chapter.

Gender Equity

At both the elementary and secondary levels, gifted girls outnumber gifted boys. For boys from poverty, this gap is even greater. Having to give up one's friends for academics is difficult for many students, but for the gifted from poverty it is an even greater sacrifice. The role of males in poverty is that of a fighter and lover. That role is not compatible with giftedness. Gifted boys are frequently subjected to name-calling by other boys. Words such as "nerd," "geek," "dork," "wimp," "weirdo," "teacher's pet," and "fag" are not uncommon descriptors heaved upon gifted boys. For gifted boys from poverty, these are fighting words. When these words come from boys within one's own neighborhood, the trauma associated with such name-calling leaves the school boundary and enters the home environment. Students ask, in effect, "Why would I want to be in a program that causes this kind of pain and humiliation?" Enduring such name-calling is difficult for any student, but gifted boys from middle-class are more likely to have a support system than are boys from poverty. Compounding this issue is a "Boy Code" in our culture that "Big boys don't cry" (Pollack, 1999). The result of this for many gifted boys from poverty is anger and aggression. (These issues are addressed in greater depth in Chapter Nine.)

Check Your Statistics		
Using your campus or district data, calculate the percentages of boys and girls from poverty for each of the following:	**# Boys %**	**# Girls %**
1. Discipline referrals		
2. Suspensions		
3. Identified ADD and ADHD students		
4. Students in alternative schools/boot camp, in-school suspension program		
5. High school dropouts		
6. Those identified for Special Education		
7. High school seniors in the top 10% of their graduating class		
8. Members of the junior high or high school National Honor Society		
9. Identified gifted students		
10. Male/female teachers		
TOTALS		

At this time in our culture, gifted females are more likely to pursue mathematics and science than they were 10 years ago. They also are more likely to have a support system within the school than boys because of the research and a heightened sensitivity to the needs of females. This awareness and

sensitivity toward the needs of males, however, is not there.
For the gifted boys from poverty who may be the class clown,
who are more aggressive in their social interactions with their
peers, and who use casual register to voice their emotions,
being acknowledged as a bright, gifted student rarely happens.

Equity between gender groups is lacking in most gifted
programs. When the element of poverty is added, this inequity
is even greater. Further discussion about the emotional needs
of gifted boys from poverty appears in Chapter Nine.

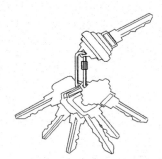

**To achieve equity for gifted
students from poverty, a
program must be able to
deliver …**

- **Highly enriched curricula and learning
  experiences that offset the home environment.**

- **Assignments that always include visual and
  verbal components.**

- **Direct-teaching of abstract processes and
  mental models.**

- **Mentors who share common interests and
  talents with students.**

- Meaningful relationships with adults and other students.

- Academic, physical, and emotional support systems:
    ◇ Small-group work.
    ◇ In-class projects and homework.
    ◇ Materials and supplies furnished.
    ◇ In-class and out-of-class tutors available.
    ◇ Teacher-directed affective lessons.

- Adequate resources for learning and meeting academic expectations, such as calculators, computers, and reference books.

- Time allotments dictated by student needs.

- Comprehensive Fine Arts curriculum as an integral part of the program.

- Teachers trained in the special needs of the gifted from poverty.

- School personnel trained to recognize and deal with special needs of gifted boys from poverty.

Chapter Eight:

Curriculum for the Gifted from Poverty

From Tragedy to Success
Vicente Rosas, Age 18

During his freshman year at Lee High School in Houston, Texas, Vicente was shot in a gang-related skirmish. When the doctors told him he would not walk again, Rosas reflected on his past crimes and failing grades and decided this was not the way he wanted his future to go. "We didn't have anything to do back then but get into trouble," Rosas said, admitting to a few brushes with the law, and a bout of experimenting with illegal drugs and stealing.

A wheelchair user after the shooting, he worked at home with a tutor and caught a glimpse of how knowledge could change his life. When he returned to school, Rosas changed the F's and D's on his report card to A's and B's and received a $500 a semester college scholarship from A Window of Opportunity Foundation in Houston for being the "most improved junior" in 1997-98. With his dedication to physical therapy and his determination, he also went from a wheelchair to walking with a cane.

He promised to be the first member of his family to graduate from high school and college. Although many of his neighborhood friends dropped out by the ninth grade and half of them are in jail, Rosas has remained outside the grasp of drug pushers and other criminals who dominate his neighborhood. He gets up each morning and takes the hour-long Metro bus ride to school. He has traded gym class and an SAT prep class to take calculus and physics. Rosas can boast of making perfect scores on four final exams last year.

In 1999 the University of Oklahoma offered him a $16,000 minority engineering scholarship for the next four years. Despite his IQ of 144 and SAT of 1020, college was still just a dream without money. A school counselor sought out the scholarship opportunity at OU. During his first year at OU, a tutor will be provided to help him maintain the 3.0 grade point average that is required of him. He also will receive counseling twice a month. Transitioning to college because of his background is Rosas' most difficult challenge. His high school counselor says she plans to call Rosas regularly at college to remind him to pick up his financial aid and discuss any problems he might be having.
                    - **Heather Saucier,** *Houston Chronicle* (p. 24A), April 19, 1999

CHAPTER EIGHT:

CURRICULUM FOR THE GIFTED FROM POVERTY

A differentiated curriculum for gifted students from poverty must be a blend of what is known about students from poverty and what is known about giftedness. The concept of differentiation, grounded in Special Education, is about modifying the curriculum so that it aligns more closely with how certain groups of children learn and process information. The curriculum that is modified is not a different or separate curriculum from what is used with all students. It is the district's regular curriculum that is adapted. In this case, it's adapted to the needs of the gifted. With the further dimension of poverty, differentiation takes on additional features. To understand more fully the implications of differentiating curriculum for gifted students from poverty, this chapter addresses the following:

- General guidelines for differentiating curriculum for gifted students.
- Curriculum guidelines for students from poverty.
- Merging what is known about poverty and applying it to what is known about differentiating curriculum for the gifted.
- Instructional methods and strategies necessary to deliver the differentiated curriculum effectively.

The intent of this chapter is not to provide an in-depth how-to model for developing curriculum for the gifted. Rather, it's to look at some essential components and principles of differentiating curriculum for gifted students. When the dimension of gifted students from poverty is added to that of a differentiated curriculum, another level of modifications become essential in order to meet the needs of these specific gifted students.

Differentiating the Curriculum for the Gifted

Curriculum that aligns with the needs of the gifted must take into account those attributes of the gifted that set them apart from other students. Gifted students have a set of attributes that are to a greater degree and dimension than their less-gifted counterparts. Three major differences emerge from the literature that distinguish gifted students from non-gifted students. They are:

1. The ability to learn at a faster rate (Keating, 1976).
2. The ability to find, solve, and act on problems (Sternberg, 1985).
3. The ability to manipulate abstract ideas and make connections (Gallagher, 1985).

Therefore, an appropriate curriculum for the gifted would address these differences. Though individual gifted students may vary in their abilities in these areas, the teacher's job is to make modifications within the curriculum to accommodate these individual and collective differences through planned learning experiences.

VanTassel-Baska (1988, pp. 9-16) identifies three curriculum models that have proved successful with gifted populations. They are:

- **The Content Model:** Emphasis is on learning skills and concepts within a predetermined domain of inquiry. Through a diagnostic/prescriptive approach, the students are encouraged to move as quickly as possible through the content area.

- **The Process/Product Model:** Emphasis is on learning investigative skills that allow students to develop high-quality products. Consultation and independent work dominate the instructional pattern.

*From **Comprehensive Curriculum For Gifted Learners**, by Joyce Van Tassel-Baska, copyright © 1994, Second Edition, by Allyn & Bacon. Reprinted by permission.

- **The Epistemological Model:** Emphasis is on students' understanding systems of knowledge. Students are exposed to key ideas, themes, issues, and principles within and across fields of knowledge so that patterns are internalized, synthesized, and amplified by future examples.

Rarely is one model used to the exclusion of the others. To be effective, the dimensions within the curriculum need to be based upon the characteristics of the learners.

Appropriate program goals for gifted students must drive the curriculum for the gifted students. Some model program goals for gifted students follow (VanTassel-Baska, 1988, pp. 28-29):

- To provide for the mastery of the basic skills in reading and mathematics at a pace and depth appropriate to the capacities of able learners.
- To promote critical thinking and reasoning abilities.
- To provide an environment that encourages divergent thinking.
- To foster inquiry and to challenge attitudes towards learning.
- To develop high-level oral and written skills.
- To develop research skills and methods.
- To develop an understanding for systems of knowledge, themes, issues, and problems that frame the external world.
- To develop self-understanding.

- To facilitate opportunities for learning that are external to the school but provide an important match to the needs of learners.
- To enhance opportunities for future planning and development.

Four major components within any curriculum that teachers would do well to address are:

- Content topics
- Process skills
- Products
- Affective needs

These four areas become the pieces of the curriculum that the teacher must differentiate for gifted students. Simply stated, these four areas are the parts of any objective for learning. An example follows. The major parts of the learning appear in bold type.

After **reading** about the U.S. Civil War from **three different sources,** the student will be able to **identify** the **five major causes of the Civil War** and give **an oral report** in which he/she defends the identified causes. The student will then identify how **differences between the North and South have impacted his/her community.**

In the this example, the major parts of the learning are:

Content: Causes of the Civil War.

Process skills: Identify and find information
from three major sources.

Product: Oral report.

Affective: Identify differences between the
North and South and their impact on
the student's community.

For learning to take place, the two essential components are
content and process skills. The student must have something to
learn and something to think about.

CONTENT + PROCESS = LEARNING

The product is an overt way the student has of showing what
he/she has learned. The affective dimension allows the student
the opportunity to transfer the learning to his/her life by
identifying in what way(s) the learning is relevant to him/her.

To differentiate the content appropriately for gifted students,
educators of the gifted need to address some key questions
(VanTassel-Baska, 1988, p. 56):

1. Is the topic worthy of the time to be spent learning
   it? Studying dinosaurs may be interesting, but they
   are dead and are not coming back. It may be cute, but

does it count? A study of causes of extinction on multiple levels would have more merit.

2. Is the content conceptually complex enough for gifted students to investigate and explore from different perspectives over time? Studying the history of teddy bears is far less complex than a study of symbols and their power to sway public opinion.

3. Is the content relevant to today's world and how it really works? A study of the judicial system has more merit than a study of fashion trends.

4. Is the content interesting to the students and viewed as relevant? What students are interested in sometimes is difficult to determine when they have not been exposed to particular information and experiences.

5. Could the content be taught effectively by the designated teacher? Teachers who don't know a subject have more difficulty being creative with that topic.

Certainly there is merit to students knowing about the causes of the Civil War. There is also some relevance about the causes of the Civil War to our life today. Students, however, may not see the causes of the Civil War as particularly relevant to them, nor may they have an intense interest it.

Differentiation is about taking these pieces of the learning objective and modifying them so they become more appropriate to the gifted student. An appropriate goal for gifted students is to think at higher levels and allow them the opportunity to think independently of textbooks, materials, and other resources. They need to be able to transfer their skills from one discipline to another and see connections to their personal life. The learning will include critical and creative thinking, problem-solving, and evaluation skills.

Teachers of the gifted and talented also need to facilitate product and project opportunities that require a synthesis of the larger understandings. These larger understandings are part of the learning experiences and are an evaluative indication of the learning that has taken place. For example, if the students have studied conflict, a generalization might be:

> **"Differences are a prerequisite for conflict."**

A gifted student's product should reflect this higher understanding by doing something that hasn't been taught directly in class. This forces a synthesis and a transfer of the information the student has studied. Based on his/her study of different types of conflict in different time periods and disciplines, the student might be asked to take a current conflict and analyze it in order to identify the differences that led to the conflict. The student then would report his/her findings through some overt means. Students who have sufficient opportunities to examine differences that have led to conflict should be able to transfer that knowledge to situations not studied in class. Students may produce their end products and projects individually and/or collectively.

To begin to differentiate the example mentioned previously for gifted students, the content is the first modification. To understand more fully the significance of complex content, it is helpful to understand how content within the disciplines is subsumed by the larger concepts. The following illustrates this arrangement.

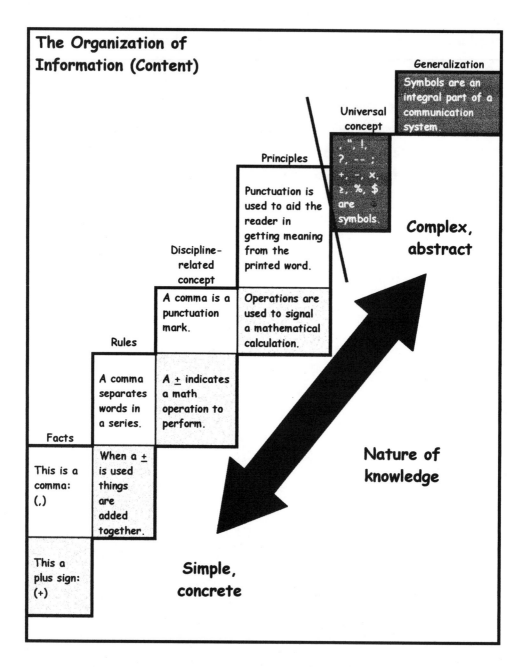

The Organization of
Information (Content)

Generalization

Symbols are an
integral part of a
communication
system.

**Universal
concept**

. " , !,
?, -- :
+, -, x,
≥, %, $
are
symbols.

Principles

Punctuation is
used to aid the
reader in
getting meaning
from the
printed word.

**Discipline-
related
concept**

A comma is a
punctuation
mark.

Operations are
used to signal
a mathematical
calculation.

Rules

A comma
separates
words in
a series.

A ± indicates
a math
operation to
perform.

Facts

This is a
comma:
(,)

When a ±
is used
things
are
added
together.

This a
plus sign:
(+)

**Complex,
abstract**

**Nature of
knowledge**

**Simple,
concrete**

Facts are at the knowledge level of thinking. When a student understands the pattern in the use of the facts, a rule can be deduced. Understanding the purposes and functions of the facts is at a comprehension level of thinking. In the previous example, mathematics and language arts are used to illustrate the parallel structure of the disciplines. In language arts, a rule for the use of the comma would be that commas separate words in a series. In mathematics, a plus sign (+) indicates "to add." As the students understand that commas and plus signs are but examples of punctuation and operations, respectively, a larger concept as it relates to the discipline is formed. Once a pattern in the application of the discipline-related concept is discerned, a principle or rule on the use of that concept within the discipline is formed. For example, commas aid the reader in deriving meaning from the printed word, and mathematical operations communicate a mathematical function or operation.

Synthesis occurs when a student understands the pattern that crosses the disciplines. This is a universal concept that supersedes all the previous information. From that understanding a generalization can be formed that explains the larger ideas and concepts. Generalizations are the explanations of the universal concepts. Complexity within the curriculum is achieved at this level. Higher-level content yields higher-level thinking.

When the content, the causes of the Civil War, is modified to become a larger concept, issue, or theme it opens up multiple bodies of knowledge and disciplines by subsuming them under a larger umbrella. The focus shifts from a study of the causes of the Civil War to a study of conflict. What was in the regular curriculum is now but one part of a larger idea, opening up the possibilities for more disciplines and more complex ideas and issues to be explored. Many types of conflict can be included in the unit of study for gifted students. Students will still study the Civil War because it's the district's core curriculum; however, it is no longer an end in itself, and it will not be enough for students to say that the Civil War was about President Lincoln freeing the slaves. The Civil War is now but one of several means to a larger end. That larger end is an in-depth study of conflict.

Such a study would be driven by a generalization about conflict to illustrate its universality. The generalizations concerning conflict allow the learning to transfer across time and place because of their universality. A generalization that teachers of the gifted and talented might use to drive a study of conflict might be:

Differences are a prerequisite for conflict.
OR
The resolution of conflict causes change.

The types of conflict that may be included in a study of conflict that are illustrative of the generalization give rise to the possible topics that students may study. Among these are:

- Supply and demand.
- Prey and predator.
- Civil-rights movement.
- Women's suffrage movement.

- Harper Lee's *To Kill a Mockingbird.*
- Opposing philosophies of artists, musicians, writers.
- Political issues and parties, forms of government.
- Genetic engineering.
- Cultural, religious, racial, and ethnic differences.

Multiple disciplines are reflected in the above examples. Many of these can be explored over time, allowing students to identify trends and patterns. Moral and ethical issues are embedded in many of these topics, allowing students the opportunity to examine personal beliefs, as well as those espoused by a culture or generation.

The process skills and product options also begin to unfold when the content is modified in this manner. Opportunities for more advanced research and investigations become available. To look at conflict in different time periods and places—and within different cultures and fields of study—paves the way for depth within the study. Allowing students to examine the interconnectedness between and among the disciplines and different time periods increases the complexity of the study. Students can participate in debates and panel discussions related to moral and ethical issues they uncover. Teachers incorporate acceleration and the independent interests of individual students when they differentiate the curriculum in this manner.

Implications for the Gifted from Poverty

Because of the lack of opportunities within the environment of gifted students from poverty, they don't come prepared to participate in a curriculum designed for gifted students who already have had an array of opportunities in the home. This lack of readiness doesn't mean they shouldn't be included in the gifted program. It does mean that the teacher working with the gifted students needs to be prepared to make modifications for the individual and collective differences that are represented in his/her classroom.

While gifted students from middle class may have many skills and experiences from which to draw, the gifted from poverty lack many of these skills and experiences. They may possess some of the skills but not know how to transfer them to, or use them in, an academic environment. For example, gifted students from poverty are survivors. Survival requires real-life problem-solving skills. Such young people may be highly verbal, yet that verbal ability could be represented in casual-register language, which is usually regarded as signifying a lack of education and intelligence. The classroom instructional program must address these issues if gifted students from poverty are going to be successful and be given the opportunity to thrive in a program for the gifted.

While teachers do well to make modifications in the curriculum, the goals and objectives for the gifted students from poverty are the same as for the other gifted students. To make the goals and objectives different would compromise equity. To provide an equitable curriculum for gifted students from poverty, they must have the opportunity to master the same differentiated curriculum as the non-poverty gifted students. To not do so would be to create an unequal education resulting in unequal opportunity and false illusions as an adult in the job market. To get gifted students from poverty to master the same differentiated curriculum as the non-poverty gifted students requires instructional strategies to be in place so they can reach the same identified expectations as their non-poverty peers.

For the gifted student from poverty, the teacher is in the unique position of building bridges because the home environment didn't build them during those early years of development. Kaplan (**Tempo**, 1999, p. 20) refers to this process as "filling in the gaps."

A bridge connects two points that are separated by something that prevents those two points from being as one. A bridge can connect two pieces of land separated by a waterway so that people can access both pieces of land as though they were one. An island is connected to the mainland by a bridge, allowing people to have equal access to both.

So what are the pieces of land—and the waterway that separates them—for gifted students from poverty? The pieces of land are the facts, skills, and knowledge that the student has and the concepts and generalizations we want the students to acquire. The waterway that separates these two are their lack of experiences that acts as a barrier between the two. The educator's job is to build the bridges between the two, allowing the students to overcome the barrier so they can access the larger, more meaningful and abstract learning.

To construct such a bridge requires quality materials and a foundation on which to put these materials. For the gifted students from poverty, their home environments create the raw material called knowledge, skills, and attitudes. The foundation on which these must be placed is their experiences—for they serve as the reference points for their knowledge, skills, and attitudes. Teachers, then, are ideally situated to help gifted students from poverty take their existing knowledge, skills, and attitudes and add further knowledge, skills, and attitudes. These will comprise the pillars that hold up the structure of the bridge. The result? A strong bridge that will allow students to connect where they currently are to where they can be. All the pieces work together in a mutually supportive way.

For students from poverty to be successful in the differentiated curriculum, teachers can help redefine the students' environment and make their skills, knowledge, and attitudes strengths on which to build. Teachers may begin this process by teaching gifted students from poverty on the "high end" of the learning, not just the lower end (Kaplan, 1999). The lower end might be where the student is. The high end—the concepts and the generalizations—is where the student is to be.

If the focus is on the lower end of the learning because the students lack "the basics," then the gifted students from poverty may never get to the higher learning. While focusing on higher learning, the teacher must fill in the gaps of information and skills needed to achieve the higher learning. By filling in the gaps, the bridge is constructed.

In a discussion of gifted and emergent English learners, Kaplan (*Tempo*, 1999, p. 20) states that the

> fill-in-the-gaps activities must be identified as inherent features of an exemplary differentiated gifted curriculum and not just as good teaching practices. Too often, limited English language learners who are gifted are either excluded from the differentiated gifted curriculum because of limited experience, or the experience is given to the students in a limited manner.

The same is true of gifted students from poverty.

So, how does the teacher fill in the gaps, teach at the high end, and build that bridge?

The brain is a pattern-seeking device. From the time a child is born, he/she tries to make sense out of chaos. Kovalik (1993) describes a child's brain as developing in stages: "Each stage is like an ever more complex template laid over the top of the previous one. At each of these stages, the brain is capable of more complex thinking, comparing, and analyzing."

Learning is also hooked to emotion. Relationships between students and teachers contribute to emotional hooks that enhance learning. An example of this follows:

> "I'm going to use a word and you tell me what comes to your mind? The word is <u>decadent</u>. Did you think of chocolate? Did you think rotten?
>
> "Whatever you thought, emotion was connected in some way. For many, a love for chocolate is what is triggered. That is an emotional hook."
>
> Virtually no one sees a picture in his/her brain that looks like this:
>
> **dec·a·dent** (dek′ə dənt), *adj* 1. Characterized by decadence; decaying; deteriorating

When there is no emotional hook, effective teachers attempt to create one because it's an important part of remembering/retention theory. Emotions associated with learning are critical. Students who feel threatened in school have feelings associated with threat; they don't remember the lesson. These emotional hooks are part of the bridging that teachers can use with gifted students from poverty.

Incoming information that requires a level of processing not yet acquired by the brain results in lack of understanding. "[Students] don't 'get it.' When things are 'ungettable,' students give up and resort to memorization. Over time, when too many things are 'ungettable,' students slowly learn not to try to understand but merely to memorize and parrot back" (Kovalik, p. 44). If school is unimportant and not perceived as relevant, the effort to memorize doesn't even take place.

Using the example of conflict from earlier in the chapter, a teacher of gifted students from poverty would need to use the students' experiences and knowledge of conflict to shed light on a more in-depth and comprehensive study of conflict. What does the student from poverty know about conflict? What does the student know about differences? Where are the emotional hooks? That which is currently stored in the student's brain about conflict can be used to help him/her understand what is studied in the classroom. The following chart shows how students from poverty and middle class might have two very different reference points on the subject of conflict, yet have some things in common.

Gifted Students from Poverty	Common Experiences	Gifted Students from Middle Class
• Conflict with the law • Conflict with social services (CPS) • Fights involving neighborhood gangs • Conflict with a landlord	• Conflict with a friend • Fights with a parent • Conflict with a school rule	• Conflict over what to wear • Conflict about telling a parent you didn't make an A on an assignment • Fights about money • Conflict between social groups

With each of these examples, students have images, pictures, emotions, and stories that are stored in the brain. It is from these experiences that students are asked to find the common attributes that each of these conflicts share. What makes them conflicts? What are the differences? What are the similarities? Once these are identified, students can transfer their knowledge of conflicts to other types of conflicts that are more abstract: conflicts that occur in different places and time periods and under different circumstances.

The moral and ethical issues that surround these studies also will be different. A student from middle class might see the pig that built his house out of bricks as very clever. A student from poverty might spend his time thinking of ways in which the wolf could have outsmarted the pig who built his house out of bricks. He also may defend the wolf's aggressive behavior.

Story Structure and Registers of Language

For children born in poverty, making sense out of an inconsistent world further complicates the learning process. The language pattern a child hears is usually in casual register. The stories are not linear and logical, they are episodic (Payne, 1998, p. 46).

> The formal-register story structure starts at the beginning of the story and goes to the end in a chronological or accepted narrative pattern. The most important part of the story is the plot. The casual-register story structure begins with the end of the story first or the part with the greatest emotional intensity. The story is told in vignettes, with audience participation in between. The story ends with a comment about the character and his/her value. The most important part of the story is the characterization.

Entertainment is more important than education and planning; goal-setting is replaced with fate and luck. For many students born in poverty, school is the first place they encounter a linear, sequential world. It is the first time many of them encounter adults on a daily basis who communicate in formal register. So, why don't the students from poverty "get it"?

Without a structure inside the brain for storing, assimilating, interpreting, and retrieving information, students from poverty will never "get it." The cognitive structures required to "get it" must be built, and the classroom is the place to do it. Payne, in *A Framework for Understanding Poverty* (1998, p. 121), explains the significance of the need for cognitive strategies as follows:

If an individual depends upon a random, episodic story structure for memory patterns, lives in an unpredictable environment, **and has not developed the ability to plan**, then ...

If an individual cannot plan, he/she **cannot predict.**

If an individual cannot predict, he/she **cannot identify cause and effect.**

If an individual cannot identify cause and effect, he/she **cannot identify consequence.**

If an individual cannot identify consequence, he/she **cannot control implusivity.**

If an individual cannot control impulsivity, he/she **has inclination toward criminal behavior.**

Teachers can address the development of these cognitive strategies in a very direct way by including gifted students from poverty in a scholastic academy. With limited cognitive strategies, gifted students from poverty will experience limited success. Random, episodic story structure must be replaced with an ability to plan. As part of virtually every instructional activity, the teacher consciously elects to help students develop a plan for attempting and completing tasks. Most students from poverty will approach tasks randomly rather than systematically; therefore, systematic constructs need to be taught. These strategies help build the bridge from where the students are to where we wish them to go. They are the connectors between existing skills, knowledge, and attitudes and the concepts, generalizations, and larger understandings students need to acquire.

Because of background void of formal-register language, students from poverty tend to think in pictures instead of words. Middle-class students who have ready access to print and formal-register language tend to think in words and symbols. School is highly dependent on students having the ability to learn by using printed language and symbols. Reading, writing, and mathematics are dependent on these processes. To help students from poverty acquire knowledge through print and formal-register language, bridges have to be built for them and with them. This requires strategies that utilize concrete images, thereby enabling the student to retrieve that information when needed. Using the concept of **conflict**, an example of moving from the concrete to a more abstract concept appears below.

- **What do all these pictures have in common? What are they about?**

- **They're all examples of a fight. Another word for a fight is CONFLICT.**

- **What is the following about?**
  John: "I think you're wrong."
  Bill: "No, I'm not. You're wrong."
  John: "Am not."
  Bill: "Are too!"

- **This is an example of a fight with words. Sometimes it's called an argument. Another word for a fight with words, an argument, is CONFLICT. These two boys have two different opinions; each has his own point of view—how something is seen.**

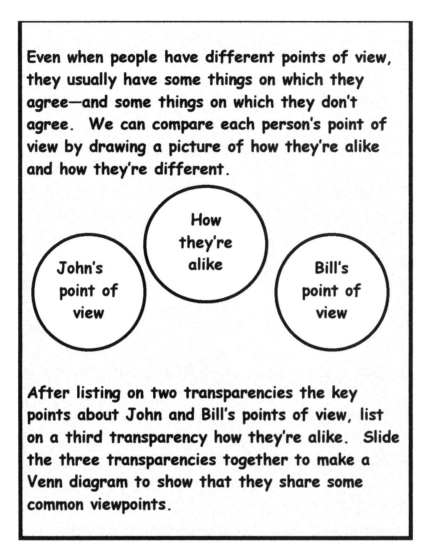

Even when people have different points of view, they usually have some things on which they agree—and some things on which they don't agree. We can compare each person's point of view by drawing a picture of how they're alike and how they're different.

How they're alike

John's point of view

Bill's point of view

After listing on two transparencies the key points about John and Bill's points of view, list on a third transparency how they're alike. Slide the three transparencies together to make a Venn diagram to show that they share some common viewpoints.

In the above example, the teacher begins with concrete pictures, then moves to more abstract symbols and words to communicate the major concepts and understandings. Students from poverty need a "plan of attack" to replace the episodic story structure. With practice and consistency, planning and cause-and-effect relationships can become tools in the learning process for the student from poverty.

> **For a more comprehensive discussion of cognitive strategies, see Payne, 1998, pp. 119-140.**

Language and achievement are connected; therefore, it is essential that teachers address casual register, discourse patterns, and story structure in school. Some suggested ways in which this can be incorporated into the daily instructional program are:

1. Have gifted students from poverty translate casual register into formal register.

2. Have students translate school information written in formal register into casual register so they can better explain the information to their parents.

3. Chart the meaning of a concept or the prerequisites necessary to acquire the skill.

4. Cluster activities so students can determine the connections among ideas and skills.

5. Write key ideas on index cards and place them on a wall. Connect related ideas by using yarn to connect the various index cards. Label the connection with an additional index card. Use different colors of yarn to make more apparent the patterns between and among ideas and facts.

6. Develop a "Key Words" dictionary using pictures and diagrams with the words (Kaplan, 1999). Key words should include, but are not limited to, the following:

kinds	types	characteristics
purpose(s)	function	attributes
conditions	issues	themes
reasons	variables	implications
factors	causes	patterns

7. Use graphic organizers to show patterns of discourse.

8. Write and rewrite stories and news events using different points of view and different language registers.

9. Use stories to explain key concepts and ideas.

It is vital to build a precise working vocabulary to describe tasks, ideas, thoughts, and feelings. The teacher is encouraged to help gifted students from poverty develop a formal register and teach them how, when, and where to use it appropriately. This is best achieved if the teacher has students think of other ways to say things. If a student said he wasn't going to "kiss up" to the teacher, the teacher would ask him what "kiss up" means. By calling the student's attention to it and informing him that "kissing up" to someone is casual register and that there's another way of saying it in formal register, the student begins to acquire the words for formal register. It's important for students to hear themselves say the words. When a teacher sends a student to the office, or the librarian sends a student back to class for inappropriate language, it's often helpful, after talking through the anger issues, to help the student practice what he/she is going to say to the teacher upon re-entering the situation. The dialogue might go something like this:

-- "Tell me what happened, John."

● "She pissin' me off. She say I was talkin', and all I was doin' was asking a question."

-- "Let me hear the words you used when you wanted to ask the teacher a question."

● "I tol' her I don't understand and she tol' me to shut."

-- "And then what did you do?"

● "I asked Fred what we suppose to do."

-- "Then what happened?"

● "She tol' me to git back to class."

-- "And did you say anything while leaving the room?"

● "No."

-- "Are you sure you didn't say anything to anyone?"

● "I tol' Fred, 'She pissin' me off' cuz I wadn't doin' nuthin wrong. I ain't said nuthin to her."

After working through the cause-and-effect issues and coming to some understanding about what John perceives happened and what the teacher might perceive, the results of the conversation would allow John to go back into the classroom with dignity and respect for himself and the teacher. To do this, John needs a picture in his head and some words to describe that picture. The dialogue might go something like this:

-- "John, how are you going to go back to class and 'kiss up' to Ms. Jones?"
• "I dunno."
-- "What do I mean when I say 'kiss up' to Ms. Jones?"
• "You're sorry?"
-- "Yes, that's right, John. It's called **an apology**. How are you going to apologize to Ms. Jones even when you think you were right and she was wrong?"
• "I'm goin' tell her I'm sorry, but she was wrong."
-- "John, have you ever had anyone apologize to you and you didn't really believe them even when they said, 'I'm sorry'?"
• "Yeah."
-- "Well, remember we talked about the teacher being the boss? So how can you tell your boss you're really sorry so the boss won't fire you?"
• "Ms. Jones, I'm sorry I was talkin' instead of listenin' to you. I shoulda listened instead of gettin' mad."
-- "Good. Now where are your hands going to be and where are your eyes going to be?"
• "I'll hold my hands in front of me and look at her when I apologize."
-- "Good. Now let's practice this. I'll be Ms. Jones, and you come back into my class to apologize."

In this example John gets an opportunity to practice several important skills. He gets to think through the incident in the classroom while being guided to identify the cause-and-effect relationship that exists between himself and the teacher. John also expands his vocabulary, develops a better understanding of formal register, realizes that two people have different perceptions of one incident, develops a plan of action, implements the plan, and, most importantly, has a reason to believe that his teacher is on his side and understands him. When knowing how to fight is part of one's code of survival, knowing who is on your side is important.

Stories are also a natural way of teaching gifted students from poverty about themselves and others. *Think Rather of Zebra* (Stailey and Payne, 1998) uses stories to teach students about poverty, wealth, role of language and story, resources, hidden rules, and choices and consequences. Teachers also can use the stories as a bridge to study historical events, social issues and problems, literature, art, music, mathematics, and science.

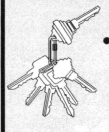

- **Gifted students from poverty must have the same opportunity to acquire the larger, more meaningful learnings that are part of the differentiated curriculum for the gifted.**

- **For gifted students from poverty to be successful in the differentiated curriculum, teachers must direct-teach thinking processes and organizational strategies, as well as create the mental models necessary to understand a more complex curriculum.**

- Teachers must build on the reference points that are part of the students' real-life experiences.

- Casual register must not be condemned. Students must be taught formal register in a direct way.

- Random, episodic story structure must be replaced with sequential, logical, cause-and-effect structures.

- Pictures and graphic symbols should be used to help students move from the concrete to the more abstract.

Chapter Nine:

Nurturing and
Keeping the Gifts

Understanding the Diversity of the Gifted

"Being gifted is like having a really nice car. But the environment in which you drive affects your forward momentum.

♦ The gifted from a nurtured, enriched background has the car with an outside accessory package. Everyone can see, admire, and serve the talents.
♦ The low-socioeconomic status gifted has the car, but may not yet have the keys to drive it.
♦ The highly gifted or prodigy gifted has the car but may only be allowed to drive within the city limits and must follow all the usual traffic signs, such as *slow, caution, speed limit*, and *stop*.
♦ The underachieving gifted has the car, but is not driving it. It remains parked in the garage.
♦ The primary gifted has the car, but is considered too young to drive it.
♦ The language-different gifted has the car, but the signs and directions are in another language so it cannot go anywhere.
♦ The ADD/ADHD gifted has the car, but the electrical ignition system is wired differently so it stays in motion when others want it to stop.
♦ The culturally-diverse gifted has the car, but it has a shrink-wrapped cover over it which clouds its potential.
♦ The physically challenged gifted has the car, but the air conditioning is broken. The mechanics are kept so busy trying to fix the air conditioning that the car never gets to be driven.
♦ The gifted female has the car, but she may self-sabotage or be around others who think she does not deserve it. Many wonder what her daddy does!

"Being gifted is like having a really nice car. Our challenge is to help all educators and parents to become sensitive to the diversity of the gifted so their cars can safely enter the high-speed freeway of learning."

Bertie Kingore, *Tempo*, *Texas Association for the Gifted and Talented, Volume 17, Number 2 (pp. 1, 6), Spring 1997*

CHAPTER NINE:

NURTURING AND KEEPING THE GIFTS

S chools may identify students from poverty as gifted and structure an academic program for them, but unless teachers and the school address their affective needs, the students will be minimally successful and/or drop out of the program. Support systems for students from poverty are essential. Gifted students from poverty bring to the school a host of issues that affect the learning process. Without clearly thought-out intervention plans, the likelihood of success in school diminishes. Issues that make the affective needs of gifted students from poverty so important include:

- Unlike their classroom peers, gifted students from poverty frequently compete in an academic environment without a support system in the home.
- They may no longer fit in with their peer group. Different values become apparent. As a result, they may feel that they must choose between academics and their friends.
- They are "different" from their peers within the neighborhood. They may feel they don't fit in at either school or home.
- They have little in common with the middle-class gifted students in their school.
- They lack many of the skills and experiences of middle-class students.
- They have few goal-setting or planning skills.

AND

- Middle-class students lack the skills and experiences of students from poverty; therefore, they don't understand them. What people don't understand they usually fear.

Neglecting the emotional development of students impacts their intellectual development. This is because emotions are a key piece of the learning puzzle. Working with the emotional development of students is affective education. Affective development pertains to the personal, social, and emotional learning that takes place in school. Areas that are involved include:

- Classroom management.
- Disciplinary procedures.
- Curriculum.
- Health and personal-hygiene issues.
- Gender and economic differences.

Though counselors need to be involved in this process, classroom teachers are in the best position to develop and implement a curriculum designed to impact positively the affective development of gifted students from poverty. Teachers and counselors play very different roles in working with these students. Van Tassel-Baska (1988, p. 338) outlines the differences between these two roles, as follows:

Affective Curriculum	Counseling Services
• Oriented toward groups.	• Oriented toward individuals.
• Usually directed by the teacher (no special training required).	• Directed by an individual trained in counseling.
• Involves self-awareness and sharing of feelings with others.	• Involves problem-solving, making choices, conflict resolution, and deeper understanding of self.

• Consists of planned exercises and activities designed by the teacher for classroom use.	• Consists of relatively unstructured private and/or group sessions in which students determine the content.
• Unrelated to therapy.	• Related to therapy.
• Students are helped to clarify their own beliefs.	• Students are helped to change their perceptions or methods of coping.
• Personalizes the curriculum, making it more relevant to the student.	• Unrelated to curriculum.

Teachers plan and implement numerous activities that foster a student's cognitive development while simultaneously contributing to his/her affective development. When teachers design lessons that call for students to work in pairs or cooperative-learning groups, they stretch the students' social development and leadership abilities. Most gifted students have confidence in their intellectual abilities but not in their social skills. Gifted students from poverty, however, may not have confidence in either of these areas. Bolstering a student's self-confidence as a learner (cognitive development) and as a productive person socially (affective) is the challenge. Because gifted students are often very intense, topics discussed on an intellectual level within the classroom can have an enormous impact on them.

Implementing instructional activities that develop the affect necessitates a philosophy that is based on respect for the uniqueness of each student's beliefs and life experiences. The teacher must make sharing optional and respect the privacy of the student.

Affective development is grounded in self-concept. Carl Rogers (1951) describes self-concept as a collection of perceptions of one's characteristics and abilities that develops out of interpesonal relationships. Since one's interaction with the world forms self-concept, it is vulnerable to feedback from others. The self then becomes the force that shapes the person's perceptions and behavior. Clark (1983, p. 108) describes the significance of self as follows:

> ... The self determines achievement and enhances or limits the development of a person's potential ... The beliefs we have about ourselves literally determine our actions and our perceptions of the world and other people. We construct our own reality from these beliefs and often operate as if this is the only view possible (Combs and Snygg, 1959; May, 1967; Rogers, 1961).

For gifted students from poverty, just as with other students, life experiences shape perceptions of the world and other people. Some of these powerful forces that are more likely to be found in poverty include:

- Struggling to survive.
- Violence in the home and/or neighborhood.
- Feeling unsafe.
- Fear of abandonment.
- Distrust of police, social workers, landlords.
- Mobility, lack of stability.
- Having to be an adult, taking care of brothers and sisters, staying home alone.
- Loss of control over one's destiny.
- Need to belong.
- Absence of play and childhood.
- Drug and alcohol abuse.
- Victimization.
- Being verbally abused.

The goal of the school is to increase the student's sense of belonging or attachment to the school. Teachers who establish firm boundaries, foster warm personal relationships in the classroom, and empower students to have an impact on their environment strengthen students' attachment to school; interest in learning; ability to control impulsive, self-destructive behaviors; and constructive behaviors.

Managing Behavior in an Instructional Setting

One way to help students be successful in the classroom is to allow them to participate in classroom decisions and responsibilities. Students, like adults, are more likely to conform to the rules if they have had an opportunity to be part of the decision-making process. Teachers might use a lesson on the U.S. Bill of Rights as a springboard to developing a "Bill of Rights for the Classroom." The teacher would begin by discussing with the students the role of the teacher and the role of the learner. What are the duties and responsibilities of a teacher? What are the duties and responsibilities of the learner? Such a discussion will generate rules stated in casual register. The teacher can help students restate the students' rules in formal register, stated in a positive manner. Students might suggest things like ...

- "I don't want nobody laughin' at me."
- "No yellin' at us."
- "No put-downs."
- "Not interrupting."

Students generally will state the common rules of a classroom. As the students exhaust the standard list of rules, the teacher might offer rules that cause them to ponder some "what if" scenarios:

- What if students could go to the restroom without asking permission?
- What if students could leave the classroom for any reason without asking permission?
- What if students didn't have to raise their hand to speak?
- What if there were no deadlines for turning in assignments?

Pondering such questions allows students the opportunity to explore the effects of rules on the larger group. It gives them a chance to talk about the need for rules that establish order for the larger whole. How are classroom rules like or different from rules at home, in the neighborhood, the church, the town? For gifted students from poverty who don't have that cause-effect pattern in the brain, such discussions become powerful learning opportunities.

When gifted students from poverty are in the same classroom with students from advantaged backgrounds, the social challenges are greater for both groups because neither group understands the hidden rules of the other. These different rules must be openly discussed, exploring the consequences for each in the context of school and the neighborhood. Activities in the classroom can help develop a deeper understanding for both groups. Ideally, activities will connect to the students' academic lessons, thus enhancing both the cognitive and affective development of the students.

The following activity (adapted from Bess, 1994, p. 46) could be included in a unit of study using children's fairy tales to illustrate how conflict is resolved. Cinderella, a rags-to-riches theme, could be used to speculate on responsibilities one has in relation to family members and others. With older students, instead of candy being used, the teacher might distribute poker chips that represent bonus points on classwork. Issues such as foreign aid, disaster-relief funds, food banks, etc., could be used to illustrate the same types of feelings that accompany giving, sharing, and receiving.

Trick or Treat

Materials: Candy
Have just enough candy, such as miniature Snickers or Milky Way bars, for each person in the classroom to have one—or not quite enough for everyone.

Objective: To develop an understanding of the difficulties, rewards, and sacrifices and emotions involved in sharing and receiving.

Activity:

- Distribute the candy randomly and unevenly among the class members. Give some three, some two, some one, and some none. Instruct the students that they are not to eat their candy until the class has had an opportunity to discuss some things.

- Ask the students for their observations. Who has candy? How much do they have? How many students are in the class? How does it feel to not have any? How does it feel to have three pieces of candy?

- Tell the students that after the lesson they will have an opportunity to eat the candy. They may share their candy or keep it, but they may not **take** someone's, nor may they eat it until the lesson is over.

- Give the students an opportunity to talk about the pros and cons of sharing or keeping their candy. Ask questions that will cause the students to identify responsibilities, if any, that they have. Ask the students who have no candy how it feels to be dependent on those who have the candy.

- Is it hard to share your candy? Discuss how it feels to share and why. Discuss how it feels to receive and why. How much does one stand to lose by giving? Is it painful to give up one's candy?

Closing: Give students one last chance to redistribute the candy if they wish. Ask the students to make connections regarding what they have just experienced to the larger unit of study.

This activity can be done many different ways using different objects that students value. A few days later repeat the activity using money. The money should be in a quantity that is sufficient for the students to buy something in the school cafeteria or pencils from the school supply closet/machine. Students usually will become more emotional about money if the teacher allows the students to identify things they can purchase with the money, calculating what it will cost, how much they have, and how much they need from others.

The hidden rules also should be talked about following this lesson. Middle class students and students from poverty may discover they have different views of their responsibility toward others. Why would some students want to save their candy/money while others would want to share it? With whom were they willing to share it? Explain to the students how various groups view sharing and receiving differently. Discuss the larger issues centered around being "my brother's keeper."

Most gifted students will experience some predictable problems as a gifted learner. These include:

- Feeling different.
- Disappointing self (perfectionism).
- Having a need to win.
- Dealing with stress.
- Having to make choices.
- Being bored.
- Feeling worried about the future of self and others.

For gifted students from poverty, the concerns are generally grouped in the following:

- Having to give up friends because they're in the gifted program.
- Having parents who don't understand "that fancy stuff," or why he/she needs to learn it.
- Wanting to achieve and not having the necessary resources within the home to achieve.
- Feeling unaccepted by the middle-class gifted students.
- Being different intellectually from their economic peer group.
- Being different economically and experientially from their intellectual group.
- Being unaware of the hidden rules of middle-class: "Why am I always screwing up no matter how hard I try?"

Because gifted students from poverty face many unique challenges, they need opportunities to talk with one another as a group without having non-poverty students present. They need to share their frustrations about their unique situation. They need to know that others are experiencing the same thing. Being in a small group also allows the students to form their own support group and collectively develop some strategies to cope with pressures within the neighborhood, at school, and in the family.

A good way to begin each day is having these students sit in a circle. Depending on the age level of the students, the teacher could call the group a variety of names (Rap Session, Jam Session, Sharing Time, Our Time, Family Circle Time, Support Time, etc.). Using some predetermined prompts, the teacher, in a non-judgmental way, allows students to respond to prompts. Students can have the opportunity to follow up the activity by writing in their personal journal. This allows the students to express things that they may not want to share with the larger group. Some possible prompts follow:

- "I feel really different when ... "
- My favorite song, movie
- My favorite singer/actor/comedian/singing group
- An adult I like most/least
- "A friend is one who ..."
- Three things that make me special
- One of the funniest things I ever did
- "If I could make a movie about one thing, it would be ..."
- "What I dislike most is ..."
- Who or what has been the greatest influence in my life?
- "I like teachers who ..."
- "I'm afraid when ..."
- "I become really angry when ..."
- "I'm very happy when ..."
- Three people who are no longer living whom I would like to have come visit me at my home
- Three characters from history or a story whom I would like to meet
- A question I have always wanted answered
- "If I could change one thing in the world, I would ..."

The teacher also can create activities that take several days to complete. Some examples are:

- Have each student observe another student for one week. Pair the students with someone different from them. Interview the student and then create an award for that person based on the special qualities discovered about that person.

- Create a "Class Mood Chart." Have the students rate their mood at three different times during the day on a scale of 1 to 10 (1 is "horrible," 10 is "euphoric"). Have students write in their journal about how and why their mood changed during the day. (This allows students to identify possible cause-and-effect relationships between their behavior, feelings, and outside forces.)

- Have students collect small objects that best describe them. Have the students describe to the class how the objects relate to them. (This enables the students to think abstractly and also form analogies, metaphors, and similes.)

- Bring some old shoes to class. Discuss with students the expression "walking in someone else's shoes." Offer several issues for the students to discuss that allow them to "walk in someone else's shoes." How does one's perspective change? Why does it change? Is one right and the other wrong? (This allows the students to explore different points of view, to look at things from a different perspective. The teacher can carry over this lesson to history; to the study of literary characters and roles people play; and to the values reflected in different time periods, age and gender groups, racial groups, economic groups.)

- Sponsor a "Bring a Buddy to Class" week. Students have to locate other students in the school who can do things they can't. They interview the student, find out about his/her strengths and talents, and then invite the person to be a guest in the class for a day.

Teachers also may use books as a springboard to talking through certain issues with students. Quality literature allows the teacher to probe a variety of situations in which people are forced to resolve a moral or ethical dilemma. Incorporating these experiences within other kinds of affective lessons increases the possibilities for affective, as well as cognitive, development.

Student behaviors are diagnostic. Virtually no student comes to school intent on giving everyone a bad day. The teacher's daily challenge is to find out what is causing the behavior that is negative—or positive. The affective curriculum is a powerful diagnostic tool. Based on students' responses, the teacher can identify ...

- Students who need to have more attention given to them and their unique situation. These students are referred to the counselor for follow-up.

- Possible methods, strategies, and activities that motivate students.
- Possible problems within the home and school that are contributing negatively to the student's development.
- Fears, anxieties, hopes, and dreams of the students.
- Significant issues with which gifted students from poverty must deal on a daily basis.

Discipline Procedures

Students have a need and a right to know the rules. Without structure, little learning takes place. Gifted students from poverty may have minimal experience in the home environment with boundaries. School is full of boundaries. Students need to know what these boundaries are and their responsibilities in relation to those boundaries. This involves consequences. If the teacher approaches the task with love and caring, showing respect and understanding of the students, they will be more likely to conform to the expectations. Behaviors that teachers can expect from gifted students from poverty include:

Behavior	Possible Strategy
• Laughing when disciplined	• Stop the discipline procedure. Wait. Ask: "How will laughing when you are being disciplined help you? How could laughing make things worse for you?" Talk about the inappropriateness of laughing while being disciplined.
• Talking loudly	• Develop a cue for when loud talk is being heard. For example, place a yellow circle on the student's desk as a reminder that he/she is too loud. Students often are unaware of their loudness.
• Using inappropriate language	• Have students come up with alternative ways of saying the same thing in formal register.
• Getting into physical confrontations	• Fighting is unacceptable at school. This is a non-negotiable matter. Help students come up with alternatives to fighting.
• Becoming angry when corrected	• Help students identify strategies and language for expressing anger and disappointment.
• Having trouble following directions	• Develop instructional "road maps" for assignments. Use the maps during the lesson so students know where they are in relationship to other tasks and events during the day or lesson.

• Showing disrespect for adults and other students	• Practice the verbal and non-verbal language for showing respect. The teacher needs to model respect for students at all times, even when angry or upset.
• Cheating and stealing	• Try to get at the cause for the cheating and/or stealing. Work privately with the student.
• Not paying attention	• Work out a system, a verbal cue, to use with the student who has difficulty paying attention that doesn't embarrass the student in front of the group.
• Refusing to wait his/her turn	• Discuss with students how not being patient with someone else is a "put-down" of that person's best efforts. This is a respect issue.
• Forgetting rules and procedures	• Have students focus on a rule for the day as part of personal goal-setting. When the list is complete, begin the cycle again.
• Losing things and assignments	• Have students research different organizational strategies by interviewing other students. Draw up a plan for organizing your desk, your day, etc.

Some guidelines for teachers to use in working on discipline issues with gifted students from poverty are:

- Speak in an adult, professional manner with students.
- Don't embarrass students in front of their peers.
- Show respect for all students at all times. Never, ever yell at students.
- Model appropriate ways of dealing with frustration and anger. Label it for the students. For example, "John, I am very angry and disappointed with you right now. I need to calm down before I can talk with you about it. When I calm down, I will speak with you about this. Would you sit over here and read your book until I'm ready to talk with you? Thank you."
- Remind yourself that all behaviors are diagnostic. Try to figure out the real issues instead of just reacting to the symptoms.
- Let the students know that you're aware of the hidden rules they must live with in their neighborhood, but note that the school uses some different rules that students must learn work to their advantage while at school. Different games are played using different rules.
- Try to resolve the issues within the classroom as much as possible. Sending students to the office can become a way for both teachers and students to avoid dealing with the real issues.

The safer and more cared about the students from poverty feel, the more likely they will stay in the program. As previously discussed, forming a significant relationship is an integral part of this effort. The students must know that the teacher is "on their side." If the teacher is viewed as the enemy, academics don't stand a chance. Classroom practices that help communicate caring and an understanding of the students' needs include:

- Furnish supplies that are needed for students to complete assignments and projects.
- Structure time within the school day for students to complete their work. Most students from poverty lack an environment conducive to doing assignments at home.
- Know the home environment and the adults in the household before calling the parent about a problem. Some parents may severely or inappropriately punish their child as a result of the school's report. When this occurs, the student may feel the teacher has betrayed him/her ("I knew she didn't like me; she got me in trouble with my mama").
- When things must be purchased, use a "barter system" that allows the student to earn the school shirt, the magazine, etc.
- Let students know that you realize there are two sides to every story. Listen to the student's side of the story, no matter how absurd the story may seem.

Since story structure for students from poverty is not usually organized in a sequential, cause-and-effect manner, it is sometimes difficult to get the facts surrounding an incident or issue. The same also is true with the parents. When a student or parent has an incident to report, a strategy that works well is having the individual tell the story using a three-step process. A workable sequence for this is as follows:

Teacher/Administrator: "I'm going to ask you to tell me your story twice. The **first time** you will tell me your story, and I will not interrupt you. I will not ask you any questions, and I will write nothing down.

"The **second time** you tell me your story, I will take notes, and I will ask you questions.

"Then I'm going to tell you your story, and you tell me if I got it right."

Using this approach achieves several objectives:

1. Listening to the story the first time allows the educator to identify any "holes" in the story and to get a sense of the story's characters and the sequence of events.

2. Hearing the story the second time allows the educator to ask questions necessary to get all the facts straight; figure out the relationships between/among the characters in the story; determine the sequence of events; and fill in relevant, missing information.

3. The third time enables the educator to tell the story in a sequential manner (modeling) so there is a cause-and-effect relationship between the event(s) and the result(s). It also allows the student and/or parent to edit any information that the educator may have misunderstood.

The result of using this process is that the parent and student leave the situation knowing they have been heard, and their concerns have been taken seriously. With young children, this strategy also works, but the educator usually finds that the story is very short the first time. It may look something like this:

> **Teacher** (teacher tells the student the sequence of telling the story as outlined above): "OK, Billy, tell me your story about what happened on the playground."
> **Student**: "Joe hit me."
> **Teacher** (after a long pause): "Billy, are you through with your story?"
> **Student**: "Yes, ma'am."
> **Teacher**: "OK, Billy, tell me your story again."
> **Student**: "Joe hit me."
> **Teacher**: "Where did Joe hit you?"
> **Student**: "On my arm."
> **Teacher**: "Where did this happen?"

This leads to a series of questions that helps the teacher identify what Billy might have done that contributed to this incident, where it occurred, who else was there, etc. The student begins to learn to elaborate his/her responses. When this approach is used consistently, students begin to benefit from the process, and their stories become more structured and sequential. They know they will be heard, asked questions, and treated with respect. Most parents also respond equally well to this format. By telling the story twice, and hearing it told to them, it is very difficult for an angry parent to retain his/her anger throughout all the steps of the process. They too know they have been heard and treated fairly.

Gifted Boys from Poverty

Of all the students identified for the gifted program, boys from poverty will experience more behavior problems than any other segment of the population. Again, their behavior is diagnostic. Unfortunately, school officials usually respond to boys' misbehavior with a mindset of "Boys will be boys" and mete out punishment with little thought about root causes of the behavior. Dr. William Pollack, a clinical psychologist with Harvard Medical School and author of **Real Boys** (1998), says it's in the public-school classroom where the most destructive effects of society's misunderstanding of boys reveal themselves.

> *Thrust into competition with their peers, some boys invest so much energy into keeping up their emotional guard and disguising their deepest and most vulnerable feelings, they often have little or no energy left to apply themselves to their schoolwork …. Over the last decade we've been forced to confront some staggering statistics.*

*From **Real Boys** by William Pollack. Copyright © 1998 by William Pollack. Reprinted by permission of random House, Inc.

From elementary grades through high school, boys receive lower grades than girls. Eighth-grade boys are held back 50 percent more often than girls. By high school, boys account for two thirds of the students in special education classes. Fewer boys than girls now attend and graduate from college. Fifty-nine percent of all master's degree candidates are now women, and the percentage of men in graduate-level professional education is shrinking each year.

Boys experience more difficulty adjusting to school, are up to ten times more likely to suffer from "hyperactivity" than girls, and account for 71 percent of all school suspensions (p. 15).

Through interviews with hundreds of boys, Dr. Pollack reports that boys comment over and over again that it's not "cool" to be too smart in school because it leads to being "labeled a nerd, dork, wimp, or fag." One boy reported, "'I'm not stupid enough to sit in the front row and act like some sort of teacher's pet. If I did, I'd end up with a head full of spitballs and then get my butt kicked in'" (Pollack, 1998, p. 16).

For boys from poverty, the trauma associated with these labels is often the "kiss of death." In neighborhoods where survival is the name of the game, doing well in school increases the odds that boys from poverty will become the hunted rather than the hunter. Complicating this is the lack of a support system in the home for boys. The home environment usually sets the stage for boys from poverty to be unsuccessful, both academically and emotionally. For many boys from poverty, they are the males living in a matriarchal household. They must be tough and responsible. Adult, male role models may ebb in and out of their lives. Fathers may be in prison, on drugs, or in the throes of alcoholism. Frequently, the security and safety of childhood are replaced with fear, feelings of abandonment, being emotionally detached, anger, and sadness. Where is the forum for gifted boys from poverty to express these feelings?

Pollack's research shows that boys will express their feelings to an adult but not in the same manner as girls. What works with boys is using games and activities that boys enjoy. While playing a game with a boy, the adult has the opportunity to dialogue by asking questions without invading his space. Allowing "wait time" and allowing the student to share when he feels safe are important elements of this process. In a classroom setting this is difficult. Most teachers don't have the time to sit with a student and play a game. Time can be created, however, that allows this strategy to work. Counselors can have times with boys in which they play a game and talk with them. Teachers can create a before- and after-school time for some students who need to spend time with a caring adult. Many students also like to help the teacher. Coming in before school to help the teacher clean off the bookshelves can provide an appropriate forum. Most boys need to have a distraction when talking. When confronted with direct questions, boys will typically respond by saying that nothing is wrong.

Robert is in third grade. He is one of four children living with his single mother. Robert has been acting out in class the last three days. Robert is usually a little loud, and he can be a class clown, but in the last three days he has stolen money from one of his classmates, refused to do his work in class, and now gotten into a fight with his best friend. After trying the usual discipline strategies, the teacher decides that she needs to create an opportunity for Robert to visit with her. She invites Robert to stay after school with her and help her put up the bulletin board. In exchange for that she will stop at McDonald's when she takes him home. The dialogue between Robert and his teacher follows:

Teacher: "I appreciate you helping me today, Robert."

Robert: "Where do you get all this stuff?"

Teacher: "Oh, I bought some of it at stores and other teachers share things with me. I bet you have some friends who share things with you."

Robert: "I have a cousin who gives me his clothes when he's done with them."

Teacher: "That's nice of him. I bet that saves your mother a lot of money."

Robert: "Yeah, I guess."

Teacher: "How is your mother, Robert?"

Robert: "She's been sick."

Teacher: "Oh, no. I'm sorry to hear that, Robert. Is she real sick?"

Robert: "She was in the hospital last week, but she's at home now. My older sister is staying home with her."

Teacher: "What was wrong with her?"

Robert: "My mama's boyfriend broke her jaw. There was a real bad fight."

Teacher: "Did your mother's boyfriend hurt you or your brothers and sisters?"

Robert: "He started to hit me, but I threw something at him and ran out of the apartment. I went next door, and they called the cops."

Teacher: "That must have been very scary for you, Robert. I can't imagine what I would do if I were in a situation like that."

Robert: "I told my mama that we should get a gun. I would shoot him if I had a gun."

Teacher: "Robert, I know you're a very brave young man, but if you did have a gun and your mother's boyfriend had found the gun, what might have happened?"

Robert: "I guess he coulda shot all of us."

Teacher: "Are you afraid your mother's boyfriend is going to come back?"

Robert: "No, he's in jail, but …

Teacher: "But what, Robert?"

Robert: "My mother has lots of bad boyfriends. I wish they'd stay away and leave us alone."

Teacher: "How do you feel about your mother's boyfriends always coming around, Robert?"

In the above scenario, the teacher has an opportunity to ask questions and interact with Robert in a non-judgmental way. She can help Robert identify options and explore his feelings related to his home situation. It also helps her understand what Robert is dealing with outside the school day. In a classroom setting or a small-group counseling session, the student likely never would have shared this information. If the teacher had confronted Robert by taking him outside the classroom into the hall, the outcome probably would have been very different, as follows:

> **Teacher:** "Robert, what is **wrong** with you? You've been in trouble all week. Is something bothering you?"
> **Robert:** "No. Nothing's wrong."
> **Teacher:** "Well, why did you and Billy get into that fight? I thought he was your best friend."
> **Robert:** "I dunno. He's still my friend."

Boys are supposed to be able to handle the situation. Whether it's Mom's boyfriend beating on them, or Child Protective Services coming to the house, or the electricity being turned off (and there is no heat) doesn't matter. If you're a boy, you've got to be strong: "Big boys don't cry. It ain't cool to cry."

Being more sensitive, persistent, and analytical than non-gifted boys makes the plight of gifted boys even more problematic. Most gifted boys from poverty are deeply conflicted about doing their best (the movie "Good Will Hunting" well illustrates this ambivalence). Even so, that "best" is driven by the hidden rules within the culture of poverty, not middle class. Boys in poverty tend to act out their feelings; they seldom verbalize their feelings. These feelings become a source of anger that give way to rage, formation of gangs, impulsivity, addictions, depression, and other self-destructive behaviors. Being driven

to be like other boys is powerful, making giftedness more of a
curse than a blessing to a boy from poverty. Though girls
certainly have their difficulties, North American culture
permits them to express their feelings without shame or guilt.
Most boys, on the other hand, feel enormous shame if they
"can't handle it." The following diagram shows these
differences between the two gender groups.

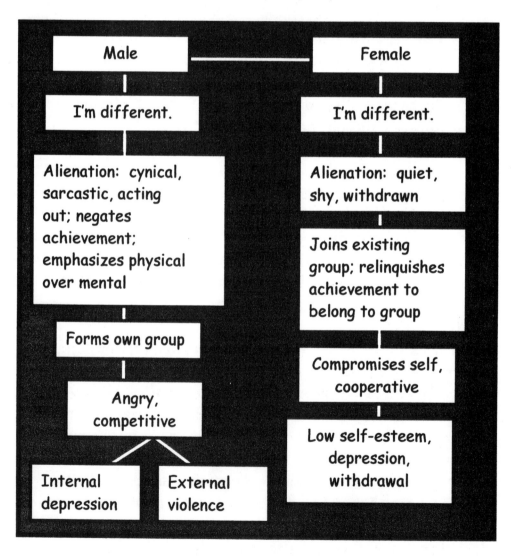

Gifted students know they're different from most of their peers. Students from poverty know they're different from non-poverty students. Giftedness and poverty together create an even greater difference. Gifted boys from poverty manifest their differences much like other boys from poverty but with a greater intensity and persistence. Students who feel different from their peer group frequently experience feelings of alienation. That difference from the peer group can be due to language, racial or ethnic orientation, gender difference, physical appearance, or economic disparity. The result is feeling alone, detached from the group.

For gifted boys from poverty, this feeling may be expressed through cynical and sarcastic behaviors, acting out in class, minimizing academic achievement, and showing off physical strength. For girls from poverty, the feeling of alienation is more likely to manifest itself in a more reserved manner. Gifted girls from poverty tend to become quiet and withdrawn.

In their quest to belong, both boys and girls from poverty seek out a group. Boys, being more competitive and independent, usually find compatible friends and form their own group. Girls tend to join existing groups and often compromise achievement in order to belong to the group. They are more willing to compromise their own personal wishes in order to "belong."

The anger, fear, sadness, and frustration that are deeply rooted in students who feel different and unaccepted by their peer group surfaces differently in boys and girls. The boys who turn their feelings inward experience varying degrees of depression. Those who turn their feelings outward tend to become more violent. Girls, on the other hand, generally become more depressed and withdrawn. Their anger can be manifested outwardly through violence, but it isn't nearly as likely for girls to respond violently.

Once students from poverty have been identified for the gifted program, it is crucial that teachers and administrative personnel work diligently to keep them in the program. To do this school officials must work with both giftedness and poverty because each is a significant part of the student. Because of the overt behaviors, hidden rules, lack of resources, and lack of skills accompanying poverty, most gifted students from poverty quickly become uncomfortable with the placement and the academic focus and challenge. Educators must work to help these students live in two very different worlds. Before teachers can effectively address these students' cognitive needs, they must understand and address their affective needs. If the student is uncomfortable and doesn't understand the feelings that this new gifted environment triggers, then very little learning will take place.

"Regrettably, instead of working with boys to convince them it is desirable and even 'cool' to perform well at school, teachers too, are often fooled by the mask and believe the stereotype; and this helps make the lack of achievement self-fulfilling. If a teacher believes that boys who are not doing well are simply

*From **Real Boys** by William Pollack. Copyright © 1998 by William Pollack. Reprinted by permission of random House, Inc.

uninterested, incapable, or delinquent, and signals this, it helps to make it so" (Pollack, 1998, p. 17).

After identifying gifted students from poverty, the school must meet their affective needs if they are to choose to remain in the program:

- Recognize that the values of poverty and those of middle class create an inner conflict for most gifted students from poverty.

- Implement disciplinary procedures that "work with" the effects of poverty rather than against them.

- Establish clear rules and involve the students in the process of establishing those rules.

- Incorporate affective lessons into the curriculum. Start each day with a group, affective activity that helps build personal relationships.

- Recognize that students' overt behaviors are diagnostic. Establish private opportunities to work with students to determine the source of covert feelings that ignite overt behaviors.

- Discuss openly with the students the hidden rules that govern them.

- Implement a "bibliotherapy" component into the curriculum. Study the lives of gifted people who came from poverty backgrounds and later achieved great things.

- Create a safe environment for students from poverty by showing them they can achieve in school and also be "cool"—both in school and in the neighborhood.

- Create opportunities for gifted boys to talk without the pressures of a peer group.

Chapter Ten:

The Systemic Challenge

Systemic Commitment Produces Individual Achievement

In 1991 Tony Robbins, a well-known seminar leader and author of self-help books, made a promise to a group of fifth grade students at Stovall Academy Elementary School in the Aldine Independent School District in Houston, Texas. If they stayed off drugs and alcohol, maintained a B average, and performed 25 to 50 hours of community service per year until they graduated from high school, they would receive a college scholarship.

Of the 103 students who signed up to meet the "Champions of Excellence" challenge, 20 students succeeded. On June 5, 1999, 20 graduates received a $16,000 scholarship. One student received additional money for achieving a high grade point average. Another received an additional $1,000 for doing 400 hours of community service beyond the required 300 hours.

When the students graduated from the elementary school, the principal organized mentors at the students' receiving middle and high schools to help her keep up with the students' progress. One student had moved out of state but continued in the program. The elementary principal visited with the students yearly at each level of school. The principal commented, "The students and I had a very unique relationship that I just absolutely treasure. I have literally watched these children grow up."

A parent reported, "Tony made us focus more as a family. He taught us to be more personal and to think things out. This really helped us contribute with the kids."

In addition to the scholarships, the students also received laptop computers, color printers from Epson, and four years of Internet service from American Online. The students also will attend a five-day seminar conducted by Tony Robbins entitled "Date with Destiny."

- *Houston Chronicle* (pp. 1D and 10D), June 9, 1999

CHAPTER TEN:

THE SYSTEMIC CHALLENGE

If the school system is going to identify and serve gifted students from poverty, it must be responsive to the issues that surround poverty. Without a sensitivity to the needs of students from poverty, the system cannot get to the point that it can identify and serve such students with any degree of success. If the system cannot be successful with students from poverty in the mainstream instructional program, how can it possibly be successful with them in a special program?

While working to become more efficient in identifying and serving gifted students from poverty, the system must engage in a process of self-examination and correct attitudes, practices, and procedures that tend to be obstacles in the identification of gifted students from poverty. This chapter explores some the systemic problems that make the task of identifying and serving gifted students from poverty more difficult at the district, campus, classroom, and personal levels.

Educators need to become aggressive in the education of parents and teachers on the unique needs of gifted students. The image the schools project to the public is that gifted students are middle or upper class, make good grades, and are not a discipline problem. The fact that this myth has prevailed is an indication that the system has not done a good job in identifying gifted students from poverty—gifted students who are bilingual, who have handicapping conditions, or who may have a combination of all of these. Because educators haven't identified these special subgroups efficiently, parents persistently fight to get their child included in what they perceive to be the "best program for the best students."

The lack of understanding about the needs of students from poverty has perpetuated myths about these students as well. Myths such as "their parents don't care" and "they can't learn" plague students from poverty. Between the myths about giftedness and the myths about poverty, the stereotypes about both groups continue. The result is practices and procedures within the system that make the gap between these two groups even wider.

The following are true stories. They illustrate the overall lack of understanding and empathy within systems and communities. There are no "bad people" in any of these stories. Their overt actions, however, reflect the deeper covert attitudes, beliefs, and lack of knowledge that hurt children.

THE NEIGHBORHOOD SCHOOL

In one suburban community the school system had a large number of students from poverty in its schools. Because of the demographic growth patterns within the community over many years, students from poverty were physically located in certain parts of the town. For several years children from these poverty neighborhoods were bused to schools in the school district that were outside the immediate neighborhood in which the students lived. As a result, the receiving schools had more students from poverty than they would've had were these students not bused out of the neighborhood. With school district growth came the need for more schools. The result? The district built a new school in a poor neighborhood to serve the students in that neighborhood.

Because of numerous administrative and community meetings to discuss the issues related to building the school in this neighborhood, the special needs of the students surfaced. Upon completion of the new school, 98% of the students would be from poverty. Among the identified needs for the students in the new school were:

- Social workers and psychologists.
- Washers and dryers for students to wash their own clothing.
- Showers for students with personal-hygiene needs.
- Additional planning time for the teachers.

- Tutorial sessions for students before and after school.
- Lower pupil-teacher ratios.
- Special training for teachers to work with students from poverty.
- Clothes closet for students.
- School supplies to be furnished by the school.
- More computers.
- Highly skilled nurse.
- Parent education.
- Highly trained counselors.

All of these students had been in the school system. They had been attending schools outside of their neighborhood. Now that the political machinery was turning, these students were being looked at as having special needs.

The Moral of the Story

When the students were bused out of their neighborhood, their needs went with them. No matter how many teachers talked about what the students could not do and did need, the system didn't change. Every campus was treated the same. The campus that had a 25% low-socioeconomic population received the same per-pupil allocation in its budget as the campus that had an 85% low-socioeconomic population. Pupil-teacher ratios were the same everywhere in the system. Equity was traded off for equality. Only when the students returned to their neighborhood, attended a beautiful new school surrounded by poverty, and the community demanded more for their children, did the system respond to the issue of equity.

THROW OUT THE YEARBOOKS

In another suburban school district the Parent-Teacher Organization sold yearbooks as one of its fund-raisers. Forty percent of the school's population qualified for the district's free-lunch program. Many of these students couldn't afford to purchase a yearbook. The principal, in an effort to help those families who couldn't afford a yearbook, organized a program whereby the students could earn money to buy a yearbook. Yet the program wasn't large enough to include all the students who wanted to participate. The principal asked the PTO president if the students could buy the yearbooks at a reduced price. The answer was no because "that wouldn't be fair to the other students who were able to pay."

A patron came to a top-level administrator's office one afternoon carrying a box filled with the school's yearbooks. The patron asked the administrator why a box of yearbooks was in the district's trash bin. The administrator said he didn't know, but he would call the principal and inquire.

Upon calling the principal, who also was unaware of the discarded yearbooks, the administrator discovered that the PTO had 35 yearbooks that didn't sell. Rather than give them away to the students who couldn't afford them or to the principal for her special Earn-a-Yearbook project, the PTO discarded them.

The Moral of the Story

Well-meaning parents chose to throw away the yearbooks because students who could afford to purchase yearbooks had purchased one. This parent group felt it would not be "fair" to charge some students less or to give them away. Treating all students equally became more important than equitable treatment of unequals, and no one asked if it was "fair" that some students are poor and others are not.

SANTA COMES FOR A FEW

In another school district, a new elementary school located in an upper-middle-class community also served some students from a poor community a few miles from the school. The Parent-Teacher Organization raised more than $20,000. One of its activities was to have a Santa come to the school on a Saturday for the students. The PTO officers decided that they wanted only the children who lived in the immediate upper-middle-class neighborhood of the school to attend the Christmas party. This would exclude those students who were bused to the school from the lower-socioeconomic neighborhood. To achieve this, the parent group had to approach members of a private group and ask them to rent the school facility for the Christmas party and be the official sponsors of the event. This way the event couldn't be classified as a school-sponsored event.

Fortunately, when the principal became aware of the situation (and even though the school facility had been rented to the private organization), the event ultimately was opened up to all children who attended the school.

The Moral of the Story

Personnel within the school district and the school board must be the advocates for those children whose parents seldom act overtly. The parents of the students living in the immediate neighborhood were active advocates for their children. The children who resided outside the immediate neighborhood had no one to come forward to speak for them. It is usually the school employees who must be the advocates to make sure these children are treated fairly and equitably.

MONEY EVERYWHERE AND NOT A DIME TO SPEND

Schools that serve more affluent neighborhoods tend to have very active parent organizations. These organizations typically raise thousands of dollars to fund field trips, parties, and special events for students. Schools in less affluent neighborhoods don't have parents who can generate the amounts of money that the more affluent neighborhoods can.

In one school district, two affluent schools had a very active Parent-Teacher Organization. The parents in these two schools had Certificates of Deposit totaling nearly $25,000. One of the two schools raised that amount of money the first year the school was open. In addition to the CDs, the PTO hired a landscape architect and paid for new playground equipment. Another school in the same school district that serves more low-socioeconomic students than the other two campuses was doing well if it could raise $2,000 in a year.

The Moral of the Story

Students who come to school with more tend to have parents who see to it that their children get even more. Those who come to school with less tend to have parents who are working two jobs and don't have the time or energy to see to it that their children are treated equitably. In fact, the code of poverty reinforces "That's just the way it is." Parents who give their children more at home also give their children more at school. Allowing each Parent-Teacher Organization in a school system to do its own fund-raising is fair, but it doesn't create a more equitable system. Indeed, the opposite generally is true.

When the school district doesn't allow for more resources for those campuses that serve the larger numbers of children from poverty, the system is contributing to the inequity. The district has an obligation to offset the lack of resources for those campuses that obviously have little.

THE MYTH

A campus with 90% of its students on free lunch had no identified gifted students using the district's process. When teachers were asked to nominate students for the gifted program, they stated that the students they taught were not gifted. As one teacher commented, "We're just trying to get them to pass and from killing each other."

A campus in the same school system in a more affluent section of the town had quite another problem. The mean score on the Iowa Test of Basic Skills was the 75th percentile. Most of the parents thought their child was gifted. Teachers, reluctant to tell a parent any differently because so many of the students had A's on their report cards, did not challenge the parents' perceptions. Special classes were formed to appease the parents of high-achieving students who weren't identified as gifted.

The Moral of the Story

When all of the gifted students are coming from the more affluent sections of town, something is very wrong with the system. Opportunity, rather than giftedness, is being identified. The myth that gifted students make straight A's, please teachers, and aren't discipline problems is just that—a myth. It is very easy for a system to get caught in the politics of giftedness and lose sight of the purpose of the gifted program.

THE GIFTED LOOK

A school district developed an identification process for its gifted program that specified that students who make below an 80 on their report card would be placed on probation for six weeks. If after the six-week period the grade didn't improve, the student would be removed from the program. This same district also specified that misbehavior could be cause to dismiss gifted students from the program. The philosophy was that gifted students should be eager learners who made good grades and are model students for other students.

The Moral of the Story

Special programs exist because there is a special need. Gifted students from poverty will have needs that manifest themselves differently from gifted students from non-poverty backgrounds. When a system imposes a stereotypical image of a gifted student on the program, the system is setting up the gifted student from poverty for failure.

Two major criteria should be used to consider removing a child from a program. These two criteria are exercised after much effort has been made to correct the situation. The criteria are:

1. Is the program hurting the student? For whatever reasons, is the program causing more harm than good?

2. Is the student hurting the program? Is the student harming the instruction and learning process to the detriment of the other students in the program?

Would the school system terminate a Special Education student because he/she had a problem? Would a bilingual student be released from a program because he/she couldn't speak English? Then why would a gifted student from poverty be discharged from the gifted program because he/she experienced an academic problem or a behavioral problem? Is it because of the mythical image of perfection that we have placed on giftedness?

Where to Start

Districts must begin to look at the equity issues within their own system. Campuses that have more resources because of contributions from community members should not penalized. No child within the school system should be penalized for affluence, but neither should a child suffer because of his/her poverty. Students don't choose their economic status. The system must protect and provide in the absence of resources in the home.

 As a school system, the challenge is ...

- Look at the gifted/talented identification practices within the system. Are the identified students coming from one economic group to the exclusion of others? Are some campuses identifying only a few gifted students while other campuses are battling with parents who say, "But my child makes all A's and is bored"?

- Are all campuses allocated the same of resources regardless of the population they serve? Treating all campuses alike is equality, but it is not equity.

- Are parent-teacher organizations supplementing campus budgets while other parent-teacher organizations struggle to raise a few dollars to purchase minimums for the students? How is the system assisting the campuses with the minimums?

- Are there provisions within the school system to provide additional, specialized training for teachers who work with students from poverty? Are campuses that have low numbers of poverty students also included? The need for training is there regardless of the percentage of poverty students.

- Are teachers trained to recognize giftedness in poverty? What does it look like, and how is it different from giftedness in non-poverty environments?

- Are there provisions for lower pupil-teacher ratios on those campuses with high numbers of students from poverty? Has the district provided them with additional resources—such as social workers, psychologists, health-care workers, etc.?

- When new schools are being built that serve students from poverty, are there provisions for showers and a washer and dryer, so that students can be taught more responsibility for their own personal hygiene?

- Are mentors available for students from poverty?

- Does the system require removing gifted students from the program if they don't maintain a certain grade-point average or conform behaviorally?

This process must begin by awakening the larger public to the need. The middle- and upper-class individuals in the above stories would eagerly buy a coat for any child who needed one. Their collective behaviors within the larger system, however, communicate another message. It joins the ranks of all the other subtle "isms" in our culture. **This time it's classism.** One class must be better than, look better than, have more of, and stand out from all others. It's a put-down that hurts everyone.

Chapter Eleven:

Conclusion

DOORS

Each of our destinies depends on finding a door in the wall, or overcoming the obstacles that block our pathways. For some people finding the door takes forever and others no time at all. But once you have found it, you must open it.

You spend your whole life trying to open doors. Sometimes we find a door and we do not even realize it. Often, we see a door and pass it because we do not wish to open our eyes and face the door. We will have go back to it, and the longer we wait the harder that door is to open. Once your first door is opened, you can use it to find others.

We never open all our doors because new ones are being placed in our lives all the time. But don't despair, keys are also made.

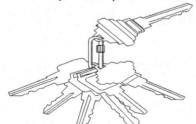

**Wendy Bourgeois, Grade 6
Vidor, Texas, 1981**

CHAPTER ELEVEN:

CONCLUSION—OPPORTUNITY KNOCKS

To identify and serve gifted students from poverty requires the commitment of educators throughout the entire school system. Teachers must be aware of the unique packaging of gifts that students from poverty bring to the classroom. Shedding stereotypical middle-class images of giftedness is as difficult for teachers as shedding effects of poverty is for students from poverty. The lack of resources, and opportunities, along with the hidden rules, creates a complex and forbidding mask.

Educators cannot change the home environments of their students. They can, however, understand them, accept them, and consider the experiences they bring with them to the instructional program. Expecting less of students from poverty is not the answer. Offering the kind of support they need to meet the expectations is the answer. To survive in poverty requires great strength. The obstacles within that environment can also be great teachers. When looking at the obstacles that some people from poverty have overcome in order to achieve greatness, one must ask: "Was it because of, or in spite of, the poverty that he/she achieved? Was it because of, or in spite of, the abuse, the alcoholism, the drug addiction, the abandonment, the handicap, etc., that the person ultimately triumphed?" Painful though they may be, adverse circumstances also can become the sources of energy that move one forward.

The equitable treatment of students from poverty is essential if these students as adults are to have equal economic opportunities. To overlook the brightest students from poverty because they are different, because they lack the opportunities and resources within their environment is unacceptable and morally wrong. Finding the gifted students in poverty and serving them appropriately necessitates systemic changes. Not attempting to meet this challenge is an abdication of the educator's duty.

No one can guarantee that these students will be successful when they are identified and served appropriately. Breaking the cycle of poverty is no small feat. Education, however, is a key component in this endeavor. Ultimately, the student must choose, but without opportunity, the student has no choice!

Identifying gifted students from poverty and serving them more appropriately and efficiently must be a priority for all school systems. Giftedness does not exist just within the middle and upper classes. Gifted programs do not exist only for the more affluent and politically vocal.

The challenge is here. The knowledge is here. The time to apply it is now. The answers to questions and the solutions to problems are found in the trying. The opportunity for equity for gifted students lies with educators who have the courage and commitment to see beyond the mask of poverty. Behind the mask are myriad gifts to be developed. If those gifts are developed appropriately, the student will be empowered to remove the mask.

If educators don't attempt to see beyond the mask of poverty and remove it, who will?

- **If not you, who?**
- **If not now, when?**

Change for gifted students from poverty begins with you.

Research Notes

Authors' Note: The following research notes have been selected to support the content in this book. This information does not replace the Bibliography, it supplements it. The authors hope that this information will motivate further study regarding the special needs of gifted students in poverty.

CHAPTER ONE: THE PARADIGM

"... [E]quality, or the condition of being the same as something else, is inconsistent with the principles of equity. Equity results from providing different educational environments, services, and programs to those who have different needs for them."

Frase, Larry E., English, Fenwick W., and Poston, William K. Jr. *The Curriculum Management Audit*. Lancaster, PA: Technomic Publishing Company, Inc., 1995. p. 162.

When examining a school system's programs and services for equity, the goal is to close "unreasonable gaps in performance and opportunity."

Ibid. p. 173.

Exclusion of underidentified and under-served Hispanic children has three main implications: "First, it sends a negative message to this underrepresented population in district gifted programs. It implies that they are somehow less able than those in other populations. Opinions such as 'there are just no gifted minorities' or 'minority children are in need of academic remediation, particularly those who are limited English proficient' are common even among teachers who work with these populations" (Davis & Rimm, 1989).

Lara-Alecio, Rafael, Irby, Beverly, and Walker, Melissa Vickery. Identification of Hispanic, Bilingual, Gifted Students. *Tempo*. Texas Association for the Gifted and Talented, Spring 1997. p. 24.

"Second, the very act of exclusion is contradictory to the American principles of

Ibid.

egalitarianism (Gintis, 1988). The task of providing equitable service for the gifted is made more difficult by the lack of uniformity in objective identification procedures and in appropriate needs-based curriculum services. Uniformity does not preclude the use of multi-dimensional approach to the identification of giftedness."

"Third, practitioners must be advocates for changes in identification procedures and programmatic services that respond to the characteristics of the Hispanic-bilingual-gifted students. Curriculum and instruction cannot be discussed, developed, or delivered in isolation of the conceptualization of giftedness of the particular ethnic group being served. Finally, a screening process is necessary as well as an effective curriculum and instruction that is sensitive to the characteristics or attributes of the Hispanic-bilingual-gifted student population.

Ibid.

"Chaos theory suggests that an organism must be looked at as a whole. The theory relies on the study of deterministic patterns that are nonlinear. Given the nature for human beings, the assessment of children for gifted programs should be multidimensional. The singular reliance on quantitative measures provides only limited information. Reliability and validity in standardized instruments allow for comparison, but they provide only a limited understanding of a child" abilities."

García, Jamie H. Nonstandardized Instruments for the Assessment of Mexican-American Children for Gifted/Talented Programs. Chapter 4. Garcia, S. B. Editor. *Addressing Cultural and Linguistic Diversity in Special Education: Issues and Trends.* Reston, VA: The Council for Exceptional children. 1994. p. 55.

"There has been a greater realization that there are many students who are gifted but whose talents, for a variety of reasons, go unrecognized. These students represent a vast loss of potential for themselves, their community, and ultimately the nation. One of the major objectives for educators of gifted students is to find and provide appropriate educational services for this group of students."

Gallagher, James J., and Gallagher, Shelagh A. *Teaching the Gifted Child* (4th Edition). Needham Heights, MA: Allyn and Bacon, Inc., 1994. p. 393.

"The reasons why giftedness may go unnoticed are numerous. These students may come from a culture different than that of middle-class America."

Ibid.

"... [E]ven in the most troubled and troublesome of learners the genius is still alive—somewhere. It may be buried under loads of put-downs, negative evaluations, low grades and test scores, delinquent behavior, self-hatred, and more, but like the seed in winter that lies dormant while braving the toughest storms and coldest arctic spells only to blossom with the sun's warmth in the spring, this genius too can survive if you will take the time to study the optimum conditions for its growth in the classroom."

Armstrong, Thomas. *Awakening Genius in the Classroom.* Alexandria, VA: Association for Supervision and Curriculum Development, 1998. p. 48.

CHAPTER TWO: ENVIRONMENTAL OPPORTUNITIES

"Children who had spent one to three years of their adolescence in a family below the poverty line were about 60% less likely to graduate from high school than children

Teachman, Jay D., Paasch, Kathleen M., Day, Randal D., and Carver, Karen P. Poverty During who had never been poor. Children who had spent four years of their adolescence living in a family below the poverty line were about 75% less likely to graduate from high school ... On average, children who spent some or all of their adolescence living in poverty obtained between 1.0 and 1.75 fewer years of schooling than other children."

Adolescence and Subsequent Educational Attainment. Duncan, Greg J., and Brooks-Gunn, Jeanne, Editors. *Consequences of Growing Up Poor.* New York, NY: Russell Sage Foundation, 1997. p. 388.

"Poor parents have less schooling, on average, than do nonpoor parents, and schooling may affect parents' abilities to encourage and help their children to get an education."

Corcoran, Mary, and Adams, Terry. Race, Sex, and the Intergenerational Transmission of Poverty. Duncan, Greg J., and Brooks-Gunn, Jeanne, Editors. *Consequences of Growing Up Poor.* New York, NY: Russell Sage Foundation, 1997. p. 463.

Causes of poverty include poor education, obsolete skills, ill health, divorce, desertion, alcohol, and drugs.

Dicks, Lee E. The Poor Who Live Among Us. Penchef, Esther, Editor. *Four Horsemen: Pollution, Poverty, Famine, Violence.* San Francisco, CA: Canfield Press, 1971. p. 118.

"... [F]ew doubt that children in low-income families are in developmental jeopardy because of the conditions that often accompany or foster poverty, such as low parent education levels, family disorganization, limited opportunities, rundown housing, bad schools and hazardous neighborhood conditions."

Zill, Nicholaus. "The Changing Realities of Family Life." *Aspen Institute Quarterly,* Winter 1993. Volume 5. Number 1. p. 38.

Without literacy skills, a child will probably be unable to break out of the "intergenerational cycles of poverty."

Lewis, Anne C. "Breaking the Cycle of Poverty." *Phi Delta Kappan,* November 1996. Volume 78. Number 3. p. 186.

Knowledge gained through formal education provides "the tools for achieving freedom—by permitting [men] to control situations and by furnishing [them] with access to a greater set of roles in life."

Sennett, Richard, and Cobb, Jonathan. *The Hidden Injuries of Class.* London/Boston: Faber and Faber, 1993. First published in U.S.A. in 1972 by Alfred A. Knopf, Inc., New York, NY. p. 30.

The extended family:
♦ Provides the basis for interdependent relationships with regard to (1) calling upon relatives in times of financial or marital difficulties; (2) child-rearing duties; and (3) economic discussions, such as buying a house.
♦ "[I]s a defense that has sheltered both black and white poor in cities."
♦ While helpful, it can also be binding—"others are always in one's personal affairs."

Ibid. pp. 106-107.

"Psychologists know that basic language patterns are formed very early, with the basic language structures in place by age 5. We learn language, perhaps the most complex of all of our systems of knowledge, by imitation rather than prescription. That is, we make sentences and follow the patterns of language long before we can explicitly state the rules of grammar or syntax, if we are ever able to do so. Childhood errors are replaced, usually with instruction, with standard forms because

Ibid. p. 240.

the child hears the language used by adults. Children in environments where SAE is the language spoken will develop patterns of that dialect themselves and will do so very early in their lives."

The definitions of class by each group: People at the bottom define class by your amount of money; people in middle class value education and your line of work almost as much as money; at the top, people emphasize "taste, values, ideas, style, and behavior"—regardless of money, education, or occupation.

Fussel, Paul. *Class.* New York, NY: Ballantine Books, 1983. p. 3.

"If it's grammar that draws the line between middles and below, it's largely pronunciation and vocabulary that draw it between middle and upper."

Ibid. p. 178.

The farther down socially one moves, the more likely that the TV set will be on.

Ibid. p. 100.

"Middle class is characterized by 'correctness' and doing the right thing."

Ibid. p. 34.

"A sign of middle class: desire to belong and to do so by a 'mechanical act,' such as purchasing something."

Ibid. p. 35.

Middle class: believes in the "likelihood of self-improvement."

Ibid. p. 37.

Upper middle class: The emphasis of cookbooks, and books about food and food presentation addressed to them, was about "elegance." At their dinner parties, their guests are an audience.

Ibid. p. 111.

"At the very top, the food is usually not

Ibid. p. 113.

very good, tending, like the conversation, to a terrible blandness, a sad lack of originality and cutting edge."

Middle class is the main clientele for mail-order catalogs; "the things they buy from them assure them of their value and support their aspirations."

Ibid. p. 132.

A sign of the upper classes is silence; proles are identified by noise and vociferation.

Ibid. p. 196.

"The economic traits which are most characteristic of the culture of poverty include the constant struggle for survival, unemployment and underemployment, low wages, a miscellany of unskilled occupations, child labor, the absence of savings, a chronic shortage of cash, the absence of food reserves in the home, the pattern of frequent buying of small quantities of food many times a day as the need arises, the pawning of personal goods, borrowing from local money lenders at usurious rates of interest, spontaneous informal credit devices *(tandas)* organized by neighbors, and the use of second-hand clothing and furniture."

Lewis, Oscar. The Culture of Poverty. Penchef, Esther, Editor. *Four Horsemen: Pollution, Poverty, Famine, Violence.* San Francisco, CA: Canfield Press, 1971. pp. 137-138.

"Families in poverty must spend so much time during the day seeking adequate food, shelter, clothing, and other basics, that there is no energy available for nurturing the child's curiosity, creativity, and inventiveness. The very fact of the family's poverty often creates emotional stress that further depresses the joy and vitality of the child."

Armstrong, Thomas. *Awakening Genius in the Classroom.* Alexandria, VA: Association for Supervision and Curriculum Development, 1998. p. 31.

CHAPTER THREE: WEIGHING THE OPPORTUNITIES

There is a direct correlation between the level of formal education of the mother and the level of education the child reaches: "The educational level of mother is the most important influence on the educational attainment of children."	Lewis, Anne C. "Breaking the Cycle of Poverty." *Phi Delta Kappan,* November 1996. Volume 78. Number 3. p. 186.
Many studies indicate that the presence of a caring relationship is a key component of learning. Greenspan indicates that no learning occurs without a relationship.	Greenspan, Stanley I. *The Growth of the Mind and the Endangered Origins of Intelligence.* Reading, MA: Addison-Wesley Publishing Company, Inc., 1997. P. 53.
When print is in the home for the child, the child tends to have higher achievement in school because of the exposure to written and oral language. Most books are written in formal register.	Caldwell, Bettye M., and Bradley, Robert H. *Home Observation for Measurement of the Environment (HOME).* Little Rock, AR: University of Arkansas, 1984. p. 13-14.
The amount of light and the use of color in the home are indicators of school achievement and well-being.	Ibid. p. 15.
Formal register is an indicator of success in school because it is the language of the abstract and representational systems upon which school success is measured.	Payne, Ruby K. *A Framework for Understanding Poverty* (Revised Edition). Baytown, TX: RFT Publishing Co., 1998. p. 43.
Violence in a neighborhood is directly	Ibid.

correlated to the number of adult men who permanently live in the households in that neighborhood. The presence of violence disrupts educational opportunities.

"The amount of parental time available while growing up (including the presence of two parents in the home) and having fewer siblings is positively correlated to educational attainment."	Haveman, Robert, Wolfe, Barbara, and Wilson Kathryn. Childhood Poverty and Adolescent Schooling and Fertility Outcomes: Reduced-form and Structural Estimates. Duncan, Greg J., and Brooks-Gunn, Jeanne, Editors. *Consequences of Growing Up Poor.* New York, NY: Russell Sage Foundation, 1997. pp. 441.
"Family income is usually a stronger predictor of ability and achievement outcomes than are measures of parent schooling or family structure."	Duncan, Greg J., and Brooks-Gunn, Jeanne. Income Effects Across the Life Span: Integration and Interpretation. Duncan, Greg J., and Brooks-Gunn, Jeanne, Editors. *Consequences of Growing Up Poor.* New York, NY: Russell Sage Foundation, 1997. P. 597.
The ability to structure time and tasks is a key skill required for success in school and in work. The ability to structure time in an abstract fashion (hours, minutes, days) rather than emotionally (how it feels) is a key factor in success. If one cannot structure and sequence time abstractly, then one cannot identify sequence.	Payne, Ruby K. *A Framework for Understanding Poverty* (Revised Edition). Baytown, TX: RFT Publishing Co., 1998. pp. 69, 121.

Without sequence, cause and effect cannot be assigned.

"The breakup of a marriage (or the parents' failure to marry) increases the chance that a child will be poor during childhood, may lead to psychological distress, may reduce parental supervision, and may limit the child's role models for marriage and work. The distress, lack of supervision, and lack of role models could in turn lead children to be poor as adults."

Corcoran, Mary, and Adams, Terry. Race, Sex, and the Intergenerational Transmission of Poverty. Duncan, Greg J., and Brooks-Gunn, Jeanne, Editors. *Consequences of Growing Up Poor.* New York, NY: Russell Sage Foundation, 1997. p. 463.

"... [P]oor families are also more likely to be headed by a single parent, a parent with low educational attainment, an unemployed parent, a parent in the low-wage market, a divorced parent, or a young parent. These familial conditions might account in large measure for the association between low income and less favorable outcomes for children."

Brooks-Gunn, Jeanne, Duncan, Greg J., and Maritato, Nancy. Poor Families, Poor Outcomes: The Well-being of Children and Youth, Duncan, Greg J., and Brooks-Gunn, Jeanne, Editors. *Consequences of Growing Up Poor.* New York, NY: Russell Sage Foundation, 1997. p. 1.

"The demographic trends in family patterns and individual behavior—changes in marriage and divorce rates, nonmarital fertility rates, and unemployment rates (especially for less educated and younger adults)—help explain the relative increase in the proportion of children in poverty."

Ibid. p. 4.

"... [C]hildren who grow up with only one biological parent are less successful, on average, than children who grow up with both parents. These differences extend to a broad range of outcomes and they persist

McLanahan, Sara S. Parent Absence or Poverty: Which Matters More? Duncan, Greg J., and Brooks-Gunn, Jeanne, into adulthood" (McLanahan and Sandefur, 1994; Haveman and Wolfe, 1991; Cherlin and Furstenberg, 1991; Amato and Keith, 1991; Seltzer, 1994).

"Death, divorce, desertion, and illegitimacy deprive many families of a male breadwinner, and this unquestionably contributes to poverty."

"Among other things, family factors have implications for childhood poverty, welfare dependency, injury, illness, premature death, adolescent childbearing, developmental and mental health disorders in children, delinquency and violent behavior in young adults, alcoholism and substance abuse. Cause and effect relationships underlying these associations have not always been clearly established, but there is certainly enough evidence to warrant public policy focus on family factors."

In the section on *Recent Trends in Poverty*, Zill writes, "Childhood poverty is also more common in families lacking full-time, year-round workers; in families in which parents have low achievement test scores and education levels; in young families; and in minority families. Studies indicate that the increase in child poverty is due to *both* the growth of single-parent families and the deteriorating earning power of young parents, especially those with limited educations."

Editors. *Consequences of Growing Up Poor.* New York, NY: Russell Sage Foundation, 1997. p. 37.

Dicks, Lee E. The Poor Who Live Among Us. Penchef, Esther, Editor. *Four Horsemen: Pollution, Poverty, Famine, Violence.* San Francisco, CA: Canfield Press, 1971. p. 120.

Zill, Nicholaus. "The Changing Realities of Family Life." *Aspen Institute Quarterly,* Winter 1993. Volume 5. Number 1. p. 32.

Ibid. p. 37.

"Economic conditions have changed such that, in order to ensure a decent standard of living and avoid poverty, a child needs to have both parents working. Yet, because of increases in divorce and unmarried childbearing, and a decline in the propensity of single mothers to marry or remarry, fewer young children are living with both parents in married-couple families. Moreover, payment of child support is typically minimal and irregular. Indeed, fewer poor children have even one parent working. Hence, today's young children in poverty are more likely to be persistently poor. In addition, more poor children, especially those in central cities, are living in high-poverty neighborhoods where the risks to their development are particularly severe."

Ibid.

"Technological developments, the globalization of the U.S. economy and changes in the distribution of income and assets have made it harder for young families, especially those in which the parents have only a high school education or less, to work and earn enough to support themselves and their children."

Ibid. p. 48.

"A promising line of research has begun to link poverty to the emotional well-being of children (McLeod and Shanahan, 1993). Elder et al. (1992) have shown that economic loss is associated with shifts in parenting practices, with negative consequences for the emotional well-being of children. Family stress and the lack of learning resources that are associated with poverty probably dampen the likelihood of high school completion."

Haveman, Robert, Wolfe, Barbara, and Wilson, Kathryn. Childhood Poverty and Adolescent Schooling and Fertility Outcomes: Reduced-form and Structural Estimates. Duncan, Greg, J., and Brooks-Gunn, Jeanne, Editors. *Consequences of Growing Up Poor.* New

York, NY: Russell Sage Foundation, 1997. p. 415.

An example of two girls who were promiscuous in New Haven was given: "When the girl from Class I [the rich] was arrested, she was provided with bail at once, newspaper stories were quashed, and she was taken care of through private psychotherapy. The girl from Class V [the poor] was sentenced to reform school. She was paroled in two years, but was soon arrested again and sent to the state reformatory."

Harrington, Michael. *The Other America.* New York, NY: Simon & Schuster, 1962. p. 128.

"In the slum, conduct that would shock a middle-class neighborhood and lead to treatment is often considered normal. Even if someone is constantly and violently drunk, or beats his wife brutally, people will say of such a person, 'Well, he's a little odd.' Higher up on the class scale an individual with such a problem would probably realize that something was wrong (or his family would). He will have the knowledge and the money to get help."

Ibid. p. 129.

"... [T]he family of the poor lives cheek [by] jowl with other families of the poor. The sounds of all the quarreling and fights of every other family are always present if there happens to be a moment of peace in one household. The radio and television choices of the rest of the block are regularly in evidence. Life is lived in common, but not in community."

Ibid. p. 136.

In a study that "made use of data from two national surveys of families with children," it was found "that only about one-third of

Ibid. pp. 38-39.

children in low-income families received stimulation and support from their parents comparable to that received by most children in families that were neither poor nor welfare dependent."

"The analysis of the data supports that the degree of quality of the learning stimulation provided within the home of the high-achieving kindergarten students was significantly different from that provided in the homes of the low-achieving kindergarten students."

Slocumb, Paul D. *The Relationship Between Achievement of Five-Year-Olds and Parents' Report of Home Environment Characteristics.* A dissertation study. Houston, TX: University of Houston/University Park, Houston, TX, 1987. p. 94.

"[P]arents of high-achieving kindergarten students encouraged their children to talk and interact with others to a greater degree and quality than did the parents of the low-achieving kindergarten students. Unlike the home environments of low-achieving kindergarten students, the conditions and events within the home environment of high-achieving kindergarten students fostered language development."

Ibid. pp. 99-100.

"The home environment of the low-achieving kindergarten students was frequently dimly lighted, crowded, and located in neighborhoods that were not aesthetically pleasing. These neighborhoods also presented unsafe conditions, such as a junkyard across the street, old refrigerators, and junk cars beside neighboring houses. Overcrowding was prevalent in the home of the low-achieving

Ibid. p. 101.

students. It was found that less than 100 square feet per person in the household existed in the home of the low-achieving students."

"The difference in the degree and quality of warmth and acceptance between the high-achieving students and low-achieving groups was significant. Parents in the high-achieving students were more interactive, verbally and physically, than were the parents of the low-achieving students."

Ibid. p. 103.

"The items in which high-achieving ... [kindergarten students scored] considerably higher than the low-achieving group were: trips away from home, trips to museums, the child's artwork being on display, and eating meals together as a family. Therefore, the students in the high-achieving group were provided a greater variety in learning experiences than those students in the low-achieving group. This difference was significant in this study and supports related studies that have concluded that variety of learning experiences contributes to higher IQ test results and/or achievement" (Bradley and Caldwell, 1976; Carew, 1975).

Ibid. p. 110.

"Traditional evaluation instruments, purporting to measure intelligence and achievement, have been deemed inappropriate for minority or culturally diverse students" (DeLeon, 1983; Markheady, Towne, and Algozinne, 1983; Renzulli, 1970).

Lara-Alecio, Rafael, Irby, Beverly, and Walker, Melissa Vickery. Identification of Hispanic, Bilingual, Gifted Students. *Tempo*. Texas Association for the Gifted and Talented, Spring 1997. p. 24.

"A major concern in assessment has been variance in standardized scores between and among populations. Education has been centered on the concepts of reliability and validity as the tools by which decisions are made, thus neglecting valuable assessment data. Using instruments built on linear sequential models (i.e., statistics) to assess multidimensional nonlinear phenomena (i.e., human beings) has resulted in decisions that are questionable at best. Gleick (1987) stated that 'a statistician uses the bell-shaped curve the way an internist uses a stethoscope, as the instrument of first resort.' In education, the bell-shaped curve as applied to instrumentation has been used as the first and last resort."

García, Jaime H. Nonstandardized Instruments for the Assessment of Mexican-American Children for Gifted/Talented Programs. Chapter 4. García, S.B., Editor. *Addressing Cultural and Linguistic Diversity in Special Education: Issues and Trends.* Reston, VA: The Council for Exceptional Children, 1994. p. 55.

"Research has shown that students identified for gifted programs by means other than intelligence tests perform as well as those identified through the use of intelligence tests (Torrance, 1982). The field of gifted education will continue to be accused of being elitist if children from culturally and linguistically diverse populations continue to be missed. The challenge is to employ and refine procedures to ensure that children are assessed in such a manner that their educational needs are identified and addressed."

Ibid. p. 56.

"Adult illiteracy in the family—caused by lack of access to adequate educational opportunities (see Kozol 1991, 1995)—makes it less likely that the children in the family will receive verbal and other forms of intellectual stimulation. In addition, problems such as poor prenatal care,

Armstrong, Thomas. *Awakening Genius in the Classroom.* Alexandria, VA: Association for Supervision and Curriculum Development, 1998. pp. 31-32.

malnutrition, and other factors commonly associated with poverty can damage the child's brain from the start of life, thereby limiting the potential to develop natural genius qualities."

CHAPTER FOUR: STUDENT PRODUCTION

The portfolio is "a useful tool with children from culturally and linguistically diverse backgrounds since the products contained in the portfolio did not have to depend on language or directly reflect academic achievement. Since its development, the portfolio has been recognized as a tool that can be used with children of any age."

García, Jaime H. Nonstandardized Instruments for the Assessment of Mexican-American Children for Gifted/Talented Programs. Chapter 4. García, S.B., Editor. *Addressing Cultural and Linguistic Diversity in Special Education: Issues and Trends.* Reston, VA: The Council for Exceptional Children. 1994. p. 47.

"Research currently being conducted to examine the predictive validity of portfolios is showing that portfolios are a better predictor of future student achievement than most instruments (Johnson, Ryser, & Doughtery, 1993). The identification procedures evaluated in Johnsen and colleagues' study included an intelligence test, a creativity test, teacher rating, and portfolios. A stepwise regression examined the accuracy of each instrument in predicting future achievement as shown by achievement test scores. The findings indicated that

Ibid. p. 48.

portfolios were a better predictor than the other instruments. However, the variance was small. It would appear that when properly implemented, the portfolio can be a valuable tool in the assessment of children from all populations for gifted programs."

"Among the benefits of the portfolio are the limited use of language if necessary and its facility in allowing the child to self-select examples of his or her best work. Another benefit is that growth over time can be observed, since the items in a portfolio are collected over a period of at least 2 months."

Ibid.

"We have found remarkable consistency in the test profiles of underachievers: high scores in vocabulary, abstract reasoning, spatial reasoning, and mathematical analysis coupled with low scores in tasks requiring sequencing ..."

Silverman, Linda. Family Counseling. *Handbook of Gifted Education.* Cogangelo, Nicholas, and Davis, Gary, Editors. Boston, MA: Allyn and Bacon, Inc., 1990. p. 312.

CHAPTER FIVE: INFORMANT DATA

"Behavioral checklists used in the identification process for gifted programs have by and large been considered ineffective in the hands of teachers. Accuracy in identification using teacher checklists ranges from 10% at the primary level to 50% at the high school level (Nelson, 1982). With training, however, a significant improvement in the quality of teacher evaluations has been noted. For Mexican-American children and children

García, Jaime H. Nonstandardized Instruments for the Assessment of Mexican-American Children for Gifted/Talented Programs. Chapter 4. García, S.B., Editor. *Addressing Cultural and Linguistic Diversity in Special Education: Issues*

from other ethnic and cultural groups, the problem has been exacerbated by the linguistic, cultural, and socioeconomic factors that come into play."	*and Trends.* Reston, VA: The Council for Exceptional Children, 1994. p. 49.
"Attempts to ameliorate this problem include checklists that are defined in terms of how children from various ethnic and cultural groups exhibit gifted behaviors. There is evidence that use of culture-specific or culture-sensitive checklists can improve the quality of data gathered on these children."	Ibid.
"... High and Udall (1983) found that even in the school where the majority of the students are from another ethnic or cultural background, the children are nominated for gifted programs at a lower rate than children from the dominant culture. This, combined with the problems associated with teacher ratings, points to the need for training in the use of behavioral checklists in order to determine the best educational placement for children. Training should include, but not be limited to, models and definitions of giftedness, characteristics of gifted children, socioeconomic differences, and behavioral indicators of giftedness for the children represented in varied populations."	Ibid. pp. 49-50.
"... [D]ata gathered from parents can provide insight into a child's abilities. One method that has been proposed to collect information more accurately from parents is the interview."	Ibid. p. 50.
"There is growing support for the inclusion	Ibid.

©RFT Publishing Co. •1-800-424-9484

of peer nomination in the assessment process. As any person who works with children can note, children accurately assess each other's abilities and can tell one much about their peers."

"When tedium rules in a classroom, students divert their attention from the lesson plan and take their curiosity inside ... They activate their imagination to more interesting areas of their lives ... and deploy their inventiveness in sneaky tricks like getting a friend's attention without being seen by the teacher."

Armstrong, Thomas. *Awakening Genius in the Classroom.* Alexandria, VA: Association for Supervision and Curriculum Development, 1998. p. 40.

"Their creativity may pop up in doodles in their notebooks, or little songs they're playing in their head, or romantic poems passed to a love interest. It takes a certain amount of genius to act as if one is involved in a lesson when one has absolutely no interest at all!"

Ibid.

CHAPTER SIX: COGNITIVE/LANGUAGE SKILLS

"The most glaring observation by this observer was the blank look on the faces of so many of the parents of the children in the bottom quartile when this interviewer asked questions related to academics. The researcher consistently experienced the feeling that the parents of the low-achieving students simply did not know that it was important to help a child learn shapes, to have children's books in the home, to hold your child and to talk with your child each day, to play counting games, and the many other things that contribute

Slocumb, Paul D. *The Relationship Between Achievement of Five-Year-Olds and Parents' Report of Home Environment Characteristics.* A dissertation study. Houston, TX: University of Houston/University Park, 1987. p. 94.

to the stimulation of cognitive development in young children."

"The high-achieving kindergarten students had greater opportunities to go on trips and outings, had parents who used a large vocabulary and talked in more complex sentences ..."

Ibid. p. 113.

"At the core of the problems of those on or nearly on welfare is the inadequacy of the schools' efforts to teach what they should first and foremost—language." Children must learn to read, write, speak, and listen.

Lewis, Anne C. "Breaking the Cycle of Poverty." *Phi Delta Kappan,* November 1996. Volume 78. Number 3. pp. 186-187.

How do we break the cycle? Start literacy enrichment in the delivery room; cognition research and infant development studies show "that early language stimulation—from the moment of birth—influences brain development and later learning success."

Ibid. p. 187.

"A more recent study by Márquez, Bermúdez, and Rakow (1992) found that the Hispanic community also perceives gifted children within that community as having an interest in reading. There is general consensus through observational data that gifted children have a propensity toward superior verbal behaviors that are expressive, elaborate, and fluent (Renzulli and Hartman, 1971). The results of our study support similar observations among Hispanic students and their exceptional abilities to verbally express themselves in their native language."

Lara-Alecio, Rafael, Irby, Beverly, and Walker, Melissa Vickery. Identification of Hispanic, Bilingual, Gifted Students. *Tempo.* Texas Association for the Gifted and Talented, Spring 1997. pp. 20-21.

"... [L]anguage is a great determiner of the perception of an individual's ability. As

García, Jaime H. Nonstandardized

such, ... sensitivity and appreciation of diverse communication styles can result in inappropriate assessment."

Instruments for the Assessment of Mexican-American Children for Gifted/Talented Programs. Chapter 4. García, S.B., Editor. *Addressing Cultural and Linguistic Diversity in Special Education: Issues and Trends.* Reston, VA: The Council for Exceptional Children, 1994. p. 51.

"A pragmatic analysis of the child's language production (Domico, 1985), either written or oral (dictated), may also assist in the interpretation of data collected. Unlike discrete point tests, pragmatics examines the way an individual uses language. An understanding of this may be useful when the assessment process includes writing samples, standardized intelligence test scores that were verbally loaded, and/or achievement subtests with strong-language-dependent components."

Ibid.

"If an instrument requires the use of a particular cognitive style and the cognitive style of the child is different, observed scores may be skewed."

Ibid.

"... [L]anguage is anything but logical, full of often absurd twists and turns, accidents and usages, and words and phrases that have dozens of different meanings in various uses. Nor is listening to speech more sequential than listening to music."

Hart, Leslie A. *Human Brain and Human Learning.* Village of Oak Creek, AZ: Books for Educators, 1983. pp. 41, 43.

CHAPTER SEVEN: DESIGNING FOR EQUITY

There should be "support networks" to help young parents from poor means in developing their child's language abilities.	Lewis, Anne C. "Breaking the Cycle of Poverty." *Phi Delta Kappan,* November 1996. Volume 78. Number 3. p. 187.
"My mother in her broken English could remedy few of the injustices, but she tried."	Rodriguez, Luis J. *Always Running.* New York, NY: Simon & Schuster, 1993. p. 21.
"In school, they placed Rano in classes with retarded children because he didn't speak much English."	Ibid.
The author says when he went to school he was put in the back of the classroom to play with blocks because he couldn't speak English.	Ibid. p. 26.
He didn't want to be misunderstood, so he seldom asked questions.	Ibid. p. 27.
"The fact was I didn't know anything about literature. I had fallen through the chasm between two languages. The Spanish had been beaten out of me in the early years of school—and I didn't learn English very well either."	Ibid. p. 219.
"This was the predicament of many Chicanos."	Ibid.
"We could almost be called incommunicable, except we remained lucid; we got over what we felt, sensed and understood. Sometimes we rearranged words, created new meanings	Ibid.

and structures—even a new vocabulary. Often our everyday talk blazed with poetry."

"Our expressive powers were strong and vibrant. If this could be nurtured, if the language skills could be developed on top of this, we could learn to break through any communication barrier. We need to obtain victories in language, built on an infrastructure of self-worth."

Ibid.

"But we were often defeated from the start."

Ibid.

"Another dimension of the struggle between excellence and equity is that the further along in the educational system one proceeds, the more excellence comes to the fore as a priority. We establish, without apology, schools for 'gifted' students at the professional level that would be severely criticized at the elementary-school level. What are our law schools, our medical schools, our advanced graduate programs, except programs for gifted students? These are well accepted by our society and we are enormously proud, justifiably proud, of the great contribution these institutions make to our nation. But if we suggest that a similar amount of special attention be paid to these same students when they are eight or nine years of age, we hear cries of special privilege ..."

Gallagher, James J. *Teaching the Gifted Child* (3rd Edition). Newton, MA: Allyn and Bacon, 1985. p. 74.

"One of the issues not sufficiently discussed in the development of special

Ibid. p. 81.

programs for the gifted is the fundamental issue of how much time is available for their instruction."

"The bringing together of gifted students allows the teacher to spend a *proportionally greater* amount of time on developing inquiry skills and discussing abstract ideas and systems than would be possible in a class of slow learners."

Ibid. p. 83.

"... [U]nusual early accomplishment requires something more positive than merely not interfering with the development of the gifted child. It requires positive encouragement and training along a certain line of development."

Ibid. p. 85

"Schools can change the *content* of the lessons to be taught; they can change the *special skills* they wish the child to learn; and they can change *learning environment*, which is supposed to facilitate the learning of special systems of knowledge and skills."

Ibid.

"... [M]any observers feel that there are some school climates that also can be considered a high-risk environment, where youngsters who tend to be underachievers will certainly be hastened to these nonproductive patterns. Rimm has pointed out two such climates:

Gallagher, James J., and Gallagher, Shelagh A. *Teaching the Gifted Child* (4th Edition). Needham Heights, MA: Allyn and Bacon, Inc., 1994. p. 403.

1. *An anti-intellectual school atmosphere that sets high priorities for athletics or social status, but not intellectual attainment or preparation for higher education.*

2. *An anti-gifted atmosphere that considers gifted programming to be elitist and emphasizes the importance of all students being 'well-adjusted' and 'fitting into a mold." (1991).*

CHAPTER EIGHT: CURRICULUM FOR THE GIFTED FROM POVERTY

"[T]he basic purpose is to see to it that the gifted child masters systems of knowledge and search strategies so ... [he/she] can be as creative and productive and enthusiastic a student and citizen as possible."	Gallagher, James J. *Teaching the Gifted Child* (3rd Edition). Newton, MA: Allyn and Bacon, Inc., 1985. p. 85.
"Because the gifted child demonstrates a manifest ability to handle a complexity of ideas far beyond his or her age, one of the natural school adaptations is a program providing content that stresses a greater complexity of ideas and higher levels of abstraction than can be mastered by the average student of that age. Passow (1979) points out that the curriculum can be changed in at least three ways: (1) in breadth or depth, (2) in tempo or pace, and (3) in kind."	Ibid.
Commonalities shared by gifted students from whatever culture they might come include: 1. "The ability to meaningfully manipulate some symbol system held valuable in the subculture 2. The ability to think logically, given appropriate information 3. The ability to use stored knowledge to solve problems 4. The ability to reason by analogy	Gallagher, James J., and Gallagher, Shelagh A. *Teaching the Gifted Child* (4th Edition). Needham Heights, MA: Allyn and Bacon, Inc., 1994. p. 409.

5. The ability to extend or extrapolate knowledge to new situations or unique applications
[T]he way in which these abilities might express themselves differ (e.g., in one culture through language, through another in drawings and paintings) but the essence of their operation remains the same."

"Generalizations are statements of conceptual relationship that transfer across examples."	Erickson, H. Lynn. *Concept-Based Curriculum and Instruction.* Thousand Oaks, CA: Corwin Press, Inc., 1998. p. 86.
"Principles are always true and have significant roles on a discipline."	Ibid.
"Essential questions are a critical driver for teaching and learning. They engage students in the study and create a bridge between performance-based activities and deeper, conceptual understandings."	Ibid. p. 90.
"It is the conceptual focus that achieves this goal of integrated curriculum. Without the focus concept, we are merely 'coordinating' facts and activities to a topic, and we fail to reach higher-level curricular and cognitive integration."	Ibid. p. 63.
"Central to any vision of comprehensive curriculum for the gifted is the focus on the ideas that have guided the development of civilizations as we know it. These large concepts, issues, and themes are those that dominate all areas of knowledge exploration, yet have specific connotations within a given discipline of thought."	VanTassel-Baska, Joyce, Feldhusen, John, et al. *Comprehensive Curriculum for Gifted Learners.* Needham Heights, MA: Allyn and Bacon, Inc., 1988. p. 57.

"So the task of educators of the gifted is to seek out those ideas that can be best utilized with gifted learners at various stages of development both within and across traditional fields of inquiry."	Ibid.
"The brain detects, constructs, and elaborates patterns as a basic, built-in, natural function. It does not have to be taught or motivated to do so, any more than the heart needs to be instructed or coaxed to pump blood."	Hart, Leslie A. *Human Brain and Human Learning.* Village of Oak Creek, AZ: Books for Educators, 1983. p. 60.
"In practice our pattern-detecting ability depends on clues from vision, hearing, touch, or other senses, on the behavior and relationships, on the situation. In short, *the ability depends heavily on our experience, on what we bring to the act of pattern detection and recognition.*"	Ibid. p. 64
"But more common is the detection and recognition of patterns *within* patterns, which leads to finer discriminations, or what can be called *categorizing down,* a most important aspect of learning. Thus, one can detect the pattern 'animal,' then categorize it down to 'dog,' and then to 'Afghan hound.'"	Ibid.
"This learning process, being natural, appears effortless, but ... it requires much random, fortuitous exposure and experience—*input.*"	Ibid. p. 67
"Pressures of tradition have blinded education to what, once seen, stands obvious: 1. The brain is by nature a magnificent	Ibid.

pattern-detecting apparatus, even in early years.

2. Pattern detection and identification involves both features and relationships, and is greatly speeded up by the use of clues, and categorizing down procedure.
3. Negative clues play an essential role.
4. The brain uses clues in probabilistic fashion, not by digital 'adding up.'
5. Pattern recognition depends heavily on what experience one *brings* to a situation.
6. Children and youngsters must often revise the patterns they have extracted, to fit new experience."

"Again and again teachers find students have specific learning only because of a family trip, the mother's political activities, the father's occupation, what has been seen recently on television or read, or some chance event."	Ibid. p. 57
"Since we learn individually in different, multipath sequences, with previous *individual* experience as the foundation to which more learning is added, logical group-instruction inevitably produces a large degree of failure."	Ibid.
"From the vast information stored, answers or tentative answers get pulled out, then assembled, compared, and interpreted by, if possible, extracting a pattern. The whole miraculous procedure bears no relationship to linear processing; ..."	Ibid. p. 52
"The brain does not usually learn in the sense of accepting or recording information	Ibid. p. 78.

from teachers. The brain is not a passive consumer of information. Instead, it actively constructs its own interpretation of information and draws inferences from it. The brain ignores some information and selectively attends to other information."

"Effective teachers understand the cultures of students in their classrooms and adapt curriculum and instruction accordingly."

Zeichner, Kenneth M. Educating Teachers to Close the Achievement Gap: Issues of Pedagogy, Knowledge, and Teacher Preparation. Williams, Belinda, Editor. *Closing the Achievement Gap.* Alexandria, VA: Association for Supervision and Curriculum Development, 1996. p. 59.

"Scaffolding consists of constructing a set of supports that enables students to relate school to experiences at home and vice-versa" (Mehan and Trujillo, 1989).

Ibid.

"Starting with Vygotsky's 'zone of proximal development,' some cognitive scientists have shown that children—given support and scaffolding—are able to construct and understand concepts earlier than once believed."

Hyerle, David. *Visual Tools for Constructing Knowledge.* Alexandria, VA: Association for Supervision and Curriculum Development, 1996. p. 14.

"Visual tools are a strong link between teaching content and facilitating and guiding thinking processes."

Ibid. p. 15.

"With visual tools, students begin to visually integrate their own holistic forms with the

Ibid.

tightly wound structure of information and thus integrate text."

"Visual brainstorming webs, task-specific organizers, and thinking-process maps thus provide a bridge between their own forms and the structures that are embodied in the text but hidden in the guise of linear strings of words." | Ibid.

"Low-road transfer is attained through a developed automaticity in the use of a cognitive process, such as classification, by way of repetitive use of the skill in a variety of content learning contexts. High-road transfer is attained when the student is able to consciously transfer a learned, abstract principle from one situation to another." | Ibid. p. 73.

"And because most television programming, computer games, and Internet fare are not being created by geniuses to awaken curiosity, wonder, or wisdom, but are being fashioned by individuals more interested in making money and serving the lowest common denominator, our students' inborn genius is likely to find little nourishment from such influences." | Armstrong, Thomas. *Awakening Genius in the Classroom.* Alexandria, VA: Association for Supervision and Curriculum Development, 1998. p. 41.

"Beyond the violent content of television and video games—which has received the greatest attention and has a huge research base demonstrating its harmful effects on children (see, for example, Singer and Singer, 1981, Huesman and Eron, 1986, Comstock and Paik, 1991)—at least three other more subtle but nevertheless devastating threats to the genius of students seem to emanate from the vast | Ibid. p. 42.

majority of TV, video, and Internet fare that kids are exposed to. These threats are (1) stereotypical images, (2) insipid language, and (3) mediocre content."

"The end result of this homogenization of language is heard in students whose speech patterns are replete with phrases like 'Yeah right, ...' and 'You know, then he went, like, you know ...' and the ubiquitous, all-purpose response to society's complexities: 'Whatever.' Absent from these linguistic black holes is any attempt at playfulness, flexibility, imagery, humor, or other qualities that are the hallmark of real genius."

Ibid. p. 44.

CHAPTER NINE: NURTURING AND KEEPING THE GIFTS

"While a young girl might seek attachment with her schoolteacher by complimenting the teacher on her special outfit, a young boy might make a connection with the teacher by asking her whether he can stay after class and help out by erasing the blackboards. On the whole, boys tend to seek attachment less through asking for it directly and more by trying to bring it about indirectly or through action."

Pollack, William. *Real Boys.* New York, NY: Henry Holt and Company, Inc., 1999. p. 67.

"For many years, traditional psychologists thought that exquisite sensitivity to shame was mostly characteristic of girls, especially at somewhat older ages. But what I have found after years of working with boys and their families is that the same kind of shame that silences girls from expressing their true voice as adolescents takes its inhibiting and self-expressing toll

Ibid. p. 33.

on their brothers at a much earlier age. And while girls may be shame-sensitive, boys are shame-*phobic*. They are exquisitely yet unconsciously attuned to any signal of 'loss of face' and will do just about whatever it takes to avoid shame."

"Men, for instance, may be more ashamed of shame than women, especially given the performance pressures that are typically placed on them and the expectation that they will rise above fear, pain, and self-doubt."

Karen, Robert. "Shame." *The Atlantic Monthly,* February 1992. p. 55.

"What we really need for boys is the same upswing in self-esteem as learners that we have begun to achieve for girls—to recognize the specialized academic needs of boys and girls in order to turn us into a more gender-savvy society."

Pollack, William. *Real Boys.* New York, NY: Henry Holt and Company, Inc., 1999. p. 16.

"... [G]irls not only outperform boys academically but also feel far more confident and capable. Indeed the boys in my study reported, over and over again, how it was not 'cool' to be too smart in class, for it could lead to being labeled a nerd, dork, wimp, or fag. As one boy put it, 'I'm not stupid enough to sit in the front row and act like some sort of teacher's pet. If I did, I'd end up with a head full of spitballs and then get my butt kicked in.'"

Ibid. p. 16.

"If a teacher believes that boys who are not doing well are simply uninterested, incapable, or delinquent, and signals this, it helps to make it so. Indeed when boys feel pain at school, they sometimes put on the mask and then 'act out.' Teachers, rather

Ibid. p. 17.

than exploring the emotional reasons behind a boy's misconduct, may instead apply behavioral control techniques that are intended somehow to better 'civilize' boys."

Fox and Zimmerman suggest five key questions that teachers and administrators should ask to help guard against gender bias:

1. "Are approximately equal numbers of boys and girls identified? Are the selection procedures biased or the provisions more attractive to one sex than the other?
2. Do girls and boys who participate in educational provisions for the gifted achieve equally well? If not, why not?
3. Are efforts made to use non-sexist instructional materials and language laid down in the program? If not, why not?
4. Are girls and boys encouraged to participate in intellectual and risk-taking to the same degree? If not, why not?
5. Are the expectations, aspirations, and confidence levels of boys and girls in the classes about the same? If not, why not?"

Fox, L.H., and Zimmerman, W.Z. Gifted Women. Freeman, Joan. Editor. *The Psychology of Gifted Children: Perspectives on Development and Education.* New York, NY: Wiley, 1985. p. 237.

"Despite the variations in the procedures used to determine underachievement from one research study to another, there is remarkable consistency in the literature concerning those characteristics that set gifted underachievers apart from gifted achievers. These characteristics were:
A lack of self-confidence
The inability to persevere
A lack of integration to goals
The presence of inferiority

Gallagher, James J., and Gallagher, Shelagh A. *Teaching the Gifted Child* (4th Edition). Needham Heights, MA: Allyn and Bacon, Inc., 1994. p. 393.

feelings."

"The clear implications of [the findings related to underachievement] is that unless some major attempt is made to counteract these trends at an early age, these underachievers will turn out to be relatively nonproductive members of society, to the detriment of both society and themselves."

Ibid. p. 401.

"The child, with few positive role models and many negative emotions, appeared to drift into a pattern of chronic underachievement in the schools. This does not mean ... that the school is helpless or that the school environment is irrelevant to the situation, but full recognition of the total pattern of coping problems that the child is revealing could be helpful in putting the problem in a context."

Ibid. p. 403.

"The research literature is also beginning to suggest that the emotional and supportive quality of the parental home rather than its structure or composition most strongly influences a child's sense of self-worth" (Demo and Acock, 1988; Raschke, 1987).

Axinn, William, Duncan, Greg J., and Thornton, Arland. The Effects of Parents' Income, Wealth, and Attitudes on Children's Completed Schooling and Self-Esteem. Duncan, Greg J., and Brooks-Gunn, Jeanne, Editors. *Consequences of Growing Up Poor.* New York, NY: Russell Sage Foundation, 1997. p. 521.

Family structure has an effect on: test scores, grade-point average, and years of school—modest effects; behavioral-problem indicators like skipping school and early childbearing—more substantial effects.

McLanahan, Sara S. Parent Absence or Poverty: Which Matters More? Duncan, Greg J., and Brooks-Gunn, Jeanne, Editors. *Consequences of Growing Up Poor.* New York, NY: Russell Sage Foundation, 1997. p. 37.

Regarding educational attainment, children in stepfamilies do better than those in single-parent families, but they do worse in the areas of behavioral and psychological problems.

Ibid. p. 47

What He/She Says
"I think I would like to be a jet pilot, a movie star, or a politician."
What He/She May Mean
"I want to do thrilling and glamorous things, but I cannot stand a position with a long period of training preceding it or where sustained hard work is needed (e.g., surgeon, electrical engineer, or president)."
What He/She Says
"Some people are lucky and some aren't. I wish I could hit it lucky for once. I dream about breaking the bank at Las Vegas."
What He/She May Mean
"If life is a game of chance, I am less personally responsible for my ultimate success or failure."
What He/She Says
"Future? What future? The bomb will take care of our future. If not, things will work out somehow."

Ibid.

What He or She May Mean

"To think of the future requires planning and effort. These are too painful because I have failed too often before. I prefer to ignore it and to trust luck to make things come out all right."

"The teachers or school system that attempts to suppress or routinize emotion in students, or take a group rather than an individual approach, is flying in the face of deep human needs."

Hart, Leslie A. *Human Brain and Human Learning.* Village of Oak Creek, AZ: Books for Educators, 1983. p. 107.

"... [I]t becomes plain that *absence of threat is utterly essential to effective instruction.* Under threat, the cerebrum downshifts—in effect, to greater or lesser extent, it simply ceases to operate. To experienced teachers, this shutting down of the newest brain is an old story and a familiar frustration. The threatened child ... 'freezes,' seems unable to think, stabs wildly at possible answers, breaks into tears, vomits, or acts up, perhaps to the point of violence."

Ibid. p. 109.

CHAPTER TEN: THE SYSTEMIC CHALLENGE

"Decisions about augmenting educational programming should consider not only differences among schools but the effects of any augmentation upon the difference."

Frase, Larry E., English, Fenwick W., and Poston, William K. Jr. *The Curriculum Management Audit.* Lancaster, PA: Technomic Publishing Company, Inc., 1995. p. 173.

"Time allocations and utilization must

Ibid. p. 171.

reflect fair and reasonable comparability across the system and for all clientele."	
"It is not uncommon for support services to be allocated and assigned on formula factors, like enrollment count irrespective of school needs. Allocations based on factors other than diagnosed need may not meet the variable demands for individual services."	Ibid. p. 175.
"Delivery of services should be structured to insure that unequal populations of student clientele receive what they need, not merely the same as other schools or by some haphazard means."	Ibid.
"... [S]taffing allocations should reflect various demographic and program needs. The level of teacher skill should match up with student needs, and staffing must be adequate to properly deliver instruction."	Ibid. p. 176.
"The more experienced, skilled teachers normally should be assigned to work with students of greater challenge, such as with at-risk students."	Ibid.
"In some systems, seniority transfer rights have facilitated the 'flight' of senior, experienced teachers to the higher socioeconomic areas, leaving the poor, minority students to junior, less experienced colleagues."	Ibid.
"... [I]nequity or inefficacy can result if teacher assignments are not carefully made and based upon student characteristics and needs. Parents have been known to complain that some schools have become a	Ibid.

'dumping ground' for poorer teachers. Administrators have been heard to indicate that 'better teachers are with better students, and poorer teachers are with poorer students.'"	
"... [I]t is not uncommon ... that older schools (often in high at-risk student neighborhoods) have library book collections that are older and more dilapidated than found in newer schools in upscale neighborhoods."	Ibid. p. 171.
"It is occasionally revealed that the older school and schools located in poor neighborhoods are less well maintained than other schools in the same district. Moreover, some schools are often better equipped than others, especially in terms of idiosyncratic situations, such as highly motivated building-level administrators, preferential treatment, or simple age of the buildings."	Ibid. pp. 171-172.
"... [A]n energetic parent organization may raise money and equip its neighborhood school with additional special equipment. If the procurement creates a disparity and said disparity creates unequal access to educational opportunity, issues arise about fairness and equity. Parent groups should have the option to provide additional resources to their schools, but if such resources exacerbate inequity, the school system may have to provide compensatory resources to ameliorate inequitable conditions."	Ibid. p. 168

CHAPTER ELEVEN: CONCLUSION—OPPORTUNITY KNOCKS

"Yet the role of the educator or social worker or employer is not to save the individual, but rather to offer a support system, role models, and opportunities to learn, which will increase the likelihood of the person's success. Ultimately, the choice always belongs to the individual."

Payne, Ruby K. *A Framework for Understanding Poverty* (Revised Edition). Baytown, TX: RFT Publishing Co., 1998. p. 148.

"There is [in the culture of poverty] a freedom of verbal expression, an appreciation of individual personality, a heightened and intense emotional experience, and a sensual, kinesthetic approach to life usually not found in middle class or among the educated. These characteristics are so intertwined in the daily life of the poor that to have those cut off would be to lose a limb. Many choose not to live a different life."

Ibid.

"... [I]t is the responsibility of educators and others who work with the poor to teach the differences and skills/rules that will allow the individual to make the choice. As it now stands for many of the poor, the choice never exists."

Ibid.

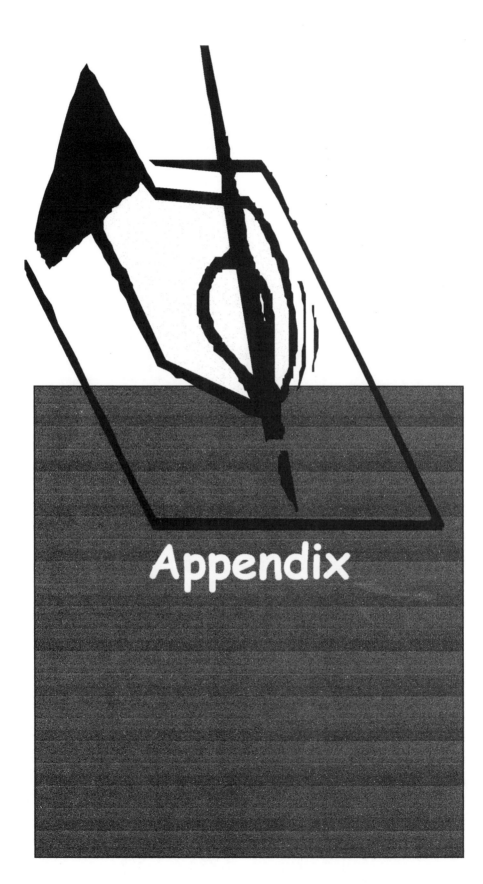

Appendix

Preponderance of Evidence
Environmental Opportunities Profile
Developed by Paul D. Slocumb, Ed.D., and Ruby K. Payne, Ph.D.
©RFT Publishing Co., 1999

I. Student Production

A. Math replication		
3	2	1

B. Story replication		
3	2	1

C. Spatial/problem-solving		
3	2	1

D. Portfolios				
	3	2	1	Avg.
Critical thinking				
Creative thinking				
Total				

II. Informant Data

A. Slocumb-Payne Teacher Perception Inventory		
12	8	4

B. Peer Perception Inventory			
5+=12	4 = 5	3 = 6	2 = 4

II. Informant Data, continued

C. Student interview		
12	8	4

III. Cognitive/Language Skills

A. Writing sample			
4	3	2	1

B. Reading sample			
4	3	2	1

C. Mathematics sample			
4	3	2	1

SUMMARY OF DATA

	I	II	III	IV	
A.					
B.					
C.					
D.		NA	NA	NA	Totals
Subtotal			NA		
EOP points					
Totals					
Valid (Y/N)					
G/T (Y/N)					

NA = Not applicable

IV. Standardized Testing Data

A. Standardized data			
%ile	%ile	&ile	%ile
4	3	2	1

B. Academic recognition: state competency tests	
Yes = 3	No = 0

C. Mastery of all state competency subtests	
Yes = 3	No = 0

Anecdotal comments:

_____
_____
_____
_____
_____
_____
_____
_____
_____
_____
_____
_____
_____
_____
_____
_____
_____
_____
_____
_____
_____
_____
_____
_____
_____
_____
_____
_____
_____
_____
_____
_____
_____
_____
_____
_____
_____
_____

**Directions for Completing the Preponderance of Evidence
Environmental Opportunities Profile
Developed by Paul Slocumb, Ed.D., and Ruby K. Payne, Ph.D.
©RFT Publishing Co., 1999**

I. **Student Production**

A. **Math replication:**
   - If the student develops a plan and works the problems correctly using his/her plan, the student receives 3 points in Section I-A of the Summary of Student Data form.
   - If the student does a plan, but works the problems incorrectly, or if the student works the problems correctly but does not develop a plan, he/she receives 2 points on the Summary of Student Data form.
   - If the student does not develop a plan and does not do problems correctly, he/she receives 1 point, which is recorded in the Summary of Data section of the Preponderance of Evidence grid.

B. **Story replication:**
   - If all the components of the task are included, the student receives 3 points in Section I-B of the Summary of Student Data form. There must be a plan and a written story (could be pictorial at the primary grades), and it must illustrate one of the themes specified.
   - If two of the three components are included, the student receives 2 points in Section I-B of the Summary of Student Data form.
   - If the student has only one of the three components, the student receives 1 point in Section IB of the Summary of Data section.

C. **Spatial/problem-solving:**
   - Students are to use 6 crayons to do this activity. Each square is to be colored, and no color can touch itself on any side of the square. The point distribution is as follows:

- Students who develop a plan and complete the task, adhering to the rule at least 75% of the time (do 75% of them correctly), receive 3 points in Section I-C of the Summary of Data section.
- Students who develop a plan and complete the task, adhering to the rule at 50% to 75% of the time, receive 2 points in Section I-C of the Summary of Data section.
- Students who do the task, getting less than 50% correct and not developing a plan, receive 1 point in the Summary of Data section. Students who develop a plan and still get less than 50% of them done correctly also receive 1 point in the Summary of Data section.

D. **Portfolio:** Each student's portfolio is rated as a 3, 2, or 1, based on the rubric for the activities selected to use with the students. A minimum of three activities that foster critical thinking and three that foster creative thinking should be used. An overall rating score for the three should be determined. Maximum total points for the portfolio is 6 points.

II.   **Informant Data**

A.   **Teacher Perception Inventory:**   After completing the **Slocumb-Payne Teacher Perception Inventory** (A *Rating Scale for Students from Diverse Backgrounds*), the overall score is entered in the Summary of Data section as follows:
- **Scores from 57-76 = 12 points**
- **Scores from 56-38 = 8 points**
- **Scores from 36-19 = 4 points**

B.   **Peer Perception Inventory:**   Students whose names appear on the Peer Perception Inventory receive points in the Summary of Data section, as follows:
- **A name appearing 5 or more times = 12 points**
- **A name appearing 4 times = 9 points**
- **A name appearing 3 times = 6 points**
- **A name appearing 2 times = 4 points**

III. **Cognitive/Language Skills**

    A. **Writing sample:** A 4-point rubric is developed for a writing sample that is appropriate for the grade level being considered. After completing each of the categories, the teacher gives the student an overall rating by adding up the rating for each descriptor and then averaging them. The final average is rounded off to the nearest whole number. Students' scores are entered in the Summary of Data section as a 4, 3, 2, or 1.

    B. **Reading sample:** Using the reading rubric for the appropriate grade level of the student, the teacher has the student read a story from a book written at that grade level. Using the descriptors included in the rubric, the teacher rates the student as a Beginning, Developing, Capable, or Expert reader. After completing each of the categories, the teacher gives the student an overall rating by adding up the rating for each descriptor and then averaging them. The final average is rounded off to the nearest whole number. Each student is categorized as a Beginning, Developing, Capable, or Expert reader.

       A score is entered on the Summary of Data section form as follows:
- Beginning = 1 point
- Developing = 2 points
- Capable = 3 points
- Expert = 4 points

    C. **Mathematics sample:** A locally developed mathematics sample is developed and administered to students. The activity should assess understanding of mathematical concepts. A distribution of points is earned based on a rubric. The distribution is as follows:

- High Performance = 7 points
- Above-Average Performance = 5 points

- Average Performance = 4 points
- Below-Average Performance = 3 points

IV.   **Standardized Testing Data**

    A.   **Standardized data:** Scores from a criterion-referenced test (CRT) or a norm-referenced test (NRT) are distributed in the Summary of Data section. A range of scores should be established that allows for students to receive 1, 2, 3, or 4 points.

    B.   **Academic recognition:** Students who receive academic recognition on the state competency test are noted in this section. Students receiving academic recognition should have a check in the box under the word Yes and receive 3 points.

    B.   **Mastery of state competency test:** Mastery or non-mastery of the state's competency test should be noted by checking either Yes for mastery or No for non-mastery. Mastery of all parts of the state competency test must be made to receive a Yes and to receive 3 points.

Environmental Opportunities Profile:

Students receive points based on the opportunities they have or do not have in their environment. This information is gleaned from school records and interviews with the primary caregiver of the student. Using the *Environmental Opportunities Profile,* students receive points in each of the categories.

- **Student Production**
  Minimum points possible = 5   Maximum points possible = 15

- **Informant Data**
  Minimum points possible = 12   Maximum points possible = 36

- **Cognitive/Language Skills:**
  Minimum points possible = 5   Maximum points possible = 15

NOTE: Standardized testing data that are included in Section IV of the Summary of Student Data form may be considered _INVALID_ if a student receives 33 or more points on the _Environmental Opportunities Profile_. If the data included in Sections I, II, and III are high, and the data in Section IV are low, the standardized testing data may not be reflecting the student's actual performance ability. Look for patterns in the data. When inconsistencies occur, ask why and try to account for the discrepancies.

Summarizing the data:

- The data are summarized in the grid box at the bottom of the last column labeled Summary of Data. The totals for each section (Sections I-IV) are entered in the appropriate column and rows (Rows A-D). The total for each section is entered in the subtotal row. The subtotal row is added together and entered in the Totals column at the end of the row.
- The points from the _Environmental Opportunities Profile_ are entered for each section.
- The total number of EOP points are added to those in the subtotal row, adding both down and across in the row labeled Totals.
- Based on the information gathered, the person charged with the responsibility of getting the data together places a Y (yes) or an N (no) for each of the sections indicating that the scores appear to be valid or invalid for that section. If for some reason some of the information collected is invalid, anecdotal comments may be made on the back of the form, explaining the circumstances surrounding that item(s). Scores may be considered invalid for a variety of reasons. Among these are:
    - The student may have copied the work of another student.
    - A teacher may have rated all students very low—or very high—on the **Slocumb-Payne Teacher Perception Inventory**, making his/her ratings questionable.
    - A family member other than the primary caregiver may have responded to the _Environmental Opportunities Profile_.
    - The student refused to answer questions during the student interview.

Distribution of Points on the Preponderance of Evidence

Points on the EOP and points gleaned from Student Production, Informant Data, and Cognitive/Language Skills balance and/or offset one another to achieve a balance. This is the equity component inherent in this identification process. The following shows the minimum and maximum points that can be earned in the various categories.

Category Points	Student Production	Informant Data	Cognitive/ Language Skills	Standardized Testing
Minimum	5	12	5	1
Maximum	15	36	15	10
Environmental Opportunities Profile				
Minimum	5	12	5	NA
Maximum	15	36	15	NA

Determining the Preponderance of Evidence:

Using the sum total (EOP points combined with the subtotals), do a frequency distribution of the scores for each of Sections I-IV, ranging from high to low. After reviewing the range of scores, determine the number of scores the campus will use to identify its gifted and high-achieving students. Use this procedure for each of the columns to determine if the score in the Subtotal 2 rows for each section are to be classified as Gifted or Non-Gifted on that campus. Total up the number of "Yes" Gifted and the number of "No" Not Gifted for each row and enter the number in the Totals column at the end of the row. Looking at the two totals, plus the anecdotal data included on the back of the form, school officials make their decisions based on the preponderance of evidence.

Example of Two Hypothetical Students

A Non-Low-Socioeconomic Student

	I.	II.	III.	IV.	Total
A.	3	12	4	4	23
B.	3	12	4	3	22
C.	3	12	7	3	25
D.	6				6
Subtotals	15	36	15	10	= 76
EOP points	5	12	5		= 22
Totals	20	48	20	10	= 98
Valid (Y/N)	Y	Y	Y	Y	
G/T	X	X	X	X	4
Non G/T					0

A Low-Socioeconomic Student

	I.	II.	III.	IV.	Total
A.	1	4	1	0	6
B.	1	4	1	0	6
C.	1	4	3	0	8
D.	2				2
Subtotals	5	12	5	0	= 22
EOP points	15	36	15		= 66
Totals	20	48	20	0	= 88
Valid (Y/N)	Y	Y	Y	NO	
G/T	X	X	X	X	4
Non G/T					0

In the above examples, the 10-point difference between the low-socioeconomic student and the non-low student is in the area of the standardized testing data (Sections IV-A, B, and C). Assuming the low-socioeconomic student scored high on the EOP, receiving the maximum number of points on the EOP, the student's standardized test scores would be considered invalid.

Math Replication
Primary

In math, a person can get an answer faster if he/she multiplies numbers rather than adding the numbers together. Suppose a person wants to know how many pieces of candy he/she has. Thinking of pieces of candy on plates can help him/her come up with the answer.

For example: In the multiplication problem 3 X 3, it would mean a person has three plates with three pieces of candy on each plate.

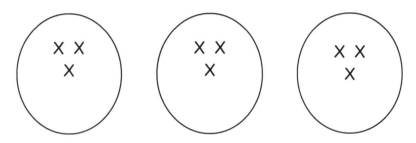

How many pieces of candy does he/she have? She has 9. So, multiplying 3 X 3 means that she has a total of 9.

___

TASK: Now **you** do the following two problems. Before you begin, develop your plan for doing the problems.

Write your plan in this box.

1. What does 6 X 6 equal?

2. What does 7 X 5 equal?

Math Replication
Intermediate

In math, an exponent is used to tell you how many times the number is multiplied against itself. For example, 8^4 means 8 is multiplied against itself 4 times. In other words, it means

$$8 \times 8 \times 8 \times 8 = 4096$$
$$64 \times 64 = 4096$$
$$8^4 = 4096$$

TASK: Now **you** do the following two problems. Before you begin, identify your plan for doing the problems.

Write your plan in this box.

1. What is 4^2 ?

2. What is 10^3 ?

Story Replication
Primary

Stories have themes or main ideas that the writer of the story wants the reader to understand. For example, in the cartoon series Anamaniacs the theme or main idea is about a person who believes that he is smarter than everyone else (the Brain), and every episode he has this big idea that is going to take over the world. He always gets Pinky (his friend) to help him, and his ideas never work. The theme of the cartoon series is simply that no one is smart enough to take over the world by himself. For example, in the story Cinderella the theme is "rags to riches theme." A poor girl who does what is right eventually gets everything, including a handsome man, riches, and the respect of her stepsisters.

Here are some common themes that are in movies and stories:

1. Good wins over bad.
2. By sticking to a cause or purpose, the person will win, in spite of trouble.
3. The good guy or girl wins, even if he or she is not perfect and makes mistakes.
4. You can never make a person love you.
5. A poor person goes from rags to riches because he/she is really a good person.
6. A person can control what happens to him/her.

TASK: Choose one of these themes. Write a story, or draw a cartoon strip using one of these themes, or you can tell your story out loud.

> **Every task needs a plan. A plan is how you will get the task done. Write down what you will do first, second, and so on.**

Story Replication
Intermediate

Most video games come in a story format. In most video games, the primary theme is good against evil. Most video games involve fighting and often, as part of the theme, the good guy or girl rescues a person from the land of a bad person.

In the video magazines, the stories are laid out in a format that combines picture and narrative (particularly for role-playing games). An example is attached.

TASK: You need to develop a video-game preview for a magazine using those examples as a format. (This example is taken from the *Game Informer*, January 1999, p. 58). You must identify three characters, give a short description and drawing of each, and briefly tell the main points of the story.

Before you begin you must make a plan—in other words, what you will do first, second, third, and so on. You must identify three characters, give a short description and drawing of each, and briefly tell the main points of the story.

```
Write your plan in this box.




```

It's Got Spirit, How 'Bout You?
(From: *Game Informer*, January 1999, p. 58)

"If you are a fan of Prairie View or the University of Minnesota, you'll probably have no interest in this game. After all, these horrible teams are accurately portrayed in GameBreaker '99. Slow, shallow, and with few skills to rely on, these basement dwellers of Division 1A college football can be pummeled easily by teams like Ohio State and Florida State. However, even though they have little chance of winning in the real season, you can change that in GameBreaker '99. If you're up to the challenge. Sure, it's possible to produce the big upset immediately, but by building your team with patience and persistence, you can turn your favorite underdog into a collegiate juggernaut.

"Of course, you can create a player and have him walk on to any campus in the country to help boost the talent pool. But in GameBreaker '99 you can also try your hand at team management. Go recruiting for the top players in the country and if enough of the top players commit, you'll be well on your way to turning the program around.

"Many other things will draw the diehard college football fan to this game, including the sounds of marching bands playing in the background. Another is the Heisman trophy award presented at the end of each season. Getting your prime offensive star to accumulate the stats needed for that prestigious award can become a game in itself. Other aspects of the college football experience included in GameBreaker '99 are Bowl games and, more importantly, the electric sounds of Keith Jackson coming out of the microphone. Does GameBreaker '99 have enough spirit to capture football fans?"

Spatial Problem-Solving

DIRECTIONS: You are to use six crayons for this activity. You are to color each square. There is one rule for this task. **No color can touch itself on any side of the square and you must use all six colors at least once.** You are to color all 36 squares as they are drawn. You may not change the size or shape of the squares.

To do any task, it helps to have a plan. A plan tells how you are going to get the job done using the rules. Please write your plan here before you begin the task. You may use the back of this page if you need more space for your plan.

Slocumb-Payne Teacher Perception Inventory
A Scale for Rating Superior Students from Diverse Backgrounds
Developed by Paul D. Slocumb, Ed.D., and Ruby K. Payne, Ph.D.
©RFT Publishing Co., 1999

Student's name_____ Date_____

School_____Grade_____Age_____

Teacher/person completing this form_____

How long have you known this student? _____years _____months

Directions: This scale is designed to obtain a teacher's perception of a student's characteristics as a potentially gifted/talented student. This is not a recommendation form; it is a perception of a student within the context of a classroom or school. Since each classroom is as unique as the teacher conducting that classroom, one teacher's perception of a student may vary considerably from that of another.

The items are derived from the research literature dealing with characteristics of gifted and creative persons. A considerable number of individual differences can be found within any student population; therefore, the profiles are likely to vary a great deal. There is no right answer to any question.

Each descriptor item in each row should be read from the left and from the right, and then circle the applicable number that best describes your perception of the student as he/she relates to that descriptor. **You are to circle only one number in each row.** Each descriptor is designed to be "two sides of same coin." Persons completing this instrument may find it helpful to first read the descriptor on the left, then the one on the right, and then place a check mark beside the descriptor that best aligns with your perception of the student under consideration. Then, using that descriptor, circle the number that most closely describes your perception of the student in relation to the descriptor.

One descriptor item per row (either the one on the left or the right) is to be rated as follows:

- 1 = Seldom or Never
- 2 = Occasionally
- 3 = Frequently
- 4 = Almost Always

Slocumb-Payne Teacher Perception Inventory
A Rating Scale for Students from Diverse Backgrounds
Developed by Paul D. Slocumb, Ed.D., and Ruby K. Payne, Ph.D.
©RFT Publishing Co., 1999

Perception of attributes	Seldom or never	Occasionally	Frequently	Almost always	Frequently	Occasionally	Seldom or never	Perception of attributes
1. Curious about information; inquisitive; doesn't accept information at first glance; questions and pushes for more information	1	2	3	4	3	2	1	1. Obnoxious with questions; likes to "stump" people with hard questions; enjoys questions with "shock value"; questions authority; unwilling to follow rules
2. Stubborn; avoids tending to other things that need to be done just because he/she is not through with his/her priority	1	2	3	4	3	2	1	2. Sticks to task; gets job done; doesn't give up easily even when things are difficult
3. Finds it hard to wait for others; unwilling to do detail work; shows reluctance to do some assignments because he/she already "knows" content or skill	1	2	3	4	3	2	1	3. Learns at faster rate than his/her peer group; absorbs more with less practice; able to accelerate his/her learning; displays eagerness to do work
4. Understands subtleties of language in his/her primary language; uses language in powerful way; displays unique sense of humor; able to use language to build personal relationships	1	2	3	4	3	2	1	4. "Smart mouth"; master at put-downs of others; uses humor in destructive manner; unable to relate to peers because his/her sense of humor isn't as sophisticated; class clown

5. Thirsts for knowledge; seeks answers to questions; motivated to do research to find answers to questions; likes rhetorical questions; curious about ideas	1	2	3	4	3	2	1	5. Shows little interest in what is to be learned; wants to pursue only those things that spark his/her curiosity; is more curious about people than events
6. Has difficulty completing tasks; unaware of deadlines; oblivious to those around him/her; very focused on and committed to his/her priorities	1	2	3	4	3	2	1	6. Commits to long-range projects and tasks; focused; goal-oriented; strives to meet high standards
7. Loves ambiguity and dislikes being given specific directions and/or parameters; unable to be specific with other people who need specific direction; comes across as highly creative/inventive	1	2	3	4	3	2	1	7. Able and willing to ascertain and solve problems; does not need specific directions; may set own goals that surpass teacher's expectations
8. Deeply interested in many things; is good at many things; loves to learn new things	1	2	3	4	3	2	1	8. Unable to make decisions—or makes decisions quickly without regard for consequences; may hop from one thing to another without experiencing closure in anything; appears random
9. Develops high standards and expectations of self; self-starter who needs little supervision; has self-control	1	2	3	4	3	2	1	9. Perfectionist; nothing is ever good enough; can't finish something because it still isn't correct; may display low self-image about academic performance

10. Has trouble listening while others talk; interrupts others to point of rudeness; talks at inappropriate times; may be reluctant to write; very expressive in casual register	1	2	3	4	3	2	1	10. Excellent facility with language; can elaborate on thoughts and ideas; uses formal register when communicating with others
11. Highly developed social conscience; concern for social issues and problems; awareness of global issues; has internal locus of control	1	2	3	4	3	2	1	11. Overconcern for social problems and issues to extent that depression results; doomsday view of life; overwhelmed with despair in world/community; sees self as victim
12. Able to comprehend complex ideas and thoughts; able to learn advanced and more complex content	1	2	3	4	3	2	1	12. Out of touch with reality, day-to-day routines; bored by simpler things in life; unwilling or unable to abide by basic requirements and/or rules
13. Unwilling to learn facts to support generalizations; can be great "talker" but is unable to produce because work lacks substance	1	2	3	4	3	2	1	13. Sees patterns in things; can transfer learning to new situations; sees big picture; discovers new information; supports generalizations with facts/details
14. Makes connections; sees relationships between/among diverse ideas and events	1	2	3	4	3	2	1	14. Difficult to stay focused because of random thoughts/ideas; highly creative but perceived as "weird" by peers
15. Shows clever, unique responses to questions and problems; often responds with humor or offers "silly" response to questions	1	2	3	4	3	2	1	15. Generates large number of ideas or solutions to problems and questions; often offers unusual, unique, clever responses

16. Appreciates color; likes to doodle and draw; has affinity for graffiti	1	2	3	4	3	2	1	16. Sensitive to beauty; tunes in to aesthetic characteristics of things
17. Uninhibited in expressions of opinion; sometimes radical and spirited in disagreement; tenacious	1	2	3	4	3	2	1	17. Uninhibited in expressions of opinion; sometimes appears radical and disagreeable; may show anger when disagreeing with others
18. High risk-taker in academic endeavors; is adventurous and speculative in his/her thinking	1	2	3	4	3	2	1	18. Risk-taker; dares to break rules and then challenges authority when caught; unafraid to challenge others
19. Criticizes openly; unwilling to accept authoritarian rules and procedures; orally and openly condemns them; may irritate others	1	2	3	4	3	2	1	19. Criticizes constructively in socially acceptable manner; unwilling to accept authoritarian pronouncements without critical examinations
Add each column; enter totals here								
Sum total of all 7 columns								

Student Interview

Developed by Paul D. Slocumb, Ed.D., and Ruby K. Payne, Ph.D.
©RFT Publishing Co., 1999

Student_____ D.O.B. _____Grade level__

Teacher_____ School_____

Interviewer_____ Date of interview_____

OVERALL RATING: 1   2   3

1. One day when you arrive at school, you discover that your teacher is ill and will be out of school for the remainder of the school year. Your new substitute teacher enters the room. Much to your surprise, your new teacher is a robot. Your robot teacher says that she can do many things that your regular teacher couldn't do. How would you like your robot teacher to be different from your regular teacher? What would you like your robot teacher to do that your regular teacher does not do? **(Listen for connection to technology, sense of fairness, magic, personification, humor. Push the student to elaborate his/her answers.)**

2. You turn the television on and there is a movie on. The movie is about you. Tell me what you think is happening in that movie about you. It's your movie; you can make it do anything you want. **(Push for a plot to be revealed. Does his/her story have other people, things, or ideas out of the ordinary?)**

3. If you could fix one thing in your neighborhood, what would you fix and how would you go about fixing it? **(Listen for scope and abstraction. With older and/or more affluent children, substitute town, state, United States, or world for neighborhood.)**

4. Would you consider yourself an "expert" on a subject that is not taught in school? Why are you an "expert" in this? How did you become an expert? **(If students do not understand what an expert is, explain to them what an expert is. Ask probing questions if the student can't think of anything (example: "What is something your friends always ask you to do because they know you can do it better than anyone else?").**

5. What is the easiest way for you to learn something new? **(Push for an elaboration of a method or rate of learning.)**

6. Have you ever been bored? Tell me about what happens when you get bored. How do you handle it? **(Listen for creative ways in which he/she handles boredom. Listen for problem-solving strategies.)**

7. You just won a new television set. This TV is different from some others. You can schedule the shows you want to watch between 7 and 8 o'clock each night without using a VCR. You also can make them last 15 minutes, 30 minutes, 45 minutes, or one hour in length without commercials. Which shows would you want to watch during that hour on Monday night? What about on Tuesday night? Wednesday night? Etc. **(If the student names the same shows for several days, stop the questioning. Listen for a theme as to the types of shows the student is selecting. Ask the student if he/she would always watch them in the same order.)**

8. What do you think being gifted means? Can you give me the names of at least two people whom you believe to be gifted? These can be people you know, people you have read about, or even people who are not alive anymore. Describe for me why you think they are gifted. **(If the student doesn't have a personal definition of gifted, talk about gifted people as those who**

have some exceptional abilities. **You can use fairy tales or fictional characters as examples.)**

9. Your two best friends are having a problem. They are mad at each other. You like them both and want the three of you to play like you used to. How would you go about getting your two best friends to stop being mad at each other and be best friends again? **(Listen for problem-solving strategies. Ask other questions that will cause the student to speculate on possible strategies he/she might use. Example: "Well, what if that didn't work? What would you try next?")**

10. If you could invent one thing that would help another person, what would you invent and why? **(Listen for a creative response that shows an awareness of others and their needs. The student could refer to a group rather than an individual.)**

Peer Nomination
(Elementary)

Think about the other students in your class and other students you know in this school. Who would you go ask if …

1.   You wanted the best ideas about how to find a lost puppy?

2.   You wanted to get the computer working?

3.   You needed advice about a friend?

4.   You needed all the words to a popular song.

5.   You needed to know the steps to a dance?

6.   You didn't have any lunch money?

7.   You needed to know what happened on the last three episodes of a TV show?

8.   You needed help with your math?

9.   You needed a good drawing?

10.   You needed someone who could help you win an argument with someone else?

11.   You needed the secrets to winning a video game?

12.   You needed your backpack fixed?

13.   You needed a personal problem explained to the teacher?

14.   You wanted to hear a good story?

15.   You wanted someone to make you laugh?

Reading Rubric: Grade 1

Student name:_____   School year:_____

Campus:_____   Grade:_____

	Beginning	Developing	Capable	Expert
Fluent	Decodes words haltingly Misses key sounds Identifies most letter sounds Identifies short vowels Says/recognizes individual words	Decodes sentences haltingly Knows conditions for long vowels (vowel at end of syllable, eg, me, he) Identifies blends and consonants Decodes digraphs and r-control vowels (or, ar, er, etc.) Reads at rate that does not interfere with meaning	Knows vowel teams (ea, ee, oa, etc.) Identifies common spelling patterns Uses word-attack skills to identify new words Reads sentences in meaningful sequence Reads with expression	Decodes polysyllabic words Decodes words in context of paragraph Decodes words accurately and automatically Reads paragraphs in meaningful sequence Reads with expression, fluency, appropriate tone, and pronunciation
Constructive	Predictions are incomplete, partial, and unrelated Predictions indicate no or inappropriate prior knowledge	Predicts what might happen next Makes minimal links to personal experience/prior knowledge	Predicts story based on pictures and other clues Relates story to personal experience/prior knowledge	Can predict possible endings to story with some accuracy Can compare/ contrast story with personal experience
Motivated	Does not read independently Concentrates on decoding	Reads when teacher or parent requests Eager to utilize acquired skills (words and phrases)	Will read for specific purpose Uses new skills frequently in self-selected reading	Self-initiates reading Reads for pleasure

Strategic	Does not self-correct Uncertain as to how parts of story fit together	Recognizes mistakes but has difficulty in self-correcting Can identify characters and setting in story	Has strategies for self-correction (reread, read ahead, ask questions, etc.) Can identify characters, settings, and events of a story	Analyzes self-correction strategies as to best strategy Can talk about story in terms of problem and/or goal
Process	Cannot tell what has been read	Does not sort important from unimportant	Can determine with assistance what is important and unimportant	Organizes reading by sorting important from unimportant

Reading Rubric: Grade 2

Student name:_____   School year:_____

Campus:_____   Grade:_____

	Beginning	Developing	Capable	Expert
Fluent	Misses key phonemic elements Rate of reading interferes with meaning New vocabulary impairs understanding	Knows basic phonetic structure of vowels: short, long, r-control, vowel teams Occasionally rate of reading interferes with meaning Mispronounces unfamiliar words	Uses word-attack skills to identify new words in section Says sentences in meaningful sequence Uses contextual clues to determine pronunciation of new words	Decoding not an issue; it is taken for granted Analyzes selection and uses most effective reading rate Enjoys new words and practices using them in his/her vocabulary
Constructive	Makes some use of clues to determine what text will be about May mention character	Can predict what character might do next Remembers general characters but not detail	Can predict possible outcomes from selection Can identify main character	Connects personal experience to predict outcomes Can give detailed accounting of

	he/she read about previously Skips over new words	New vocabulary impairs understanding	For new word, can give example but not definition	character and motive Can generate definition or synonym for new word
Motivated	Has limited interaction with or response to reading Reads only when asked	May be involved in or identify with portion of story Self-initiates reading	Responds on personal basis to selection Has criteria for selecting reading materials	Tells others about what he/she has read Analyzes personal choices and determines new selections to explore
Strategic	Is uncertain as to how all parts fit together but can identify parts of selections	Has structure for story reading	Understands criteria of expository piece	Differentiates fiction from non-fiction by structure of piece
Process **Before**	Simply begins reading; does not know purpose	Has purpose for reading but relies heavily on pictures	Demonstrates some knowledge of clues to use before reading (looks at graphics, predicts, asks questions)	Applies strategies before reading that help better understand what text will be about
During	Keeps reading if he/she does not understand	Has only external strategies (will ask for help)	Uses some strategies during reading*	Applies appropriate strategies while reading; can self-correct**
After	Cannot verbalize what he/she read	Can identify which part he/she liked best	Can summarize with assistance/ direction	Summarizes accurately

*Reading strategies: Summarizes, retells events; makes mental picture of what author says; predicts next event; alters predictions based on new information.

**Self-correction or "fix-up" strategies: Looks back, looks ahead, rereads, slows down, asks for help.

Reading Rubric: Grade 3

Student name:_____   School year:_____

Campus:_____   Grade:_____

	Beginning	Developing	Capable	Expert
Fluent	Mispronounces common words Decodes sentences haltingly	Sees word root and endings separately Decodes words accurately and automatically	Understands that prefixes, roots, and suffixes are "changeable parts" Decodes words in context of paragraph	Analyzes pronunciation using analogy to known words and word parts Reads with expression, fluency, appropriate tone and pronunciation
Constructive	New vocabulary impairs understanding Predicts story based on pictures and other clues	Can generate an example or synonym for new word Identifies parts of story in relation to his/her own experience	Can generate synonyms, definition, or antonym for new word Connects personal experience to clues and text	Uses new and unusual words in writing or speaking Can compare and contrast previous personal experience to parts of story
Motivated	Reading is initiated by teacher. Holds as much beginning information as possible and forgets rest Does not read for information	Reading is initiated by student May describe what selection is about and provide some detail Reads for information if teacher-initiated	Reads for pleasure Identifies main idea Uses appropriate text for needed information	Reads for pleasure and information as needed Identifies main idea and supporting information Compares/ contrasts one piece of reading with/to another
Strategic	Has difficulty differentiating	Knows important parts exist but	Can identify important	Can identify and store important

		important from unimportant	cannot always identify	information	information and discard unimportant
		Does not self-correct	Recognizes mistakes but has difficulty in self-correcting	Has strategies for self-correction**	Analyzes self-correction strategies as to best strategy
Process	Before	Prereading strategies involve number of pages and size of print	Identifies purpose for reading	Identifies purpose and applies strategies before reading that help better understand what text will be about	Determines strategies needed to understand selection
	During	Calls words and skips words if they cannot be understood or pronounced	Some aspects of text are connected to prior knowledge/ experience	Uses some strategies during reading*	Applies appropriate strategies while reading; can self-correct**
	After	Summaries are retelling of as much as is remembered	Needs help with summary; can identify which part he/she liked best	Has strategy for categorizing and summarizing information	Organizes reading by sorting important from unimportant and relating it to purpose and structure

*Reading strategies: Summarizes, retells events, makes mental picture of what author says; predicts next event, alters predictions based on new information.

**Self-correction or "fix-up" strategies: Looks back, looks ahead, rereads, slows down, asks for help.

Reading Rubric: Grade 4

Student name:_____   School year:_____

Campus:_____   Grade:_____

	Beginning	Developing	Capable	Expert
Fluent	Mispronounces common words Decodes words haltingly	Sees word root and ending separately Decodes words in context of paragraph	Understands that prefixes, roots, and suffixes are "changeable parts" Decoding is non-issue	Analyzes pronunciation using analogies to known words and word parts Reads with expression, fluency, appropriate tone and pronunciation
Constructive	Can predict what character might do next New vocabulary impairs understanding	Can predict possible endings to story Can generate example or synonym for new word	Can predict more than one ending/solution Can generate synonyms, definition, or antonym for new word	Can predict endings to story and explain advantages and disadvantages for author in using various endings Uses new vocabulary in writing or speaking
Motivated	Little understanding of reason for reading Limited interaction with or response to reading	Reads text because teacher said to May mention character he/she has read about previously	Establishes clear purpose for reading Compares/ contrasts one piece of reading with/to another	Evaluates purpose for reading Analyzes personal choices and determines new selections to explore
Strategic	Does not have enough information to ask questions	Has difficulty asking questions Can use structures to	Can ask questions about what was read Uses structures	Asks questions that tie this text and other reading together

		Has difficulty differentiating important from unimportant Some difficulty differentiating structure of fiction from non-fiction	identify important information Differentiates fiction from non-fiction by structure of piece	to assign order, remember characters, and identify problem/goal Can differentiate among structures used in fiction***	Uses structure to determine most important aspects of text to remember Can differentiate among non-fiction structures****
Process	Before	Prereading strategies involve number of pages and size of print	Identifies purpose for reading	Applies strategies before reading that help him/her better understand what text will be about	Determines strategies needed to better understand selection
	During	Calls words and skips words if not understood	Some aspects of text are connected to prior knowledge/ Experience	Uses some strategies during reading*	Applies appropriate strategies while reading; can self-correct**
	After	Summaries are retelling of as much as is remembered	Can identify part he/she likes best but needs help with summary	Has strategy for categorizing information	Organizes reading by sorting important from unimportant and relating it to purpose and structure

*Reading strategies: Summarizes, retells events, makes mental picture of what author says, predicts next event, alters predictions based on new information.

**Self-correction or "fix-up" strategies: Looks back, looks ahead, rereads, slows down, asks for help.

***Fiction structure (examples): Flashbacks, chronological, episodic, story within story.

****Non-fiction structure, (examples): Topical, cause and effect, sequential, comparison/contrast, persuasive.

Reading Rubric: Grade 5

Student name:_____   School year:_____

Campus:_____   Grade:_____

	Beginning	Developing	Capable	Expert
Fluent	Rate of reading interferes with meaning	Occasionally rate of reading interferes with meaning	Analyzes selection and uses most effective reading rate	Can articulate the demands of the reading task
Constructive	Has trouble understanding meaning of text Vocabulary slows reader	Can understand text but has difficulty formulating questions Can use text to make meaning of new vocabulary	Can explain why text is important and can summarize main points Can ask questions over text	Assigns meaning and relates information in a larger context of knowledge Vocabulary applied outside of text and used to refine understanding
Motivated	Does not read for information; concentrates on decoding Can provide some details about selection Reading is initiated by teacher	Holds as much beginning information as possible and forgets rest May describe what selection is about and provide some detail Reading is initiated by student	Identifies main idea; determines fact from non-fact Compares and contrasts information to other events or experiences Shares reading with others	Knows the specific information he/she needs from text Develops questions unanswered by selection Actively seeks reading opportunities
Strategic	Differentiates fiction from non-fiction by structure of piece	Can differentiate among structures used in fiction***	Can differentiate among non-fiction structures****	Can articulate and analyze author's use of structure
Sorting	Can remember some of	Uses structures to assign order,	Uses structures to determine	Discusses how structures

		remember characters, and identify problem/goal	most important aspects of text to remember	assist reader in sorting important from unimportant
Asks questions	Does not have enough information to ask questions	Has difficulty asking questions	Can ask questions about what was read	Asks questions that tie this text to others
Self-correction Strategies	Does not self-correct	Recognizes mistakes but has difficulty self-correcting	Has strategies for self-correction**	Analyzes self-correction strategies as to best strategy**
Identifies Purpose	Little understanding of reason for reading	Reads text because teacher said to	Establishes clear purpose for reading	Evaluates purpose for reading
Process **Before**	Does not predict	Has some difficulty making predictions	Applies strategies before reading that help better understand what text will be about	Predicts and identifies how author or genre tends to end selections
During	Keeps reading if he/she does not understand	Uses some strategies during reading*	Applies appropriate strategies while reading; can self-correct**	Analyzes own reading and thinking while reading
After	Summaries are retelling of as much as is remembered	Has strategy for categorizing information	After reading, revises schema/ conceptual organization	Develops more clarity in thinking as result of reading

*Reading strategies: Summarizes, retells events, makes mental picture of what author says, predicts next event, alters predictions based on new information.

**Self-correction or "fix-up" Strategies: Looks back, looks ahead, rereads, slows down, asks for help.

***Fiction structures (examples): Flashbacks, chronological, episodic, story within story.

****Non-fiction structures(examples): Topical, cause and effect, sequential, comparison/contrast, persuasive.

Writing Rubric: Kindergarten

	Scribble/ Drawing/ Pre-phonemic	Early Phonemic	Phonemic	Standard
Oral fluency	Talks about characters; response may ramble; may tell part of story; includes irrelevant information	Can tell story with beginning, middle, and end	Gives details about characters and has meaningful story	Has richly developed story with detailed characters and unusual word choice
Written fluency	Uses drawings and scribbles to resemble written forms; left-to-right progression not evident	Draws pictures and writes series of letters that resemble sentence or complete thought	Writing resembles specific words; uses inventive spellings; story can be ascertained	Story has several sentences with more-standard spellings and makes sense
Elaboration	Detail in pictures; details may be confused	Detail in oral language	Uses pictures and language for details in writing	Uses language for details in writing

This rubric represents developmental stages.

Writing Rubric: Grade 1

First Semester: Narrative/Expressive

	Below Expectations	Minimum	Mastery	Excellent
	1	2	3	4
Stays on topic	Lacks narrative purpose Words or phrases about topic	Narrative purpose may be questionable Some information that is related to topic	Evidence of narrative purpose Most information is related to topic	Narrative purpose is clear Several sentences related to topic

Organization and structure	Student writes words or phrases Student can write/list story elements from story read orally	Student attempts story with two to three sentences Evidence of at least one story element	Student begins simple story with several sentences Some evidence of story line	Story with several sentences—beginning, middle, and end Story line is apparent
Language control	Meaning is not clear Words and phrases are primary form of language used	Some clarity of thought Attempts sentences	Some evidence of language control Uses simplistic sentences	Language control evident but may interfere with meaning occasionally Sentences used appropriately
Support and elaboration	Descriptions are not apparent	Student uses at least one descriptive word (could be size, color, quantity)	Students uses two or more descriptive words	Student includes some description in story
Mechanics, grammar, and conventions*	Words do not follow conventional progression Unable to differentiate words from random letters Inventive spelling cannot be read by others	Left-to-right progression evident Some evidence of spacing between words Inventive spelling may be difficult to read	Conventional use of left-to-right progression Spacing between words is acceptable Inventive spelling rarely interferes with meaning	Conventional use of left-to-right progression Appropriate spacing utilized throughout story Inventive spelling does not interfere with meaning

*Teacher should model and encourage appropriate capitalization and punctuation. This should be assessed second semester.

Writing Rubric: Grade 1

Second Semester: Narrative/Expressive

	Below Expectations	**Minimum**	**Mastery**	**Excellent**
	1	2	3	4
Stays on topic	Some information included that is unrelated Narrative wanders	Most information isrelated Narrative is about topic	Nearly all information related Narrative is on topic	All information related Additional information provided
Organization and structure	Has beginning but not necessarily middle or end; contains list-like phrases Lacks story line	Has beginning, middle, and end Story line is apparent	Has beginning, middle, and end Story line is apparent with evidence of problem	May have unique features (surprise ending, cause/effect, or dialogue) Includes most story elements (setting, characters, problem, events, conclusion)
Language control	Meaning may not be clear	Language control may interfere with meaning	Evidence of language control	Language control used throughout story
Support and elaboration	Descriptions are not apparent or are very weak Minimal use of descriptive words	At least one story element is extended Some use of descriptive words	Two or more story elements are extended Descriptive words enhance story	Story elements are extended Descriptive words create mental, visual pictures
Mechanics, grammar, and conventions	Evidence of incomplete sentences Inventive spelling difficult to read Little or no control of	Uses simplistic sentences Inventive spelling does not interfere with meaning Attempts appropriate use	Sentence use appropriate Capitalization and spelling do not interfere with meaning Some use of appropriate	Sentences used appropriately throughout narrative Capitalization, punctuation, and spelling do not interfere with meaning

	capitalization or punctuation	of punctuation and capitalization	punctuation	Most punctuation used appropriately

Writing Rubric: Grade 2

Narrative/Expressive

	Below Expectations	Minimum	Mastery	Excellent
	1	2	3	4
Stays on topic	Makes brief attempt to address prompt

Narrative wanders from purpose

Some information included that is unrelated | Narrative addresses the prompt

Narrative is about purpose

Most information is related | Narrative clearly addresses prompt

Narrative clarifies purpose

Nearly all information related | Narrative clearly addresses prompt

Narrative clarifies and extends presented purpose

All information related and ideas extended |
| Organization and structure | Has a beginning but not necessarily middle or end

Lacks evidence of story elements

Major gaps in order of events and lacks cause/effect | Has a beginning, a middle, and end

Story line is apparent with some evidence of a problem or goal

Events presented and some cause/effect apparent | Has purposeful beginning, middle, and end

Includes all story elements (setting, characters, problem, events, conclusion) in logical order

Events in logical order and cause/effect evident | Has clear and consistent beginning

Includes all story elements (setting, characters, problem, events, conclusion) and may have surprise ending or unique features

Extended steps presented in a logical order and cause/effect evident |
| Language control | Attempts and uses sentences | Uses complete sentences | Uses varied sentence | Uses wide variety of |

			patterns	sentence patterns
	Difficult to understand Lacks language control	Uses simple, logical sentences Language control is questionable	Events are clear and some transition evident Adequate control of language	Transitions are clear and evident Consistent/good control of language
Support and elaboration	Characters are apparent A few attributes may be given Lacks time-order	Characters are described Extends some ideas using description and detail Demonstrates use of ordinal words (first, second, etc.)	Characters and setting description is extended Descriptive words are used for setting, objects, etc. Demonstrates use of a variety of time-order words (first, then, after, next, etc.)	Detail is rich for characters and setting Uses a variety of forms of elaboration (synonyms, metaphor, simile, analogy) to enhance story Demonstrates use of unusual time-order words/phrases (in the meantime, etc.)
Mechanics, grammar, and conventions	Major errors in capitalization, punctuation, and spelling impair meaning Incomplete sentences Frequent errors in subject-verb agreement may be evident	Errors in capitalization, punctuation, and spelling Few sentences fragments Some mistakes in subject-verb agreement	Minor errors in capitalization, punctuation, spelling Consistent use of complete sentences Usually uses correct subject-verb agreement	Uses most conventional capitalization, punctuation, and spelling Use of compound complex sentences Subject-verb agreement correct

Writing Rubric: Grade 2

Informative/How-to

	Below Expectations	Minimum	Mastery	Excellent
	1	2	3	4
Stays on topic	Poorly or minimally addresses the purpose Drifts from "how-to" to another mode and may include irrelevant information	Somewhat addresses the purpose Some information off topic	Clearly addresses the purpose Stays on topic, and flow of steps apparent	Clearly addresses and extends the purpose Fluent, clear flow of information and steps
Organization and structure	Steps/elements presented in list-like manner Lacks introduction and/or conclusion Repetitive, rambling, and has major gaps	May lack some elements Brief introduction and conclusion Some organization apparent, but flow may be disrupted	Includes all elements of purpose (materials, steps, etc.) Introduction and conclusion of one to two sentences that restate the prompt Consistent organization	Includes and extends all elements Strong introduction and conclusion that clarify prompt Clear and well-developed steps in logical order

Language control	Attempts and uses sentences Difficult to understand Lacks language control	Uses complete sentences Uses simple, logical sentences Language control is questionable	Uses varied sentence patterns Events are clear with some transitions evident Adequate control of language	Uses wide variety of sentence patterns Transitions are clear and evident Consistent/good control of language
Support and elaboration	Lacks explanation of elements (materials, steps, etc.) Lacks elaboration of steps Repetitive word choice	Elements are somewhat explained/ descried Steps are somewhat elaborated or extended Limited word choice	Elements are clearly explained/ described Contains a variety of elaborated steps Effective word choice provides support	Elements are clearly explained, described, and extended Fully developed steps with elaboration and rich detail Vivid and unusual word choice enhances purpose
Mechanics, grammar, and conventions	Major errors in capitalization, punctuation, and spelling impair meaning Incomplete sentences Frequent errors in subject-verb agreement may be evident	Errors in capitalization, punctuation, and spelling Few sentence fragments Some mistakes in subject-verb agreement	Minor errors in capitalization, punctuation, spelling Consistent use of complete sentences Usually uses correct subject-verb agreement	Uses most conventional capitalization, punctuation, and spelling Uses compound/ complex sentences Subject-verb agreement correct

Writing Rubric: Grade 3

Narrative/Expressive

	Below Expectations	Minimum	Mastery	Excellent
	1	2	3	4
Stays on topic	Student makes brief attempt to address prompt May drift to another purpose and include irrelevant information	The narrative addresses prompt Digressions may occur	All information related to prompt Additional information provided to clarify events	Narrative clearly addresses prompt Fluent, clear flow of information and ideas
Organization and structure	Lacks clear flow or beginning, middle, and end Repetitive, rambling, and confusing Major gaps in defining problem/goal May list some events but lacks cause/effect relationship	Has beginning, middle, and end Story line is apparent Some evidence of problem/goal Events presented and cause/effect apparent	Has purposeful beginning, middle, and end Includes all story elements Clearly defined problem/goal Events in logical order and cause/effect evident	Clear and consistent organization with purposeful beginning, middle, and end Includes and develops story elements Unique solution to problem/goal Extended steps presented in logical order and cause/effect evident
Language control	Attempts and uses sentences Difficult to understand Lacks language control	Uses complete sentences Uses simple but logical sentences Evidence of language control	Varied sentence patterns Sentences evident with some transitions between events Consistent control of language	Wide variety of sentence patterns Clear transitions evident Consistent, strong control of language
Support and elaboration	Characters are apparent	Characters are described	Character and setting	Strong description of

	Some attributes may be given Limited word choice	Some ideas are described, but not in great detail Appropriate word choice	described Ideas are extended using description, detail, and dialogue Effective word choice supports the narrative	character and setting Uses variety of forms of elaboration (synonyms, metaphor, simile, analogy) to enhance story Unique word choice enhances narrative
Mechanics, grammar, and conventions	Major errors in capitalization, punctuation, and spelling impairs meaning Many errors in subject-verb agreement Incomplete sentences	Minor errors in capitalization, punctuation, and spelling Few mistakes in subject-verb agreement Few sentence fragments	Occasional errors in capitalization, punctuation, and spelling; they do not interfere with understanding Most subject-verb agreement correct Consistent use of complete sentences	Conventional use of capitalization, punctuation, and spelling Virtually all subject-verb agreement correct Use of compound/ complex sentences

Writing Rubric: Grade 3

How-to

	Below Expectations	Minimum	Mastery	Excellent
	1	2	3	4
Stays on topic	Poorly addresses purpose May drift to another purpose and include irrelevant information	Somewhat addresses purpose Digressions may occur	Clearly addresses purpose Additional information provided to clarify steps	Clearly addresses and extends purpose Fluent, clear flow of information and steps
Organization and structure	Lacks introduction Elements presented in a list-like manner Major gaps, repetitions, and inconsistencies	Brief introduction and conclusion May lack some elements (materials, steps) Brief gaps, digressions, and/or repetitions	Introduction and conclusion of one to two sentences that restate the prompt Includes all elements (materials, steps) Clear, logical order	Strong introduction and conclusion that clarify prompt Includes and extends all elements Clear, well-developed, logical order
Language control	Attempts and uses sentences Difficult to understand Lacks language control	Uses complete sentences Use of simple but logical sentences Evidence of language control	Varied sentence patterns Sentences evident with some transitions between steps Consistent control of language	Wide variety of sentence patterns Clear transitions evident Consistent, strong control of language
Support and elaboration	Lacks explanation of elements (materials, steps) Lacks elaboration	Elements somewhat explained and/or described Lacks variety of elaboration	Elements clearly explained and/or described Variety of appropriate elaboration	Elements clearly explained, described, and extended Variety of unique elaboration

	Limited word choice	Appropriate word choice	Effective word choice provides support	Unique and effective word choice
Mechanics, grammar, and conventions	Major errors in capitalization, punctuation, and spelling impair meaning Many errors in subject-verb agreement Incomplete sentences	Minor errors in capitalization, punctuation, and spelling Few mistakes in subject-verb agreement Few sentence fragments	Occasional errors in capitalization, punctuation, and spelling do not interfere with understanding Most subject-verb agreement correct Consistent use of complete sentences	Conventional use of capitalization, punctuation, and spelling Virtually all subject-verb agreement correct Use of compound/complex sentences

Writing Rubric: Grade 3

Classificatory

	Below Expectations	Minimum	Mastery	Excellent
	1	2	3	4
Stays on topic	Presents only one side (like or dislike) Makes a brief attempt to address topic May be more narrative	Attempts to present both likes and dislikes May stray from topic Some non-classificatory writing	Clear set of likes/dislikes Remains on topic Addresses topic	Three distinct likes and dislikes presented Specifically addressed topic Clearly addresses purpose
Organization and structure	Lacks introduction and/or conclusion Simply states likes/dislikes Major gaps,	Introduction and conclusion that restate prompt May mix likes and dislikes in same sentences/paragraph	Brief introduction and conclusion of one to two sentences that restate prompt Logical progression of	Introduction and conclusion of one to two sentences that clarify prompt Easy to read and understand likes/dislikes

	repetitions, and inconsistencies	Brief gaps, digressions, and/or rambling occurs	reasons Occasional inconsistencies	Clear sense of order and completeness
Language control	Attempts and uses sentences Difficult to understand Lacks language control	Uses complete sentences Uses simple but logical sentences Evidence of language control	Valid sentence patterns Sentences evident with some transitions between events Consistent control of language	Wide variety of sentence patterns Clear transitions evident Consistent, strong control of language
Support and elaboration	Provides little support for likes/dislikes Likes/dislikes poorly stated Lacks elaboration	Provides support for likes/dislikes Somewhat elaborated likes/dislikes Some elaboration included Appropriate word choice	Two or more extended ideas with specific details, reasons, examples Elaborated likes/dislikes Some variety in types of elaboration used Effective word choice supports the narrative	Three or more ideas elaborated using examples, reasons, details Strong elaboration of some likes/dislikes Varied types of elaboration Unique word choice enhances narrative
Mechanics, grammar, and conventions	Major errors in capitalization, punctuation, and spelling impair meaning Many errors in subject-verb agreement Incomplete sentences	Minor errors in capitalization, punctuation, and spelling Few mistakes in subject-verb agreement Few sentence fragments	Occasional errors in capitalization, punctuation, and spelling do not interfere with understanding Most subject-verb agreement correct Consistent use of complete sentences	Conventional use of capitalization, punctuation, and spelling Virtually all subject-verb agreement correct Use of compound/ complex sentences

Writing Rubric: Grades 4 and 5

How-to

	Below Expectations	Minimum	Mastery	Excellent
	1	2	3	4
Stays on topic	Poorly addresses purpose Makes brief attempt to address topic	Somewhat clearly addresses purpose May stray from topic	Clearly addresses purpose Specifically addresses topic	Clearly addresses and extends purpose Addresses and extends topic
Organization and structure	Lacks introduction and/or conclusion May lack some elements (materials, steps, caution) Major gaps, repetitions, and inconsistencies	Brief introduction and conclusion of one to two sentences that restate prompt Includes all elements Brief gaps, digression; repetitions, and/or rambling occur	Introduction and conclusion of one to two sentences that clarify prompt Includes all elements in clear, logical order Occasional inconsistencies	Strong, concise introduction and conclusion of one to two sentences Elements are tightly focused and extended Clear sense of order and completeness
Language control	Thoughts may not be connected Lacks language control Confusing sentences may be evident	Some transitions evident between elements Some control of language evident Use of complete sentences	Clear and effective transitions between elements General control provides easy understanding of process Varied sentence structure	Clear, effective transitions throughout writing Clearly defines and extends process Varied sentences, including compound/complex sentences
Support and elaboration	Lacks explanation/description of elements	Elements are somewhat explained/described	Elements are clearly explained and described	Elements are clearly explained, described, and

	(materials, steps) Lacks variety of elaboration Minimal word choice	Some variety of elaboration Some use of effective word choice	Variety of appropriate elaboration Effective word choice evident	extended Variety of unique elaboration Rich, unusual, and vivid word choice
Mechanics, grammar, and conventions	Errors in spelling, capitalization, and punctuation interfere with understanding Many errors in verb tense Frequent errors in subject-verb agreement may be evident	Some errors in spelling, capitalization, and punctuation may be evident Inconsistencies in verb tense may be evident Some mistakes in subject-verb agreement	Minor revisions may be needed in spelling, capitalization, and punctuation Usually uses correct verb tense Usually has correct subject-verb agreement	Incorporates most conventions of spelling, capitalization, and punctuation Consistently uses correct verb tense Subject-verb agreement correct

Writing Rubric: Grades 4 and 5

Classificatory

	Below Expectations	Minimum	Mastery	Excellent
	1	2	3	4
Stays on topic	Presents only one side (like or dislike) Makes brief attempt to address topic May be more narrative	Clear set of likes/dislikes May stray from topic Some non-classificatory writing may be included	Distinct likes and dislikes presented Specifically addresses topic Addresses purpose as stated	Three tightly focused likes/dislikes Addresses and extends topic Clearly addresses the purpose
Organization and structure	Lacks introduction and/or conclusion	Brief introduction and conclusion of one to two sentences	Introduction and conclusion of one to two sentences that clarify prompt	Strong, concise introduction and conclusion of one to two sentences

			Easy to read and understand likes/dislikes	Consistent and unified organization
	May mix likes and dislikes in same sentence and/or paragraph Major gaps, repetitions, and inconsistencies	restate prompt Logical progression of reasons may be interrupted by repetition Brief gaps, digression, and/or rambling occur	Occasional inconsistencies	Clear sense of order and completeness
Language control	Thoughts may not be connected Lacks language control Confusing sentences may be evident	Some transitions evident between likes/dislikes Some control of language evident Use of complete sentences	Clear and effective transitions between likes/dislikes General control provides easy understanding of likes/dislikes Varied sentence structure	Clear, effective transitions throughout writing Clearly defines and extends likes/dislikes Varied sentences, including compound/ complex sentences
Support and elaboration	Likes/dislikes stated but lack elaboration Provides little support for likes/dislikes Lacks elaboration Minimal word choice	Somewhat elaborated likes/dislikes Two or more extended ideas with specific details/reasons/ examples Some elaboration included Some use of effective word choice	Strong elaboration of some likes/dislikes Three or more ideas elaborated using examples, reasons, and details Some variety in types of elaboration used Effective word choice evident	Strong elaboration of three or more likes/dislikes Ideas fully developed using examples, reasons, and specific evidence Varied types of elaboration Rich, unusual, and vivid word choice
Mechanics, grammar, and conventions	Errors in spelling, capitalization,	Some errors in spelling, capitalization,	Minor revisions may be needed in spelling,	Incorporates most conventions of

and punctuation interfere with understanding

Many errors in verb tense

Frequent errors in subject-verb agreement may be evident | and punctuation may be evident

Inconsistencies in verb tense may be evident

Some mistakes in subject-verb agreement | capitalization, and punctuation

Usually uses correct verb tense

Usually has correct subject-verb agreement | spelling, capitalization, and punctuation

Consistently uses correct verb tense

Subject-verb agreement correct |

Writing Rubric: Grades 4 and 5

Narrative/Expressive

	Below Expectations	Minimum	Mastery	Excellent
	1	2	3	4
Stays on topic	Narrative wanders from purpose

Some information included that is unrelated

Makes brief attempt to address prompt | Narrative addresses the purpose

Most information related

Narrative addresses prompt | Narrative clarifies purpose

Virtually all information related

Narrative clearly addresses prompt | Narrative clarifies and extends purpose

All information related

Narrative clearly addresses prompt |
| Organization and structure | Has a beginning but not necessarily a middle or end

Lacks evidence of story elements

Major gaps in order of events and cause/effect | Has a beginning, middle, and end

Story line is apparent with some evidence of a problem

Some gaps in order of events and cause/effect | Has purposeful beginning, middle, and end

Story line presented in a logical order, including all story elements

Clearly defined steps in logical order using cause/effect | Clear and consistent organization with purposeful beginning, middle, and end

Includes and develops story elements with unique solution to problem/goal

Extended steps presented in |

				logical order using cause/effect
Language control	Attempts and uses sentences Difficult to understand Lacks language control	Uses complete sentences Uses simple but logical sentences Evidence of language control	Varied sentence patterns Complete sentences evident and effective transitions between events Consistent control of language	Varied sentence patterns Clear, effective transitions evident Consistent, strong control of language
Support and elaboration	Characters are apparent A few attributes may be given Limited word choice	Character are described Some ideas are described but not in great detail Appropriate word choice	Character and setting described Ideas are extended using description, detail, and dialogue Effective word choice supports narrative	Strong description of character and setting Uses a variety of forms of elaboration (synonyms, metaphor, simile, analogy) and unique solutions Unique word choice enhances narrative
Mechanics, grammar, and conventions	Error in spelling, capitalization, and punctuation interfere with understanding Many errors in verb tense Frequent errors in subject-verb agreement may be evident	Some errors in spelling, capitalization, and punctuation may be evident Inconsistencies in verb tense may be evident Some mistakes in subject-verb agreement	Minor revisions may be needed in spelling, capitalization, and punctuation Usually uses correct verb tense Usually has correct subject-verb agreement	Incorporates most conventions of spelling, capitalization, and punctuation Consistently uses correct verb tense and subject-verb agreement

Writing Rubric: Grades 4 and 5

Persuasive

	Non-Mastery	Non-Mastery	Mastery	Academic Excellence
	1	2	3	4
Stays on topic	Makes brief attempt to address position May drift from topic, purpose Information may not support position	Position stated and minimal support provided Occasionally drifts from position/reasons Information supports position	Clearly defines the position Provides three distinct reasons to support position Information focused on position	Presents position with convincing reasons in a logical, unified manner Position supported with at least three well-developed reasons Information fluent, tightly focused on topic
Organization and structure	Lacks connection between reasons Introduction/ conclusion may not be evident Major gaps, rambling, and inconsistencies	Organization apparent Brief introduction and conclusion that state position Some gaps, rambling, and inconsistencies	Paragraphs indicate use of transitions from one thought to another Introduction and conclusions that clearly state position and address audience Generally well-organized and clear enough to understand reasons presented	Paragraphs reflect effective use of transitional, introductory, and concluding elements Introduction and conclusion that clearly state position and address audience in a unique way Consistent strategy evident
Language control	Thoughts may not be connected Lacks language control	Some transitions evident between reasons Some control of language evident	Clear and effective transitions between reasons General control	Clear, effective transitions throughout paper Consistent,

			provides easy understanding of position Varied sentence structure	creative control of language supports position Varied sentences, including compound/complex sentences
	Confusing sentences may be evident	Use of complete sentences		
Support and elaboration	Insufficient elaboration to support position Brief lists of non-specific and unelaborated reasons Minimal word choice	Some elaboration and/or extension of reasons Fewer than three reasons provided Limited word choice	Elaboration may support one fully developed reason or a lengthy set of less developed ideas Three moderately elaborated reasons to support writer's stated choice Effective word choice	Elaborates in a variety of ways Three specific and well-elaborated reasons that are clear and convincing Rich, unusual, and/or vivid word choice
Mechanics, grammar, and conventions	Errors in spelling, capitalization, and punctuation interfere with understanding Many errors in verb tense Frequent errors in subject-verb agreement may be evident	Some errors in spelling, capitalization, and punctuation may be evident Inconsistencies in verb tense may be evident Some mistakes in subject-verb agreement	Minor revisions may be needed in spelling, capitalization, and punctuation Usually uses correct verb tense Usually has correct subject-verb agreement	Incorporates most conventions of spelling, capitalization, and punctuation Consistently uses correct verb tense Subject-verb agreement correct

Environmental Opportunities Profile

Developed by Ruby K. Payne, Ph.D., and Paul D. Slocumb, Ed.D.
©RFT Publishing Co., 1999

Date of interview_____ Name of interviewer_____

Name of student_____ Grade level_____

School_____ Teacher_____

Person interviewed_____ Relationship to student_____

Address_____

City_____ ZIP_____ Day phone #_____

Evening phone #_____ Emergency #_____

Additional notes from interview:

Total number of people in household:

_____

Range of family's annual income:
____Less than $10,000
____$10,000 to $20,000
____$20,000 to $30,000
____$30,000 to $40,000
____$40,000 to $50,000
____$50,000 to $75,000
____More than $75,000

Environmental Opportunities Profile
Developed by Ruby K. Payne, Ph.D., and Paul D. Slocumb, Ed.D.
©RFT Publishing Co., 1999

Section I: Student Production	Criteria	Rating
Item 1: Number of years of schooling of primary caregiver, particularly mother **Question:** How many years were you in school, starting with 1st grade?	• 16+ years of schooling • 12-15 years of schooling • Less than 12 years of schooling	☐ 1 point ☐ 2 points ☐ 3 points
Item 2: Number of years at same school **Question:** How long has your child gone to this school?	• Has spent or will spend two or more years in same school • Is and/or plans to be in same school for one year • Moves during year; is unlikely to stay for entire school year	☐ 1 point ☐ 2 points ☐ 3 points
Item 3: Child/family have medical/health benefits **Question:** Does your family have medical/health benefits that include child?	• All members are covered • Only employed parent(s) are covered • No members are covered	☐ 1 point ☐ 2 points ☐ 3 points
Item 4: Number of years in same job; stability of income **Question:** Do you and/or other adults in the household work outside the home? How long have you/they worked there?	• One or more adults are employed and have been consistently employed for two or more years with same company or type of work • One or more adults are employed and have been for at least one year with	☐ 1 point ☐ 2 points

	same company or type of work • No adult is employed or has been employed for more than six months with same company or type of work on full-time basis	☐ 3 points
Item 5: Identified as LD, ED, ADHD, ADD, 504, Title I, bilingual, etc. **Question:** Does your child receive any special services at school, such as with reading or math from a special teacher, in Special Education, special tutoring, etc.?	• No learning conditions identified • Identified learning problems; interventions appear effective; parents pleased with student's progress • Learning problems identified; interventions appear ineffective; parents displeased with progress	☐ 1 point ☐ 2 points ☐ 3 points
	Subtotal of Section I =	
Section II: Informant Data	**Criteria**	**Rating**
Item 6: Parents born in United States **Question:** Were you and your spouse born in the United States?	• Both parents born in United States • One parent born in United States • Neither parent born in United States	☐ 1 point ☐ 2 points ☐ 3 points
Item 7: Support system in home—number of adult males in household **Question:** How many adult men	• One or more adult males live in household, consistently and	☐ 1 point

live in your house?	fairly constantly	
	• One adult male on fairly permanent basis; if divorced, father exercises visitation rights regularly	☐ 2 points
	• No adult males in household, or males are not in household on regular basis	☐ 3 points
Item 8: Support system in home—number of adult females in household **Question:** How many adult women live in the household?	• One or more adult females live in household, consistently and fairly constantly	☐ 1 point
	• One adult female on fairly permanent basis; if divorced, mother exercises visitation rights regularly	☐ 2 points
	• No adult females in household, or females are not in household on regular basis	☐ 3 points
Item 9: Support system in household—number of adults in household **Question:** How many children are in the household and how many adults (ratio of children to adults)?	• Child/adult ratio is one-to-one or better	☐ 1 point
	• Child/adult ratio is two children to one adult	☐ 2 points
	• Child/adult ratio is three or more children to one adult	☐ 3 points

Item 10: Amount of light in home **Question:** Do you have lots of light in your house? Do you open the curtains during the day?	• Window coverings are open during day; three or more light fixtures and/or lamps are in major rooms in house	☐ 1 point
	• Window coverings partially open; overhead light or lamp per room	☐ 2 points
	• Window coverings closed; one or less low-wattage light bulb is used; light often comes from TV	☐ 3 points
Item 11: Use of color in home décor **Question:** What colors are in your house? Describe the colors of your walls, pictures, and furniture.	• Light-colored walls with contrasting colors in drapes and furnishings	☐ 1 point
	• Neutral shades and décor; colors complement or blend rather than contrast	☐ 2 points
	• Darker décor; random use of medium-to-dark nondescript color	☐ 3 points
Item 12: Is older or younger than classmates **Question:** When was your child born? Did he/she start kindergarten when he/she was 5? Has he/she ever been retained?	• Overage—has been retained, started school late, or has birthday within first two months of school	☐ 1 point
	• Same age range as classmates	☐ 2 points
	• Underage—has birthday one or two months prior to start date of school	☐ 3 points

Item 13: Qualifies for and/or receives free or reduced lunch **Question:** Does your child take part in the free-or-reduced lunch program at school? (Note: If this is a sensitive question to ask, check school records.)	• No assistance • Reduced lunch • Free lunch	☐ 1 point ☐ 2 points ☐ 3 points
Item 14: Child is member of dominant racial or ethnic group of campus (dominant means 50% or more of students belong to that group) **Question:** Check school records	• Member of dominant group • There is no dominant group; no group has 50% or more • Not member of dominant group	☐ 1 point ☐ 2 points ☐ 3 points
Item 15: Child is member of dominant economic group of campus **Question:** Check school records	• Member of dominant group • There is no dominant group; no group has 50% or more • Not member of dominant group	☐ 1 point ☐ 2 points ☐ 3 points
Item 16: There are general time frames for meals, TV, going to bed, taking bath, etc. **Question:** Do you have a set time that you make your child take a bath? Go to bed? Watch TV? Do homework? Etc.	• Time frames exist and are consistently followed • Time frames exist for most and are often followed • Time frames vary or are nonexistent and are inconsistently followed	☐ 1 point ☐ 2 points ☐ 3 points

Item 17: Child has spent night 50 miles or more away from home with parent or other family member **Question:** Has your child ever been 50 miles or more away from home with you or another family member and stayed overnight? If so, how many times?	• Frequently—more than once a year • Occasionally—once a year (such as family vacation) • Never	☐ 1 point ☐ 2 points ☐ 3 points
Subtotal of Section II =		
Section III: Cognitive/Language Skills	**Criteria**	**Rating**
Item 18: Significant relationships **Question:** Who is the primary caregiver of the child?	• Two or more significant relationships • At least one significant relationship • None	☐ 1 point ☐ 2 points ☐ 3 points
Item 19: Number of children's books in home **Question:** How many books does your child have that are for him/her? (Note: Books should have been purchased for him/her.)	• Two or more books per year of age • One book per year of age • Less than one book per year of age	☐ 1 point ☐ 2 points ☐ 3 points
Item 20: Presence of newspapers or magazines in home **Question:** Do you purchase newspapers or magazines on a regular basis?	• Daily newspaper and two or more magazines • Weekend newspaper or tabloid purchased on regular basis; magazines purchased at store	☐ 1 point ☐ 2 points

	• No systematic access to newspapers or magazines	☐ 3 points
Item 21: Formal register is used at home (in any language) **Question:** Observe for use of language	• Spoken and written formal register (in any language) used by all adult household members	☐ 1 point
	• Formal register spoken by all adult household members, but not written	☐ 2 points
	• Casual register used by one or more of household adults; very little writing of any kind	☐ 3 points
Item 22: Speaks language other than English **Question:** What languages are spoken in the home? (Observation)	• All adults in household speak English	☐ 1 point
	• At least one adult speaks at least one language fluently	☐ 2 points
	• Language acquisition delayed, or no dominant language; poor grammatical structures used orally	☐ 3 points
Subtotal of Section III =		
Total of Sections I, II, and III =		

Bibliography

BIBLIOGRAPHY

Armstrong, T. (1998). *Awakening Genius in the Classroom.*
Alexandria, VA: Association for Supervision and
Curriculum Development.

Bess, S. (1994). *Nobody Don't Love Nobody.* Carson City, NV:
Gold Leaf Press.

Bigelow, B. (April 1999). Why standardized tests threaten
multiculturalism. *Educational Leadership.* 56 (7), 37-40.

Buchalter, G. (April 4, 1999). A power will guide. *Parade
Magazine.* pp. 4-6.

Caine, R.N., and Caine, G. (1991). *Making Connections: Teaching
the Human Brain.* Alexandria, VA: Association for
Supervision and Curriculum Development.

Caldwell, B.M., and Bradley, R.H. (1984). *Home Observation for
Measurement of the Environment (HOME).* Little Rock,
AR: University of Arkansas.

Clark, B. (1997). *Growing Up Gifted: Developing the Potential
of Children at Home and at School* (5th Edition).
Columbus, OH: Charles E. Merrill.

Cogangelo, N., and Davis, G. (Eds.). (1990). *Handbook of Gifted
Education.* Boston, MA: Allyn and Bacon, Inc.

Combs, S.W., and Snygg, D. (1959). *Individual Behavior* (2nd Edition). New York, NY: Harper & Row.

Duncan, G.J., and Brooks-Gunn, J. (Eds.). (1997). *Consequences of Growing Up Poor.* New York, NY: Russell Sage Foundation.

Eggen, P.D., and Kauchak, D.P. (1988). *Strategies for Teachers.* Englewood Cliffs, NJ: Prentice Hall.

Elias, M.J., Zins, J.E., et al. (1997). *Promoting Social and Emotional Learning.* Alexandria, VA: Association for Supervision and Curriculum Development.

Erickson, H.L. (1998). *Concept-Based Curriculum and Instruction.* Thousand Oaks, CA: Corwin Press, Inc.

Feuerstein, R. (1991). Intervention programs for retarded performers: goals, means, and expected outcomes. In Idol, L., and Jones, B.F. (Eds.). *Educational Values and Cognitive Instruction: Implications for Reform* (pp. 139-178). Hillsdale, NJ: Lawrence Erlbaum Associates.

Fox, L.H., and Zimmerman, W.Z. (1985). Gifted women. In Freeman, J. (Ed.). *The Psychology of Gifted Children.* New York, NY: Wiley.

Frase, L.E., and English, F.W., et al. (1995). *The Curriculum Management Audit.* Lancaster, PA: Technomic Publishing Company, Inc.

Fussel, P. (1983). *Class.* New York, NY: Ballantine Books.

Galbraith, J. (1983). *The Gifted Kids Survival Guide (For Ages 11-18)*. Minneapolis, MN: Free Spirit Publishing, Inc.

Galbraith, J. (1984). *The Gifted Kids Survival Guide (For Ages 10 & Under)*. Minneapolis, MN: Free Spirit Publishing, Inc.

Gallagher, J.J. (1985). *Teaching the Gifted Child* (3rd Edition). Newton, MA: Allyn and Bacon, Inc.

Gallagher, J.J., and Gallagher, S.A. (1994). *Teaching the Gifted Child* (4th Edition). Needham Heights, MA: Allyn and Bacon, Inc.

García, J.H. (1994). Nonstandardized instruments for the assessment of Mexican-American children for gifted/talented programs. In García, S.B. (Ed.). *Addressing Cultural and Linguistic Diversity in Special Education: Issues and Trends* (pp. 46-57). Reston, VA: The Council for Exceptional Children.

Greenspan, S.I. (1997). *The Growth of the Mind and the Endangered Origins of Intelligence*. Reading, MA: Addison-Wesley Publishing Company, Inc.

Gurian, M. (1996). *The Wonder of Boys*. New York, NY: Tarcher/Putman Books.

Harrington, M. (1962). *The Other America*. New York, NY: Simon and Schuster.

Hart, L.A. (1983). *Human Brain and Human Learning.* Village of Oak Creek, AZ: Books for Educators.

Hyerle, D. (1996). *Visual Tools for Constructing Knowledge.* Alexandria, VA: Association for Supervision and Curriculum Development.

Johnsen, S.K., Ryser, G., and Doughtery, E. (1993). Teacher rating of students in relation to ethnicity of students and school ethnic balance. *Gifted International: A Talent Development Journal.* 6(3), 154-166.

Kaplan, S. (n.d.-a). *Academic portfolio.* Austin, TX: Texas Education Agency.

Kaplan, S. (n.d.-b). *The jot down.* Austin, TX: Texas Education Agency.

Kaplan, S. (1999). Teaching up to the needs of the gifted English language learner. *Tempo.* XIX (2), 1, 20-21.

Karen, R. (February 1992). Shame. *The Atlantic Monthly.* 40-70.

Kingore, B. (1993). *Portfolios: Enriching and Assessing All Students.* Des Moines, IA: Leadership Publishers, Inc.

Kingore, B. *Understanding the diversity of the gifted.* Published in *Tempo,* Spring, 1997, Volume XVII, Issue II (pp. 1, 6). Austin, TX: Texas Association for the Gifted and Talented (TAGT).

Kovalik, S., and Olsen, K. (1993). *ITI: The Model, Integrated Thematic Instruction.* Village of Oak Creek, AZ: Books for Educators.

Kozol, J. (1991). *Savage Inequalities: Children in America's Schools.* New York, NY: Crown.

Kozol, J. (1995). *Amazing Grace: The Lives of Children and the Conscience of a Nation.* New York, NY: Crown.

Lara-Alecio, R., and Irby, B., et al. (Spring 1997). Identification of Hispanic, bilingual, gifted students. In *Tempo* (pp. 20-25). Austin, TX: Texas Association for the Gifted and Talented.

Lewis, A.C. (November 1996). Breaking the cycle of poverty. *Phi Delta Kappan,* 78 (3). 186-187.

Maker, C.J. (1982). *Teaching Models in Education of the Gifted.* Rockville, MD: Aspen Publications.

Parks, S., and Black, H. (1990). *Book II: Organizing Thinking.* Pacific Grove, CA: Critical Thinking Books & Software.

Parks, S., and Black, H. (1992). *Book I: Organizing Thinking.* Pacific Grove, CA: Critical Thinking Books & Software.

Payne, R.K. (1998). *A Framework for Understanding Poverty* (revised edition). Baytown, TX: RFT Publishing Co.

Paulson, F.L., and Paulson, P.R. (April 1991). The ins and outs of using portfolios to assess performance (revised edition).

Paper presented at the Joint Annual Meeting of the
National Council of Measurement in Education and the
National Association of Test Directors, Chicago, IL.
(ERIC Documents Reproduction Service No. ED 334 250)

Pelzer, D. (1993). *A Child Called "It."* Deerfield Beach, FL:
Health Communications, Inc.

Penchef, E. (Ed.). (1971). *Four Horsemen: Pollution, Poverty,
Famine, Violence.* San Francisco, CA: Canfield Press.

Piaget, J. (1952). *The Origins of Intelligence in Children.* New
York, NY: International University Press.

Piaget, J. (1975). *The Child's Conception of the World.*
Totowa, NJ: Littlefield, Adams, and Co.

Pollack, W. (1998). *Real Boys.* Random House, Inc.

Reis, S.M. (1988). *Work Left Undone.* Mansfield Center, CT:
Creative Learning Press, Inc.

Rodriguez, L.J. (1993). *Always Running.* New York, NY: Simon
& Schuster.

Rogers, C.R. (1951). *Client-Centered Therapy.* Chicago, IL:
Houghton Mifflin.

Rogers, C.R. (1961). *On Becoming a Person.* Chicago, IL:
Houghton Mifflin.

Saucier, Heather, "*Senior turns tragedy into successes.*" (April 19, 1999), *Houston Chronicle.* p. 24A.

Sennett, R., and Cobb, J. (1993). *The Hidden Injuries of Class.* London/Boston: Faber & Faber. First published in U.S.A. in 1972 by Alfred A. Knopf, Inc., New York, NY.

Slocumb, P.D. (1987). *The Relationship Between Achievement of Five-Year-Olds and Parents' Report of Home Environment Characteristics.* Houston, TX: University of Houston/University Park.

Stailey, J.C., and Payne, R.K. (1998). *Think Rather of Zebra: Dealing with Aspects of Poverty Through Story.* Baytown, TX: RFT Publishing Co.

Strong, F. (June 9, 1999). An excellent night. *Houston Chronicle.* pp. 1D, 10D.

Swartz, R.J., and Parks, S. (1994). *Infusing the Teaching of Critical and Creative Thinking into Content Instruction.* Pacific Grove, CA: Critical Thinking Books & Software.

Tomlinson, C.A. (1999). *The Differentiated Classroom: Responding to the Needs of All Learners.* Alexandria, VA: Association for Supervision and Curriculum Development.

VanTassel-Baska, J., Feldhusen, J., et al. (1988). *Comprehensive Curriculum for Gifted Learners.* Needham Heights, MA: Allyn and Bacon, Inc.

VanTassel-Baska, J., Feldhusen, J., et al. (1994). *Comprehensive Curriculum for Gifted Learners* (2nd Edition). Needham Heights, MA: Allyn and Bacon, Inc.

Wiggins, G., and McTighe, J. (1998). *Understanding by Design.* Alexandria, VA: Association for Supervision and Curriculum Development.

Yonezawa, S., and Oakes, J. (April 1999). Making parents partners in the placement process. *Educational Leadership,* 56 (7), 33-36.

Zeichner, K.M. (1996). *Educating teachers to close the achievement gap: issues of pedagogy, knowledge, and teacher preparation.* In Williams, B. (Ed.). *Closing the Achievement Gap: A Vision for Changing Beliefs and Practices* (pp. 56-76). Alexandria, VA: Association for Supervision and Curriculum Development.

Zill, N. (1993). The changing realities of family life. *Aspen Institute Quarterly,* 5 (1), 27-51.

RFT PUBLISHING CO.
P. O. BOX 727
HIGHLANDS, TX 77562-0727
(800) 424-9484 TOLL FREE
(281) 426-5600 FAX

WANT YOUR OWN COPIES? WANT TO GIVE A COPY TO A FRIEND?
PLEASE SEND ME:

_____   COPY/COPIES OF *REMOVING THE MASK: GIFTEDNESS IN POVERTY*

BOOKS: 1-4 books $22.00/each + $4.50 first book plus $2.00 each
                               additional book shipping/handling
               5 & up books $15.00/each + 8% shipping/handling

MAIL TO:
NAME _____

ORGANIZATION _____

ADDRESS _____

_____

PHONE _____

METHOD OF PAYMENT
PO # _____

CREDIT CARD TYPE _____   EXP _____

CREDIT CARD # _____

CHECK $ _____   CHECK # _____

SUBTOTAL $ _____

SHIPPING $ _____

SALES TAX $ _____ 7.75% IN TEXAS

TOTAL $ _____